ANCIENT INDIAN TRADITION & MYTHOLOGY

Translated by
A BOARD OF SCHOLARS

Edited by
Dr. G.P. BHATT
Late Prof. J.L. SHASTRI

VOLUME 34

ANCIENT INDIAN TRADITION AND MYTHOLOGY SERIES

[PURĀṆAS IN TRANSLATION]

Volumes Released

ŚIVA 1-4
LIṄGA 5-6
BHĀGAVATA 7-11
GARUḌA 12-14
NĀRADA 15-19
KŪRMA 20-21
BRAHMĀṆḌA 22-26
AGNI 27-30
VARĀHA 31-32
BRAHMA 33-36
VĀYU 37-38
PADMA 39-48
SKANDA, PARTS I-XXII, 49-71
VĀMANA 72-73
GAṆEŚA 74-75

Volumes Under Preparation

BHAVIṢYA
BRAHMAVAIVARTA
DEVĪBHĀGAVATA
KĀLIKĀ
MĀRKAṆḌEYA
MATSYA
VIṢṆU
VIṢṆUDHARMOTTARA

BRAHMA PURĀṆA

Translated and Annotated by
A BOARD OF SCHOLARS

PART II

MOTILAL BANARSIDASS PUBLISHERS
PRIVATE LIMITED • DELHI

2nd Reprint: Delhi, 2014
First Edition: Delhi, 1985

ISBN: 978-81-208-0034-2
ISBN: 978-81-208-3827-7 (Set of 4 Vols. of Brahma Purāṇa)

MOTILAL BANARSIDASS
41 U.A. Bungalow Road, Jawahar Nagar, Delhi 110 007
8 Mahalaxmi Chamber, 22 Bhulabhai Desai Road, Mumbai 400 026
120 Royapettah High Road, Mylapore, Chennai 600 004
236, 9th Main III Block, Jayanagar, Bangaluru 560 011
Sanas Plaza, 1302 Baji Rao Road, Pune 411 002
8 Camac Street, Kolkata 700 017
Ashok Rajpath, Patna 800 004
Chowk, Varanasi 221 001

UNESCO COLLECTION OF REPRESENTATIVE WORKS—*Indian Series*
This book has been accepted in the Indian Translation Series of the UNESCO Collection of Representative Works, jointly sponsored by the United Nations Educational, Scientific and Cultural Organization (UNESCO) and the Government of India

Printed in India

by RP Jain at NAB Printing Unit,
A-44, Naraina Industrial Area, Phase I, New Delhi–110028
and published by JP Jain for Motilal Banarsidass Publishers (P) Ltd,
41 U.A. Bungalow Road, Jawahar Nagar, Delhi-110007

PUBLISHER'S NOTE

The purest gems lie hidden in the bottom of the ocean or in the depth of rocks. One has to dive into the ocean or delve into the rocks to find them out. Similarly, truth lies concealed in the language which with the passage of time has become obsolete. Man has to learn that language before he discovers that truth.

But he has neither the means nor the leisure to embark on that course. We have, therefore, planned to help him acquire knowledge by an easier course. We have started the series of Ancient Indian Tradition and Mythology in English Translation. Our goal is to universalize knowledge through the most popular international medium of expression. The publication of the Purāṇas in English Translation is a step towards that goal.

PREFACE

The present volume contains the *Brahma Purāṇa* Part II (Chapters 41-105) in English Translation. This is the thirty-fourth volume in the Series on *Ancient Indian Tradition and Mythology*.

The project was planned in 1970 by Lala Sundar Lal Jain of Messrs Motilal Banarsidass, with the aim to universalize knowledge through the most popular international medium, viz. English. Hitherto the English translations of ten Purāṇas, namely Śiva, Liṅga, Bhāgavata, Garuḍa, Nārada, Kūrma, Brahmāṇḍa, Agni, Varāha and Brahma (part 1) have come out.

The present volume contains chapters 41 to 105. It opens with the narrative of Indradyumna, king of Avanti, his performance of horse-sacrifice at the holy centre Puruṣottama and the establishment of images of Saṅkarṣaṇa, Kṛṣṇa and Subhadrā in the magnificent palace which he built there. The account extends to the forty-eighth chapter ending with the description of Puruṣottama, the centre sacred to Viṣṇu. The text then passes on to the story of sage Mārkaṇḍeya with the significant reference to Śiva's temple by the side of Mārkaṇḍeya lake which was built in A.D. 800 by Kuṇḍala Kesarin, king of Orissa. This is followed by the description of holy shrines, the procedure of worship of deities therein and the benefits of their worship. The Purāṇa expiates upon the merits of living and dying at this centre. Chapters 69 to 103 describe the narrative of Śrī Kṛṣṇa and the legends of Balarāma, Pradyumna and Aniruddha. Chapters 104 and 105 which conclude this part glorify different manifestations of the lord as well as review the path of the world of Yama.

Most of the chapters in this as well as the preceding part describe the holy places of Orissa. They seem to have been composed by one who was well acquainted with Orissa. We may, therefore, conclude that the group of chapters relating to Orissa might have sprung up in that centre.

Acknowledgement of obligations

It is our pleasant duty to put on record our sincere thanks to Dr R. N. Dandekar and the UNESCO authorities for their kind encouragement and valuable help which render this work very useful. We are grateful to Shri T. V. Parameshwar Iyer for his valuable assistance in the preparation of this work. We also express our gratitude to all those scholars who have offered suggestions for improving the same.

In fine, we avail of this opportunity to state that any critical suggestion or advice for improvement is welcome and will receive proper consideration from us.

—*Editor*

CONTENTS

PART II

ABBREVIATIONS

Common and self-evident abbreviations such as Ch(s)—Chapter(s), p—page, pp—pages, V—Verse, VV—Verses, Ftn—footnote, Hist. Ind. Philo—History of Indian Philosophy are not included in this list.

ABORI	*Annals of the Bhandarkar Oriental Research Institute*, Poona
AGP	S. M. Ali's *The Geography of Purāṇas*, PPH, New Delhi, 1973
AIHT	*Ancient Indian Historical Tradition*, F. E. Pargiter, Motilal Banarsidass (MLBD), Delhi
AITM	*Ancient Indian Tradition and Mythology* Series MLBD, Delhi
AP	*Agni Purāṇa*, Guru Mandal Edition (GM), Calcutta, 1957
Arch.S.Rep.	Archaeological Survey Report
AV	*Atharva Veda*, Svādhyāya Mandal, Aundh
Bd. P.	*Brahmāṇḍa Purāṇa*, MLBD, Delhi 1973
BG	*Bhagavadgītā*
Bh. P.	*Bhāgavata Purāṇa*, Bhagavat Vidyapeeth, Ahmedabad
Br.	*Brāhmaṇa* (preceded by name such as Śatapatha)
BS. P.	*Bhaviṣya Purāṇa*, Vishnu Shastri Bapat, Wai
BV. P.	*Brahma Vaivarta Purāṇa*, GM, 1955-57
CC	*Caturvarga Cintāmaṇi* by Hemādri
CVS	*Caraṇa Vyūha Sūtra* by Śaunaka; Com. by Mahidāsa
DB	*Devī Bhāgavata*, GM, 1960-61
De or GDAMI	*The Geographical Dictionary of Ancient and Mediaeval India*, N. L. De, Orienta Reprint, Delhi, 1971
Dh. S.	*Dharma Sūtra* (preceded by the author's name such as Gautama)
ERE	*Encyclopaedia of Religion and Ethics*—Hastings.
GP	*Garuḍa Purāṇa* Ed. R. S. Bhattacharya Chowkhamba, Varanasi, 1964

GS	*Gṛhya Sūtra* (preceded by the name of the author such as Āpastamba)
HD	*History of Dharma Śāstra*, P. V. Kane, G. O. S.
IA	*The Indian Antiquary*
IHQ	*The Indian Historical Quarterly*
JP	*Purāṇa* (Journal of the Kashiraj Trust), Varanasi
KA	*Kauṭilya Arthaśāstra*
KP	*Kūrma Purāṇa*, Veṅkaṭeśvara Press Edt. Bombay, also Kashiraj Trust Edt., Varanasi 1971
LP	*Liṅga Purāṇa*, GM, 1960; also MLBD, Delhi, 1981
Manu.	*Manusmṛti*
Mbh.	*Mahābhārata*, Gītā Press, Gorakhpur, VS 2014
MkP	*Mārkaṇḍeya Purāṇa*
MN	*Mahābhārata Nāmānukramaṇi*, Gītā Press Gorakhpur, VS 2016
MtP	*Matsya Purāṇa*, GM, 1954
MW	*Monier Williams Sk. English Dictionary* MLBD, Delhi, 1976
NP	*Nāradīya or Nārada Purāṇa*, Veṅkaṭeśvar Press, Bombay
PCK	*Bhāratavarṣiya Prācina Caritrakośa*, Siddheshwar Shastri, Poona, 1968
Pd. P.	*Padma Purāṇa*, GM, 1957-59
PE	*Puranic Encyclopaedia*, V. Mani, English, MLBD, Delhi, 1975
PR or PRHRC	*Puranic Records on Hindu Rites and Customs* R. C. Hazra, Calcutta, 1948
ṚV	*Ṛg-Veda*, Svādhyāya Mandal, Aundh
Śat. Br.	*Śatapatha Brāhmaṇa*
SC or SMC	*Smṛti Candrikā*—Devanna Bhaṭṭa
SEP	*Studies in Epics and Purāṇas*, A.D. Pusalkar, Bharatiya Vidya Bhavan (BVB), Bombay

CHAPTER FORTYONE

The narrative of Indradyumna
Description of Avanti

Brahmā said:

1. O brahmins, formerly, in the Kṛtayuga there was a glorious king who was known as Indradyumna. He was as valorous as Indra.

2. He was truthful in speech, pure in thought and efficient in work. He was most excellent among the wielders of weapons. He was handsome and fortunate. He was heroic and liberal in charitable gifts. He enjoyed pleasures and spoke pleasingly.

3. He performed many sacrifices. He was favourably disposed to the brahmins. He was truthful in utterance. He was an adept in the science of archery, Vedas and other scriptures. He was contented.

4. He was the lover of humanity and he looked splendid like the moon on the full moon-night. Like the sun he was dazzling to look at, he was terrible to the hosts of enemies.

5. He was a devotee of Viṣṇu. He was endowed with Sattva attribute. He conquered wrath and the sense-organs. He was interested in the spiritual lore. He was desirous of salvation. He was interested in virtue.

6. While that king, the repository of good qualities, ruled over the Earth he thought of propitiating Viṣṇu.

7. "How shall I propitiate Viṣṇu, the lord of Devas? In which holy centre or sacred spot or the river bank or hermitage shall it be?"

8-9. Pondering thus in his mind he thought of all holy centres on the earth. He saw them in dreamy vision. After seeing the holy centres, sacred spots and cities he mentally repaired to the holy centre Puruṣottama that bestows salvation on the devotees.

10. The king went there accompanied by his flourishing army and vehicles. He duly performed a horse sacrifice where much wealth was distributed as gift.

11-12. He got a lofty palace built there. He established the images of Saṁkarṣaṇa, Kṛṣṇa and Subhadrā therein. He constructed five holy spots there. He performed the rites of ablution, charitable gift, penance, sacrifice and the visit to the deity regularly. He devoutly propitiated the lord duly every day by the grace of the lord. In course of time he attained salvation.

13-14. O brahmins, by taking ablution in the ocean named (after) Indradyumna and visiting Mārkaṇḍeya, Vaṭa (banyan tree), Kṛṣṇa and Bala-Rāma one attains salvation certainly.

The sages said:

15-21. Formerly, why did that lord of the world, Indradyumna go to that great holy centre Puruṣottama that bestows salvation?

O most excellent one among Devas, after going there how did that excellent king duly perform horse-sacrifice and worship the lord? How did he manage to build an excellent mansion well known in three worlds in that rarest of holy centres that bestows all benefits?

How did that leading king create the idols of Kṛṣṇa, Rāma and Subhadrā endowed with all characteristic marks, O Patriarch Brahmā?

How did that king instal Kṛṣṇa and other deities who are worshipped by Devas, in that palace which was most excellent in the world?

O most excellent among Devas it behoves you to recount all this precisely and in detail, the whole narrative of that intelligent king.

We are not fully satiated by the nectar-like words of yours. We wish to hear more. Our curiosity has grown excessively.

Brahmā said:

22-23. Well done, O excellent brahmins that you have asked me about the ancient story that is holy, destructive of sins, splendid and conducive to worldly pleasures and salvation. I shall mention the story as it had happened in the Kṛta Yuga. O leading sages, listen with concentration and restraint over the sense-organs.

24. The city of Avanti[1] in Mālava, known as the most excellent one over the earth, was the capital of that monarch.

25. It was thronged by citizens who were delighted and well nourished. The rampart wall, and the arched gateway were firmly built. There were strong mechanical means of bolting the doors. The city was embellished by moats.

26. It was filled by different merchants with different articles for sale. The city was beautiful with streets and bazars. It was bedecked by triangular and quadrangular lawns.

27-31. It was full of rows of mansions with upper stories and apartments; the four cross-roads were well partitioned. Houses and towers abounded in that city which was adorned by hundreds and thousands of palaces which resembled royal swans with pure wonderful necks and which looked charming and gay. The whole city was in a joyous mood due to sacrifices and festivities; the sounds of songs and musical instruments spread everywhere. It was adorned with flags and ensigns of different colours. There were armies of elephants, horses, chariots and infantry men. The city was filled by soldiers of all kinds. It had various centres where crowds gathered together. O excellent sages, the city was rendered prosperous by the people who lived there such as the Brahmins, Kṣatriyas Vaiśyas and Śūdras. The city was embellished by great scholars who made it their permanent home. There were no dirty people there; neither fools nor weak men resided in it.

32-35. There were no sickly persons, no crippled or maimed persons. None indulged in the vice of gambling there. Men and women were always delighted and nobleminded.

The people sported about in day and night with great joy. Men were dressed well and splendidly. Their ear-rings were polished and cleaned. They were handsome and noble. They were bedecked in divine ornaments. They had all good traits and they resembled cupid in their gaiety.

---

1. *Avanti*—Ujjayinī. In the wider sense the name signifies Mālava-deśa. The town is situated on the bank of Śiprā. The renowned poets like Kālidāsa lived there. It is one of the seven cities capable of giving liberation (*moksa*).

Their hair were fine. Their cheeks were beautiful. Their faces were handsome and they wore moustaches. They were conversant with holy scriptures. They could pierce through the army of the enemy.

36. They were liberal donors of jewels and the enjoyers of riches. O excellent sages, charming women were seen in that splendid land.

37. Their mode of walking was like that of the swan or the elephant;[1] their eyes extended upto the ears; the waists were slender and the buttocks exquisite, their breasts were plump and elevated.

38. Their tresses were glossy and beautiful. Their cheeks were fine and their forelocks steady. Their teeth were like the clearly visible lightning streaks. Their faces were like the full moon. They bent their necks in exhibiting their emotions with gesticulation and charming twists; their ears were adorned with ornaments.

39. Their lips were red like Bimba fruits. They shone with their mouths coloured by chewing betal leaves. They were bedecked in golden ornaments.

40. Some were dark-complexioned, some were fair-complexioned; they had fine buttocks, their girdles and armlets produced charming sounds. They wore divine garlands and garments; they applied divinc scents and unguents over their bodies.

41. The women were clever and competent. They were lovely with attractive faces and charming limbs. They were pleasing to look at. They were endowed with beauty and good colour and form. They had smiling faces.

42. Mad and intoxicated they sported about in assemblies and quadrangular court-yards. They delighted others by songs, instrumental music and spicy conversation.

43. The chiefs of harlots, experts in dancing and singing could also be found there. They were experts in the art of conversation, scanning and scrutiny. They were endued with feminine charms and fine qualities.

---

1. The mode of ladies' walking is often compared to that of a swan or an elephant. Elsewhere it is likened to the slow-moving autumnal clouds after they have shed water.

44. There were others too, the women of noble families endowed with noble traits, chaste, fortunate and embellished by all good qualities.

45-52. The city abounded in fruit-bearing trees and flowering plants, in charming parks, splendid groves and meritorious gardens. There were divine shrines and temples beautified by different sorts of flowers. The following were the important trees:— Śālas, Tālas, Tamālas, Bakulas, Nāgakesaras, Pippalas, Karṇikāras, sandal trees, Aguru, Campakas, Punnāgas, coconuts, jack fruit trees, Sarala trees, citron, Lakucas, Lodhras, Saptaparṇas, Śubhāñjanas, mangoes, Bilvas, Kadambas, Śiṁśapas, Dhavas, Khādiras, Pāṭalas, Aśokas, Tagaras, black Karavīras, yellow Arjunas, Bhallātas, Siddhas, Āmrātakas, Nyagrodhas, Aśvatthas, Kāśmaryas, Palāśas and Devadārus. There were Mandāras, Pārijātas, Tintiḍīkas, Vibhītakas, old embyllc myrobalam trees, Plakṣas, Jambū trees, Śirīṣa trees, Kāleyas, Kāñcanāra trees, Madhus, Jambīras, Tindukas, Kharjūras, Agastyas, Bakulas, Śākhoṭakas, Harītakas, Kaṅkolas, Mucukundas, Hintālas, Bījapūrakas, and other trees. There were Ketaki groves, Atimuktas and Kubjakas.

53-60. The gardens were adorned by Mallikās, Kundas, Bāṇas, stems of plantain trees, Mātuluṅgas, Pūgaphalas, Arece palms, Pink Sindhuvārakas, Bahuvāras, Kovidāras, Badaras, Karañjakas and many other charming trees in full bloom. There were creepers and bushes in the gardens comparable to their counterparts in the Nandana[1] garden. They were always full of fragrant flowers. They bent down due to the weight of fruits. The gardens were surrounded by many domestic and wild animals. The place was resonant with the diverse cries of birds. The chief birds were Cakoras, Śatapatras, Bhṛṅgāras, Priyaputrakas, Kalaviṅkas(Partridges) Peacocks, Parrots, Cuckoos, doves, Khañjarīṭas (Wagtails), herons, vultures and pigeons. There were many other sorts of charming birds that sang songs pleasing to the ears. There were rivers, lotus-ponds and lakes. There were other sacred water-reservoirs adorned by lilies as well as blue lotuses, white lotuses, fragrant Kalhāra flowers and other beautiful flowers growing in water. They had sweet divine fragrance. The plants put forth flowers and shone in all seasons.

1. *Nandana*: name of a celestial garden.

61-65. The lakes were rendered beautiful by swans, Kāraṇḍava ducks and ruddy geese. There were Sārasa birds, tortoises, fishes, crocodiles. There were web-footed swimming waterfowls. There were other birds flying in the sky and moving about in waters. The sky was sweetly resonant with the cries and songs of birds of variegated colours. The magnificent city was rendered beautiful by divine temples and shrines. There were many beautiful birds that swam in water or flew about over the land. In the different gardens there were many flowering trees. The three-eyed lord who slew the Tripuras is seated in that city.

66-70. The deity Śiva is known by the name Mahākāla. He bestows all cherished desires upon the devotee who should take holy dip in the sacred ditch Śivakuṇḍa which is destroyer of sins. The learned devotee should perform Tarpaṇa rites for Devas, Pitṛs and sages. He shall go to the shrine of Śiva and perform three circumambulations. Restraining his sense-organs and wearing washed and dried cloth he shall enter the sanctum sanctorum and worship the deity by offering flowers, sweet scents, incenses, lights, ablution, devoutly offered Naivedyas, musical instruments, songs, circumambulations, etc. He shall propitiate Śiva by obeisance, dances, and hymns of praise.

By worshipping Mahākāla, Śiva, even for once, but duly and devoutly, the man obtains the benefit of a thousand horse-sacrifices.

71. Rid of all his sins he will ride in an aerial chariot equipped with all desirable things and go to heaven where there is the abode of lord Śiva.

72. He will become glorious and assume a divine form. Bedecked in divine ornaments he will enjoy excellent pleasures until the dissolution of all living beings.

73-74. O excellent sages, he will be devoid of old age and death in the world of Śiva. When his merits begin to dwindle he is reborn here in an excellent brahmin family. He shall be a brahmin and master of all Vedas. He shall be an expert in all sacred lores. Thereafter, he shall attain Pāśupatayoga and attain salvation.

75-76. In that city, there is a holy river Kṣiprā. He who takes bath there and performs Tarpaṇa to the Pitṛs and deities shall be liberated from sins. Seated in an excellent aerial chariot he goes to the celestial world and enjoys pleasures of all sorts there.

77. Lord Viṣṇu the overlord of Devas is also stationed there itself. He is named Govindasvāmin. He yields worldly pleasures and salvation to the devotees.

78-79. By visiting that deity the devotee obtains liberation for himself and twentyone generations of his family. He goes to the world of Viṣṇu in an aerial chariot which has solar colour, clusters of tinkling bells, is richly endowed with desirable things and can go wherever it desires to go and which is very steady. The Gandharvas will sing in praise of him. He is honoured in the world of Viṣṇu.

80-85. Devoid of ailments he enjoys various pleasures until the dissolution of all living beings. He will be blessed with good features, good fortune and happiness. In due course of time, the intelligent devotee shall be re-born as a brahmin on the earth in the house of excellent Yogins. He shall be proficient in the Vedas and other scriptures. After adopting the Yoga of Viṣṇu, he will attain salvation, with no return to this earth.

O brahmins, there itself the man shall visit Viṣṇu named Vikramasvāmin. By visiting the lord, the devotee, whether it be a man or a woman, shall attain the benefits that are mentioned before.

There are other Devas too, viz. Indra and others led by him. O excellent sages, there are Mothers who bestow their cherished desires. By visiting them, and by duly and devoutly worshipping and bowing to them the man goes to heaven. Such is the city of great beauty protected by that lion of a monarch.

86-89. It was gay and joyous with perpetual festivities like the city of Amarāvatī[1] pertaining to Indra. It consisted of

1. *Amarāvatī*. The capital city of Indra. Its location is as follows: Brahmā's world extends over 10,000 Yojanas on Mahāmeru mountain. There are eight cities—each 2,500 square yojanas in extent—of the aṣṭadikpalas in parts of this Brahmāpurī:

(i) In the centre Brahmā's city—Manovatī;
(ii) To the east of Manovatī, Indra's city Amarāvatī;
(iii) In the south-east corner, Agni's city Tejovatī;
(iv) On the southern side, Yama's city, Saṁyaminī;
(v) In the south-west corner, Nirṛti's city Kṛṣṇāñjanā;

eighteen sectors or sub-divisions. The cross-roads were extensively wide and large.

The twanging sound of bowstrings echoed everywhere. It was adorned by the presence of Siddhas. The people consisted mostly of the learned groups; the loud chanting sound of the Vedas reverberated everywhere.

O brahmins, day and night the discourses on Itihāsas, Purāṇas and scriptures and the critical reviews of poems are heard. O Brahmins, thus, the city of Avanti of excellent virtues, has been cited by me. It was here that, formerly, Indradyumna of great intellect ruled as king.

CHAPTER FORTYTWO

The Holy centre sighted

Brahmā said:

1. Administering the excellent country formerly, from that city, that king of great intellect, protected his subjects like his own bosom-born sons.

2-7 He was highly intelligent and truthful in speech. He was heroic and a veritable repository of all virtues. He was learned and richly endowed with piety. He was the most excellent among all those who wielded weapons. Possessing good conduct, truthfulness and control over his sense-organs the glorious king conquered the cities of his enemies. In refulgence he was like the Sungod; in beauty he was like Aśvins,[1] he possessed their increasing good qualities, he had the valour of Indra; adorned by all traits he shone like the autumnal moon. He performed various sacrifices such as Horse Sacrifice and others.

(vi) In the west, Varuṇa's city Śraddhāvatī;
(vii) In the north-west corner, Vāyu's city Gandhavatī;
(viii) In the north, Kubera's city Mahodaya;
(ix) In the north-east corner, Śiva's city, Yaśovatī.
(See Devī Bhāgavata, 8th Skandha)

1. *Aśvins*—Aśvinīkumāras, Aśvinīdevas viz. Satya and Dasra. The two were the sons of Sūrya. They became physicians of Devas.

There was no other king equal to him in charitable gifts, sacrifices and austerities.

At every sacrifice, he gave the leading brahmins much wealth consisting of gold, jewels, pearls, elephants and horses. There was no limit to the wealth possessed by him such as elephants, horses and prominent chariots, blankets, deer-skins and garments, jewels, cash and food-grains.

8. Thus endowed with riches and adorned by good qualities the king administered the excellent kingdom with his mind assured of realizing all cherished desires.

9. Once he pondered over this, in mind—"How shall I propitiate Viṣṇu, the lord of all Yogas? How shall I propitiate lord who bestows worldly pleasures and salvation?"

10-12. He pondered over the scriptural texts, Tantra texts and extensive Āgamas. He poured over the Itihāsas, Purāṇas, the ancillaries of the Vedas, Dharmaśāstras, codes of law propounded by the sages, Vedāṅgas, Scriptural texts and all source-books of the extant lores. After assiduously resorting to his preceptors, the brahmins who had mastered the Vedas, he attained the highest point of learning and became fully contented.

13. After realising the greatest entity, the unchanging lord Vāsudeva, he passed beyond all illusory knowledge.[1] Restraining his sense-organs, he became a seeker of liberation.

14-16. He thought thus—"How shall I propitiate the eternal lord of Devas? He is yellow-robed. He has four arms. He holds a conch, a discus and an iron-club. His chest is covered with garlands of Sylvan flowers. His eyes are large like the petals of a lotus. He has the scar Śrīvatsa in his chest. He appears splendid with crown, shoulderlets and other ornaments.

Having thought thus, the king set-off from his city Ujjayini, accompanied by a large army, his priest and his servants.

17. The Charioteer-soldiers followed him in chariots resembling aerial vehicles. They were decorated with flag-staffs and fanners. The soldiers carried weapons in their arms.

---

1. *bhrānti-jñāna*—illusory knowledge, such as the knowledge of "snake in rope or of silver in a shell". This is known as the prātibhāsika jñāna.

18. The cavalry men followed the king with horses on a par with the wind. They carried javelins and iron clubs.

19-20. The (brave warriors) experts in wars of conquests followed him with Himālaya-born elephants in their rut. These elephants were comparable to mountains. They had trunks like the poleshafts. They were fierce and intoxicated, of sixty years in age. Their Howdabs were golden. They were adorned with flags and ringing bells.

21-22. Innumerable infantry-men followed him. They had bows, javelins and swords. They wore divine garlands and garments. They had applied divine scents and unguents (over their bodies). They were young and they wore earings of finished gold. They were mighty heroes, experts in all weapons and missiles and eager to fight.

23-26. The women of the harem followed him. They were bedecked, richly endowed with beauty and blooming youth. They were embellished by all ornaments. They wore divine garments and were bedecked in divine garlands. They had smeared their limbs with divine scents and unguents. Their faces resembled the autumnal moon. Their waists were fine and their dress, exquisitely beautiful. Their ears were beautified by the forelocks. Their lips resembled the Bimba fruits. They had fine teeth and their eyes were large like the petals of the lotus. Their mouths were coloured by the betal leaves they had chewed. They were protected by watchmen and guards. They went ahead in high and low vehicles that were splendid and bedecked in jewels and gold. The birds sang songs in their praise. They were surrounded by men armed with weapons.

27-33. Many courtesans and harlots followed him along with their attendants. They were beautiful in every limb and they were bedecked in all ornaments. They were loving, fortunate and beautiful. They were endowed with feminine charms. Bedecked in all sorts of ornaments they rode in various vehicles and followed him. He was accompanied by brahmins who were conversant with the Vedas and their ancillaries[1] and who were

1. *Vedāṅgas*—ancillaries. They are six in number:

(i) *Śikṣā*—Science of proper articulation and pronunciation.

(ii) *Chandas*—Metre;

masters of topics in different scriptures. So also the Kṣatriyas, Vaiśyas, Śūdras of eight subcastes accompanied him. The goldsmiths, blacksmiths metal-workers, breakers of stones, jewellers, potters, cobblers, cooks, small vendors, cane-makers, artisans working on lids, barbers, those who make gourd-like supports of lutes, those who make and mend arrows, those who work in gold, sword-makers, those who prepare oblations, those who repair vehicles, those who make sweet pies, those who sell (drinking) water, garland-makers, those who make joints, those who sell all sorts of things, groups of village merchants and residents of different towns, followed him with their riches, jewels, gold, folk women and attendants.

34. There were people who sold missiles, those who sustained themselves by trading in betal leaves, the sellers of grass, the sellers of fuel.

35. All those who sustained themselves by the stage, those who sold meat, oil-mongers and cloth merchants followed him.

36. Sellers of fruits, those who sold leaves, those who transported grass and fodder and thousands of washermen (followed him).

37. There were cowherds, barbers, tailors, shepherds, goatherds and those who tended deer and swans.

38. There were people who sold foodgrains, powdered fried grains, gaggery and salt.

39. There were musicians, dancers, bards, actors, story-tellers and those who are experts in Purāṇas.

40. There were poets, versifiers, composers of poems, experts in different poems, followers of Garuḍa who dispel poison and those who test different jewels.

41. There were blacksmiths, coppersmiths, those who work in bellmetal, Rūṭhakas?, those who make scabbards, painters, turners and Pāvakas.

42. There were makers of sticks and batons, those who make swords, those who maintain by selling ale or gambling;

(iii) *Vyākaraṇa*—Grammar;

(iv) *Nirukta*—Etymology;

(v) *Jyotiṣa*—Astronomy and Astrology;

(vi) *Kalpa*—Ceremonial represented by Sūtra works.

wrestlers, messengers, Kāyasthas (accountants and clerks) and other workers.

43-44. There were physicians and surgeons on human beings, elephants, trees and cows and those who cut and burn; there were weavers, there were those who painted, those who made wicks and oil paintings, those who maintained by selling quails, partridges and other birds and animals.

45. All these citizens and those who have not yet been mentioned followed him. The entire residents of the city followed him too.

46. Just as the sons eager to see other villages follow their father who proceeds ahead so also those citizens followed him.

47. Thus the glorious king surrounded by a great concourse of people as well as (the four divisions of the army viz the elephants, horses, chariots and infantry, proceeded slowly.

48. Going ahead thus, followed by the armies the king reached the shore of the Southern sea after a long time.

49-58. There the king saw the ocean and was struck with wonder. It was beautiful and it appeared to be dancing in front of him; it was confused and agitated on account of hundreds and thousands of waves; it was filled with many living organisms and it was the abode of many jewels, it contained many waves and billows; it was full of miracles, it was the king of sacred waters, very noisy and extremely terrible, it had no other shore; it was the deep abode of crocodiles, it resembled groups of clouds;

It was full of fishes, tortoises, conches, oyster shell, crocodiles, skate fishes, porpoises, crabs and serpents of great poison.

The briny sea, the bed-chamber of Viṣṇu, is the lord of rivers, it is holy and it dispels all sins, it is the bestower of all cherished desire; it is majestic due to many whirlpools, it is the place of resort for the Dānavas, it is the divine charming wood-stick of nectar (i.e. the source of origin for nectar); it is the lord of waters of divine source of origin, it is the most distinguished supporter of the life of all living beings; it is the most sacred of all sacred objects and most auspicious of all auspicious things; it is the most sacred of all holy waters; it is the most unchanging lord of oceanic creatures, it cannot be pierced or split by any living being, it is the source of the nectar of Devas, it is the cause of origin, sustenance and annihilation; it is eternal. It is the basis of subsistence for all. It is the holy lord of rivers.

59. After reaching the sea-shore the king encamped there in a beautiful holy land endowed with the qualities of a good land.

60-68. The place was full of Śāla, Kadamba, Punnāga, Sarala, Jack coconut, Bakula, Nāgakesara, Kharjūra, Pippala, Tāla, citron, pomegranate, Amrātaka. Lodhra, Bakula, Bahuvāra, Kapittha, Karṇikāra, Pāṭala, Aśoka, Campaka, Dāḍima, Tamāla, Pārijāta, Arjuna, Prācīnāmalaka, Bilva, Priyaṅgu, Vaṭa, Khadira, Iṅgudi, Saptaparṇa, Aśvattha, Agastya, Jambuka, Madhuka, Karṇikāra, Bahuvāra, Tinduka, Palāśabadara, Nīpa, Siddhanimba, Śubhāñjana, Vāraka, Kovidāra, Bhallāta, Āmalaka Tāla, Hintāla, Kāṅkola, Karañja, Vibhītaka. Sarja, Madhu, Kaśmari, Śālmali, Devadāru, Śākhoṭaka, Nimbavaṭa, Kumbhi, Koṣṭha, Harītaka, Guggula, sandal, Aguru, Pāṭala, Jambīra, Karuṇa, tamarind, red sandal and many other trees resembling the trees of Kalpa. The trees bore flowers and fruits during all seasons.

69-71. It was resonant with the chirping sounds and divine cooings of different birds such as cuckoos, peacocks, parrots, sparrows, Hārītas, royal bees, Cātakas, Bahuputrakas, Jīvañjīvakas, Kākolas, partridges, doves, and other kinds of birds charming in appearance and sweet in voice. They were beautifully perched on the trees in full bloom and they were chirping.

72-74. There were many flowering plants such as Ketaki, the perpetually white flowers of Mallikā, Kunda, Yūthikā, Tagara, Kuṭaja, Bāṇa, Atimukta, Kubja, Mālatī, Karavīra, golden Kadalīs and various other fragrant flowers beautiful to look at. These flowers of various colours abounded in forests, parks and gardens. They were sweet-smelling.

75-84. The place was frequented by Vidyādharas, Siddhas, Cāraṇas, Gandharvas, Serpents, Rākṣasas, goblins, Kinnaras, sages, Yakṣas and various animals too. There were deer, monkeys, lions, boars, and buffaloes. There were antelopes and other animals wandering everywhere. There were tigers, elephants and wild animals too. Thus the place was full of trees, gardens and parks comparable to the Nandana park; there were creepers, hedges, bushes and different sorts of water reservoirs. There were birds such as swans, Kāraṇḍavas, Cakravākas, floating geese and the Kadambas decorated by clusters of lotuses, lilies, Kalhāra flowers etc; there were other flowers too growing in water; there were mountains with bright peaks and charming caves. They abounded in different sorts of birds and various minerals. The peaks were full of wondrous miracles; they were auspicious abodes of all living beings; they contained all medicinal herbs and the ridges were vast and variegated.

Thus, the king saw the place beautified collectively by all these beautiful things. It was a place worshipped by the three worlds. It was ten Yojanas in length and five Yojanas in width. The holy centre was endowed with all mysteries. It was extremely rare.

CHAPTER FORTYTHREE

A Review of Past Incidents

The sages said:

1-2. O Lord, was there no idol of Viṣṇu in the excellent holy centre pertaining to Viṣṇu, formerly ? Wherefore did that king go there with his army and vehicles, and established Kṛṣṇa, Rāma and Subhadrā, the bestower of auspicious things.

3. O lord of the universe, great indeed is our doubt in this matter and so also is our wonder. We wish to hear everything in detail. Tell us the reason thereof.

Brahmā said :

4. Listen you all. I shall succinctly mention the story of some past incidents. It is a story that destroys sins : Formerly, Lord Viṣṇu was asked by Lakṣmī.

5. On the wonder-inspiring golden peak of Sumeru, the lotus-born goddess bowed to the unchanging creator of all worlds, named Vāsudeva.

6-17. The peak of Meru is always rendered splendid by the presence of Siddhas, Vidyādharas, Yakṣas and Kinnaras, Devas,

Dānavas, Gandharvas, Nāgas, Apsarās, sages, Guhyakas, Siddhas, Sauparṇas, Maruts and other people residing in the abode of Devas, Sādhyas, and Patriarchs viz. Kaśyapa and others. It was made charming by the presence of Bālakhilyas[1] and others.

The peak of the Meru mountain was adorned by the glowing Karṇikāra groves which abounded in flowers of all seasons that resembled gold and which shone in brilliance like the sun.

There were many other trees such as Śāla, Tāla, Punnāga, Aśoka, Sarala, Nyagrodha, Āmrātaka, Arjuna, Pārijāta, Āmra, Khadira, Nīpa, Bilva, Kadambaka, Dhava, Khādira, Pālāśa, Śīrṣāmalaka, Tinduka, Nāriṅga, Kola, Bakula, Lodhra, Dāḍima, Sarja, Tagara, Karṇa, Śiśi, Bhūrjava and Nimba trees; there were other trees golden in colour and bent under the weight of fruits. The peak of Meru was rendered splendid by Devas and adorned by many plants endowed with fragrant flowers. They were Mālatī, Yūthikā, Malli, Kunda, Bāṇa, Kuruṇṭaka, Karavīra, Ketaki, Kubja, Kiṁśuka, Pāṭala, Agastya, Kuṭaja and Mandāra flowering plants. There were other flowers too that yielded pleasure to the mind.

The peak was rendered beautiful by many flights and flocks of different birds that chirped sweetly. It was rendered resonant by the sweet cooings of cuckoo and the excited crowings of peacocks in an intoxicated state. Thus the peak was rendered resonant and beautiful by different birds, trees and flowers. It was frequented by Devas. The unchanging lord of the universe, the creator of the universe, the maker of the worlds stationed himself there. The lotusborn goddess lowered her head in his presence with a desire for the welfare of the world and put this great question to that excellent lord.

Śri said :

18-20. Tell me, O lord of worlds, there is a great doubt lurking in my mind. The world of mortals is the land of holy

1. *Bālakhilyas* or *Vālakhilyas*—Sixty thousand hermits born to Kratu, a hermit, by his wife Santati. Everyone of them was of the size of half a thumb, but they were as bright as the blazing sun and had attained control over their senses.

rites. It is extremely inaccessible and excessively surprising; it is a great ocean of lust and fury where people are seized by the crocodiles of greed and delusion. O lord of Devas, if you consider me who have bowed down, as worthy of being blessed tell me how a devotee is liberated from this ocean of worldly existence. Excepting you, there is none else in the world who can clarify this doubt decisively.

21. On hearing those words of his consort, Viṣṇu the lord of Devas spoke with pleasure. What he said was nectarlike. It was the great essence.

The lord said :

22. O gentle lady, the well known deity Viṣṇu is stationed in the excellent holy centre. The deity is fascinating. The lord awards excellent benefits. He can be easily worshipped and propitiated.

23. There is no other God in the three worlds, on a par with him. By glorifying this lord one is liberated from all sins.

24-25. This leading holy centre has not been perfectly understood by the immortal beings, Daityas, and Dānavas. O fair-faced lady, this has been kept as a secret by me even from excellent sages Marīci and others. But I shall recount to you the leading holy centre. O fair-complexioned lady of fine buttocks, listen to it with a single-minded attention and emotional fervour.

26-27. (When the previous Kalpa comes to a close and the new) Kalpa[1] is about to begin, when the mobile and immobile beings have perished when Devas, Gandharvas, Daityas, Vidyādharas and Nāgas have been dissolved, everything was enveloped in darkness. Nothing could be seen or known. In that darkness the soul of the living beings, the Supreme Being, the preceptor of the universe is alone kept awake.

28. He is the lord and cause of Lord Śiva the three deities, viz. Brahmā the creator of the Universe, and Viṣṇu. The great lord of Yogic soul is known as Vāsudeva.

29. At the conclusion of his Yogic slumber he created

1. *Kalpa*—a period of one thousand yugas or fourteen Manvantaras.

Brahmā and unchanging being. He was in the midst of his umbilical lotus resembling the filament of the lotus.

30-36. Brahmā, lord of the world, who originated in that manner, slowly created the world constituted of five great elements. The gross elements that had their natural cause in the subtle elements were created by him. He created the mobile and immobile beings of four types viz. the oviparous, the viviparous, the sweat-formed (worms etc.) and the vegetables and trees that pierce the ground and grow. Brahmā, the patriarch, pondered over the Ātman in his mind and created the universe of mobile and immobile beings. He created different subjects. He created Marīci and other sages, Gandharvas, Nāgas, Rākṣasas, the fourteen worlds of seven heavens and the netherworlds. He created continents, oceans, Gaṅgā and other rivers. He created Yakṣas, Vidyādharas, monkeys, lions and different sorts of birds. He created people of four castes viz. Brahmins, Kṣatriyas, Vaiśyas and Śūdras. He created alien tribes and last-born (outcastes) severally. He created the entire universe of mobile and immobile beings—whatever that can be termed as living being viz. the grass, the bushy hedge and ants.

37. After thinking, he created a manly being from his right side. He created a woman from his left. He created human beings from his two parts.

38-43. Since then, the subjects are being procreated by sexual intercourse.

After thinking deeply and creating diverse forms of living beings whether of low, middle or higher order and all of my shrines, the lotus-born deity meditated upon the physical form of Vāsudeva. Immediately after being meditated upon by that lord Vāsudeva revealed himself as the glorious being with thousand eyes, thousand legs and thousand heads. His eyes resembled the lotus. His body was dark-coloured like the rain-bearing cloud. The scar Śrīvatsa was his characteristic sign. Brahmā, the grandfather of the worlds saw him, all on a sudden. After offering seats, Arghya, Pādya etc without any omission, Brahmā eulogised him with concentration, by means of high class hymns of prayer.

Thereafter, I spoke thus to Brahmā the lotus-born lord:—

"O dear one, tell me the reason why I have been meditated upon, now".

Brahmā said :

44-46. O lord of the universe, tell me about the most excellent abode on the earth, greater than all other abodes and shrines. O lord of Devas, sacrifices, charitable gifts and holy rites are pathways leading to the portals of heaven. Similarly, Yogic practice, truthfulness, penance, faith and holy pilgrimages to the various holy centres are also the causes of heavenly pleasures. But they are difficult of access to ordinary mortals. For the welfare of the Universe, tell me the easiest means for some other centres than those mentioned above.

47-49. O beloved one, on hearing the words of Brahmā I said thus,—"Listen, O Brahmā, I shall mention the rarest of holy centres on the Earth. It is devoid of impurities. It is the most excellent of all holy centres. It is the blessed shrine that enables one to cross the ocean of worldly existence. It is conducive to the welfare of cows and brahmins. It is meritorious. It is conducive to the rise of happiness of all the members of four castes. The holy centre is extremely splendid and it yields worldly pleasures and salvation unto men. O great grandfather to all those who reside there, it is extremely meritorious.

50-52. The eternal lord of holy centres originated from Him. The great and well known holy centre is resorted to in the four Yugas. The lord is the most excellent being among all Devas, sages, religious students, Daityas, Dānavas, Siddhas, Gandharvas, Nāgas, Rākṣasas, and Vidyādharas, nay of all mobile and immobile beings. Hence, it is called the best of all.

53. On the shore of the Southern ocean a place extending to ten Yojanas all round the place where there stands a holy big tree, is the rarest of all holy centres.

54. This holy fig tree does not perish when the Kalpa comes to a close and the dissolution of all the worlds starts. It remains there as before.

55. Even the sin of brahmin slaughter is dispelled merely when the holy fig tree is seen and its shadow falls on one. What doubt then in the case of other sins ?

56. All those creatures who circumambulate and make obeisance, shake off their sins and go to the abode of lord Viṣṇu.

57-58. To the north of the holy fig tree and to the south of the abode of lord Viṣṇu is a palace. It is a pious and victorious spot. The devotee should stop there. Men who visit my idol there made by the lord himself go to my world without any strain.

59. O my beloved, on seeing men (and women devotees) going thus, (God of death) came near me once, bowed to me with the bent head, and said thus:—

Yama said:

60-68. O lord, O lord of worlds, O lord of the universe, I am bowing down to the lord with all these characteristics. He stays in the milk ocean. He lies on the body of Śeṣa.[1] He is the most excellent bestower of boons. He is the lord and creator and is not created by anyone. He is the maker of all worlds. He is conducive to the happiness of all. He is the ancient Puruṣa. He is worthy of being known. He is the eternal lord manifest and unmanifest. He is the creator of the greater and lesser beings. He is the lord of worlds. He is the preceptor of the universe. There is the scar Śrīvatsa[2] on his chest. He is adorned by the garlands and sylvan flowers. He is clad in yellow robes. He has four arms in which he holds conch, discus, mace etc. He is bedecked in necklaces, shoulderlets, crown and armlets. He is fully endowed with all characteristic marks. He is devoid of all sense-organs. He stands motionless like the steady peak of a mountain. He is subtle and eternal in the form of luminary.

1. *Śeṣa*—Ādiśeṣa, Chief of the Nāgas, is the reposing bed of Viṣṇu. But he is also represented as supporting the earth at the behest of Brahmā. According to a myth, Balabhadra Rāma, the elder brother of Śrīkṛṣṇa was born from a portion of Śeṣa.

2. *Śrīvatsa*—Once sage Bhṛgu went to the abode of Mahāviṣṇu. There he saw Mahāviṣṇu in deep slumber. Seeing Mahāviṣṇu whose task is to preserve the world, sleeping like the irresponsible person, Bhṛgu gave him a kick on his breast. Viṣṇu sprang up suddenly, saw Bhṛgu standing before him. He begged pardon of the sage. He declared that he would carry Bhṛgu's footprint permanently on his chest as a sign of his repentence for having shown disrespect to him. This footprint still remains on Viṣṇu's chest and is known as Śrīvatsa.

He is devoid of both positive and negative aspects. He pervades (everything). He is greater than Prakṛti. I bow unto that lord of the universe, the lord who bestows happiness".

In this manner, Lord Yama eulogised me formerly by the side of that holy fig tree by raciting different hymns and made obeisance.

69. O highly blessed lady, on seeing him standing outside with palms joined in reverence, I asked the (God of Death) about the purpose for which I had been eulogised.

70. O Vaivasvata of long brawny arms, indeed, you are the most excellent of all Devas. Why did you eulogise me ? Tell me all in brief.

Yama said :

71. In this meritorious shrine known as Puruṣottama, there is an excellent idol made of sapphire. It bestows all cherished desires.

72. O lotus-eyed lord, by visiting it with emotional fervour and faith, even men devoid of desires go to the abode called Śveta.[1]

73. Hence, O slayer of enemies I am not able to carry on my activities. O great lord, be pleased. O lord, withdraw the idol.

74. On hearing the words of Yama I spoke to him : O Yama, I shall conceal it with sands all round.

75-76. Then, O gentle lady, that idol was concealed by me under the heap of Earth and creeping plants, so that men who seek for heavenly pleasures could not see it. O gentle lady, after covering it up with creeping plants with golden coverings and appendages, I sent Yama to his own city[2] in the South.

Brahmā said :

77-78. Every event that happened there, O brahmins, in

1. *Śveta* or *Śvetadvīpa*—Colonel Wilford identifies it with Britain—J. Dowson. Hindu Mythology and Religion p. 315.

2. The city of Yama is named *Saṁyaminī*.

that holy excellent shrine Puruṣottama, Janārdana, the lord of Devas, related fully to his splendid consort.

79-89. The lord mentioned everything immediately to her: viz. Indradyumna's departure to that place, vision and description of the holy centre, building of the palace, performance of horse-sacrifice, dream, sight of a log of wood on the shore of the briny sea; vision of Vāsudeva, the king of sculptors, O brahmins, the making of the idol with due colours in particular, the installation of idols in the palace that was most excellent in the world. O leading brahmins, glorification of Kalpa at the time of pilgrimage, episode of Mārkaṇḍeya, installation of Śaṅkara, glory of five holy centres, vision of the trident-bearing lord, that of the holy fig tree, O brahmins, and its prosperous consequence, the vision of Baladeva, Kṛṣṇa, in particular and Subhadrā there itself. Vision of Narasiṁha and the glorification of its prosperity, vision of infinite Vāsudeva, glorification of the merit, greatness of Śvetamādhava, vision of heavenly portals, vision of wide ocean, the holy dip therein, the performance of Tarpaṇa rite, O brahmins, the efficacy of holy dip in the ocean by Indradyumna, benefit of five holy centres, Mahājyeṣṭha, abodes of Kṛṣṇa and Balarāma, the benefit of entire pilgrimage, description of the world of Viṣṇu and of holy centre once again.

The great lord mentioned all these to the Goddess.

CHAPTER FORTYFOUR

Description of the Holy Centre

The sages said :

1. O lord, we wish to hear the rest of the story of the king. After going to that excellent holy centre what did the lord of men do?

Brahmā said :

2. Listen, O leading sages, I shall mention briefly the vision of the holy centre that the king had and his activities thereafter.

3. After going to the holy centre well-known to the three worlds the king saw the beautiful (surrounding) regions and the rivers.

4. There is a sacred river there which takes its source from the foothills of the Vindhya Forest. It is a splendid river that dispels sins and it is known as Vindhyāpagā.

5. This river of great current is on par with Gaṅgā. It falls into the southern ocean. That excellent river of meritorious waters is known as Mahānadī.[1]

6. She is the beloved wife of the southern ocean. Her beauty is enhanced by hundreds of tributaries. There are villages and cities on either of its banks.

7. O leading sages, these villages are full of well grown plants. They are very charming and thronged by delighted and well nourished people. They are finely dressed and bedecked in ornaments.

8. The Brahmins, Kṣatriyas, Vaiśyas and Śūdras are found there engaged in their duties. They are splendid in their traits and very peaceful.

9-10 Their mouths are filled with betal leaves. They are bedecked in garlands and necklaces. The Vedic mantras fill the mouths of the brahmins. They have learnt the Vedic Mantras along with the six ancillary subjects. They have learnt the Vedic mantras by heart in their Padapāṭha and Krama Pāṭha. Some of them are engaged in Agnihotra and some in the holy rites of Aupāsana. They are experts in the scriptural topics. They perform sacrifices distributing wealth by way of Dakṣiṇās.

11-12. In the quadrangles, the royal highways, gardens, parks, assemblies, mansions and temples of the deities, the following are heard by the common people viz. the mythological traditions, Itihāsas and Purāṇas, the Vedic Mantras with their ancillaries and the characteristically good discourses on poetry and scripture.

13-19. The ladies who resided in that land were justifiably proud of their beauty and blooming youth. They were fully

1. *Mahānadī*—a river celebrated in the Purāṇas and flowing through the region of Utkala (Orissa).

endowed with all characteristic marks. Their buttocks were ample. They were dark-complexioned but their faces resembled lotuses or the autumnal moon. They had plump and elevated breasts. Being prosperous they were beautiful to look at. They wore golden bangles and they were richly adorned by lustrous robes. They were as soft to the touch as the interior of the plantain tree. They had the lustre of the pollen dust of lotus flowers. They were lovely with the lower lips resembling the Bimba fruit and the eyes extending upto their ears. Their faces were beautiful and their tresses lovely. They were bent under the weight of necklaces. Their eyes resembled the petals of red or blue lotus. Other slender-bodied ladies had their teeth sparkling like the streaks of lightning. Their forelocks were curly. They shone with their hairs partitioned on upper side. Their necks were made beautiful due to the various ornaments. They were bedecked in garlands and necklaces. With their earings studded with jewels and the beautiful Karṇapūras (ear-ornaments) they were seen resembling the celestial women. They had splendid traits.

20-22. These excellent ladies dallied with highly blessed bride-grooms singing divine songs. They sported about with various musical instruments such as lutes, flutes, Mṛdaṅga, drums and other types of drums like the Paṇavas, Gomukhas and Dundubhis. The conches too produced sweet sounds. Sporting about with sweet musical instruments these elegant ladies delighted one another. Expertly playing in these musical instruments and singing sweetly, these excellent ladies were gay and jolly, mad and passionate, by day and night.

23. The whole of that holy centre was frequented by mendicants, recluses, Siddhas, householders, religious students, those who had mastered Mantras, those who had realised self by practising austerities and those who had become Siddhas by means of performing sacrifices.

24-25. The king, thus saw the rarest of holy centres. He thought—Here itself I shall propitiate the eternal lord Viṣṇu, the great lord, the preceptor of the universe, the sole redeemer, the supreme saviour, the infinite lord of chiefs of all, the unvanquished lord.

26-30. This is now known to me as the mental Tīrtha Puruṣottama. It is the place where the huge holy fig tree stands like the Kalpa tree. The idol having the lustre of sapphire has been hidden by the lord himself. There is no other splendid idol of Viṣṇu seen anywhere. I shall endeavour to make Viṣṇu the lord of the universe of truthful exploit visible to the eye. I shall duly observe excellent holy rites by performing sacrifices, charitable gifts, austerities, meditations, worships and observances of fasts. With the mind not resting on any other topic, with the mind dwelling on him and not thinking of anyone else, I shall begin the preliminary activities for the construction of Viṣṇu's abode.

CHAPTER FORTYFIVE

Horse-Sacrifice

Brahmā said:

1. O excellent brahmins, after thinking like this the king made the preliminary arrangements for the propitiation of Viṣṇu.

2-6. He called for experts in astronomical calculations and the masters of astrology. He got a spot of land sanctified. With great assiduity and joy he consulted the wise brahmins who had mastered the Vedas and scriptures, the ministers, counsellors and those who were experts in the science of architecture. On an auspicious day, at an auspicious hour when the combination of the moon and the constellation was good and when there was favourable beneficial influence of planets the king offered libation with faith and concentrated mind. There were shouts of victories. Auspicious sounds were raised by charming musical instruments, the chanting sounds of the Vedic Mantras and sweet vocal songs. Flowers, fried

1. *Kalpa-vṛkṣa*—a tree in paradise. It gives any object which a person desires to get.

grains and raw rice grains (were scattered). Sweet scents were offered. People accompanied him with sacred lamps and pots filled with water.

7. After duly offering libation, the king Indradyumna called the heroic rulers of Kaliṅga, Utkala and Kosala and said:

The king said :

8-9. With great concentration you go together for the collection of rocks and slabs. Take with you chiefs of sculptors and artisans expert in rocks to the extensive Vindhya Mountains splendid with many caves and caverns. Examine the ridges and peaks and get the splendid rocks chopped off. Let them be brought here on carts. Do not delay".

10. After commanding them to proceed, Indradyumna spoke to the ministers and priests.

The king said :

11-12. Let messengers go in haste, to each and every corner of the earth where there are kings and let them proclaim my order, "At the behest of Indradyumna may the kings start together with their priests, ministers and four divisions of the army, viz. elephants, horses, chariots and foot-soldiers.

Brahmā said :

13. Thus the messengers who were commanded by the noble king went to different kings and proclaimed the words of that monarch to them.

14. On hearing the words of messengers the kings came there in a hurry accompanied by their armies.

15-17. Those who had been staying in the eastern, southern, western and northern quarters, those who lived at the outskirts and border lands, the residents of the adjacent territories, the dwellers of the mountain regions and the inhabitants of all islands came there. O brahmins, on hearing the command of Indradyumna, they came with their chariots, elephants, infantry and cavalry in elaborate and extensive array.

18. On observing that the various kings had arrived with their ministers and priests, the delighted king announced the weighty task on hand.

The king said :

19-21. Listen, O leading kings, to what I am going to say. My mind is worried as to how I shall be able to perform the great Horse Sacrifice in this auspicious and excellent holy centre that yields worldly pleasures and salvation and to build a palace pertaining to Viṣṇu. O excellent kings, if you all assist me I shall carry out these things with collaboration and co-operation of all of you.

Brahmā said :

22-33. When the intelligent king of kings announced this, they were delighted. At his behest they offered the requisite things in cash and kind. They showered coins and jewels, gold pieces and pearls. They presented blankets, deerskins, auspicious antelope skin coverings, diamonds, lapis lazulis, rubies, emeralds and saphires. They supplied elephants, horses and the chariots. Innumerable materials of worship and articles of utility high and low, were supplied by them in plenty. Hundreds of jars and vessels were filled with rice grains, barleys, pulses of various kinds, gingely seeds, mustard seeds, Bengal grams, wheat, Masoor dals, rice of various kinds such as Śyāmāka, Nīvāra, Madhūka and horse gram. Other grains and foodstuffs grown in villages or forests and heaps of rice were supplied by them. Hundreds and thousands of jars were filled with ghee and various foodstuffs and unguents and whatever was needed for the holy rites. On seeing that every thing necessary for the sacrifice had been gathered, the brahmins conversant with the rules of holy rites assembled. On seeing the brahmins who had mastered the Vedas and Vedāṅgas and who were experts in the scriptural texts and the performance of holy rites, the sages, great sages, celestial sages and ascetics, religious students, householders, forest dwellers and recluses, the newly initiated brahmins and others strictly adhering to the performance of Agnihotras, preceptors, venerable teachers and others who regularly recited the Vedic passages and performed penance, and many other holy personages who were present as members of the assembly watching the proceedings—on seeing all these the glorious king spoke to his preceptor.

The king said :

34. Let learned brahmins who have mastered the Vedas go about and find out a place worthy of being used for successfully concluding the horse-sacrifice.

Brahmā said :

35-37. Thus ordered, the royal priest carried out the behest of the king. He gladly accompanied the ministers, architects and carpenters. Keeping the brahmins who were experts in the holy rites of sacrifice in front, the intelligent brahmin (the priest) converted the Fishermen's village into sacrificial chamber with lofty pinnacles and bylanes.

38. (All round the sacrificial chamber) hundreds of palaces were built. They were beautiful and they resembled the abode of Indra. They were bedecked in gold and jewels. Excellent gems enhanced their beauty.

39-40. The columns were wonderfully built of gold. There were many big ornamental gateways in and near the surroundings of the shrine of sacrifice. Solid and pure gold was used for them. The righteous king erected harems for the kings who had come from different lands.

41. He got constructed many comfortable houses and residences for the Brahmins and Vaiśyas who had come there from different lands.

42. Due to their love and affection for that king (Indradyumna), the excellent kings and their womenfolk assembled there during the festivities, bringing with them precious stones and jewels (as presents).

43. As those noble persons enjoyed themselves in their respective camps; their sound reached heaven like that of the rumbling sea.

44. O excellent sages, the king gave specific orders that food, beverages and items of bedding should be duly supplied to the visitors.

45. Delicious foodstuffs of various kinds prepared with rice, sugarcane, barley milk and milk products were served to guests. The excellent king himself approached them and ordered for the immediate supply of things they wanted.

46-49. There were many expounders of Brahman in that sacrifice. Noble and excellent brahmins came there accompanied by their disciples. The king greeted them all lovingly. He followed them to their camps. Eschewing all arrogance, the king of great splendour (did everything to their honour). The artisans and sculptors finished their work in regard to the holy altar of sacrifice and informed the king. On hearing that everything was complete the alertful unerring king experienced a joyful horripilation alongwith his ministers.

Brahmā said :

50-57. When the sacrifice began to function eloquent expounders of syllogisms discussed the causes and arguments, desirous of defeating one another.

O brahmins, everything was arranged for the guests by the lion among kings in a manner befitting even the lord of Devas. The ornamental gateways were made of gold. The various items of bedstead and seats were studded with jewels. There were chambers of crystal and pots and dishes of peculiar shape and workmanship. The king did not find any of these pots not made of gold. But the sacrificial pots were made of wood because it had been prescribed in the scriptures. Of course they were embellished with gold. O brahmins, the animals of the land and water were duly offered at the proper time. The kings saw the animals of excessive splendour present there. He saw cows, buffaloes and old ladies too. There were aquatic animals, birds and beasts of prey. There were oviparous, viviparous, sweat-born and vegetation. They also saw the mountainous people and the subsidiary grains. Thus every body was gay and jolly, due to the presence of milk animals and food-grains.

58-65. On seeing the sacrificial chamber the visiting kings were struck with wonder. Much of sweet and cooked rice was distributed among the brahmins and the vaiśyas. While a full hundred thousand brahmins were taking food there, the Dundubhi (drum) produced loud sound frequently like the rumbling sounds of the cloud. At the close of every day it was sounded many times. Thus the royal horse sacrifice increased and flourished. O brahmins, the surplus quantities of the cooked rice were scattered about. There were canals of curds and eddies of milk. The entire population of Jambūdvīpa was present there along with the people of other islands. Brahmins were seen in large numbers in that great sacrifice. O excellent brahmins, thousands of men wearing ear-rings of finished gold took the vessels with them and served the brahmins, and announced what they were serving. Other men who followed served beverages. The people gave the brahmins those of cooked food usually enjoyed by the monarch.

66-67. The king honoured the brahmins who were conversant with the Vedas and the kings, lords of the earth, who had come there as visitors. He distributed wealth by way of gifts. He welcomed kings who were great fighters in battles and who had come there from different quarters. He welcomed the actors, dancers and others who were experts in music and dance.

68-74. The king had a thousand one hundred charming wives who had plump and elevated breasts. Their eyes resembled the petals of blue lotus. Their faces resembled the autumnal moon. They were of noble birth and endowed with qualities. The beauty of the sacrificial chamber was enhanced by his excellent wives who wore garlands studded with jewels. They had necklaces of precious stones that spread the divine lustre of the moon. The chamber was beautified by flagstaffs and banners. The elephants were drenched in ichor and were pleasing to look at. They were huge, like mountains. Hundreds and crores of tuskers bedecked in ornaments beautified the sacrificial hall. The crores of excellent horses beautified the holy place. They had the velocity of the wind. They were of excellent breed hailing from the Sindhu region. They were white in colour with dark coloured ears. There were innumerable foot soldiers. They were ready to face all eventualities with different weapons lifted up. They were comparable to the sons of Devas. The king surveyed the entire sacrificial chamber (and the surroundings). He derived joy. The delighted king spoke thus.

The king said :

75-77. O Princes of good restraint, bring you, the excellent horse marked with auspicious traits. Take it all over the Earth. May the sacrifice be performed here by the learned conversant with holy rites and piety. May there be brought elephants sixty years old, black antelope, birds, bulls and cows along with the persons who tend them.

78-82. After bringing various objects along with gold plattus the king gave them to the brahmins in accordance with the injunctions and in great faith. The lord duly presented the kings residing in different lands with cash, elephants, horses, good garments and lands. He propitiated the brahmins with different sorts of jewels along with foodstuffs and edibles. He delighted the poor and the helpless persons by giving them various things they desired. The excellent king attaining gifts of their choice returned to their respective native lands.

He delighted his own family including house servants both male and female by giving them whatever they desired. Thus, the king felt contented due to the successful performance of horse-sacrifice. He felt he was blessed.

Extra verses Between verses 77 *and* 78

[May the sacrifices function and may the place pertaining to Viṣṇu (be started). Whatever the Brahmins desire in their mind may be given to them, even if the objects be women, jewels, villages and cities. Let the fertile lands or fields be given to the suppliants. So also other beautiful things be given to those who ask for them. The words "not available", should never be uttered. Let this sacrifice function as long as the ancient lord becomes visible to me, very near the venue of sacrifice.

O brahmins, after saying thus, Indradyumna the most powerful of long arms made gifts of the following articles :— Masses of gold, crores of ornaments, a hundred thousand elephants, hundred thousands of horses, a hundred million bulls, cows with their horns wrapped in gold, beautiful milch cows along with the vessels for milking made of bellmetal. He gifted these articles to the brahmins who understood the Vedas. He was glad to do this.

In that great sacrifice he gave valuable clothes, deer skin-coverings white in colour and pure in quality, and excellent corals and jewels. He gave away different sorts of jewels such as diamond, lapis lazuli, ruby, pearl, etc. He presented the brahmins with five hundred pure virgins bedecked in ornaments and eyes resembling lotuses. Many beautiful mature women were given as ladies of love to the brahmins and others who sought them. Those ladies had heavy breasts. They had covered their breasts by their bodice. They were so slender-waisted that they appeared as though they did not have the waist at all. They had good buttocks. Their eyes were as large as the petals of lotus; by bending their necks they exhibited their emotional fervour and amorous gestures. Many of them were bedecked in bangles. They wore anklets on their feet. They were clad in silk garments. O excellent brahmins, they were gifted to everyone of the suppliants among the brahmins at the horse-sacrifice. The dishes prepared were full and delicious with different ingredients appropriately added. There were many delicacies prepared from candid sugar, savouries prepared after frying them in oil, baked breads made of flour, other items of edibles prepared neatly, confectionery items fried in ghee, sweets and salted dishes, sweet pies and well cooked rice. In order to please everybody the cooked food was served again and again. There was no end to the wealth already gifted or going to be gifted.

On seeing this great sacrifice Devas, Daityas, Cāraṇas, Gandharvas, Apsaras, Siddhas, Sages, and Prajāpatis were struck with great wonder. The excellent sacrifice was very splendid. The priests. ministers and king Indradyumna were all delighted. There was no dirty person there. There was no one wretched or hungry person left. There was no calamity or casuality; there was neither mental agony nor physical ailments. There was no premature death. There was no death due to poisonous bites; there was no evil influence of adverse planets. The people were well nourished and jolly during the great festival of that king. The sages richly endowed with austerities and power of penance who had been staying there for a long time said that there had never been such a sacrifice before with the lavish display of wealth and food-grains.

Thus, O excellent brahmins, the king concluded the excellent sacrifice called Aśvamedha].

CHAPTER FORTYSIX

Extra verses at the beginning of Chapter

[*The sages said* :

O lord of the chiefs of Devas, tell us what we ask regarding the ancient incidents. How were the idols made formerly by Indradyumna ? In what manner was Viṣṇu pleased with him ? Please mention all these incidents to us. We are very eager to hear.

Brahmā said :

O leading sages, listen, to the Purāṇa that is on a par with the Vedas. I shall recount the past events and the origins of the idols.

When the great sacrifice duly functioned, when the palace was also built, he was worried over the idols day and night.

"I do not know, by what means I can see the supreme lord, the lord of Devas, the lord of all, the sanctifier of the world, the cause of creation, sustenance and annihilation".

The king was extremely worried. He never slept either at night or by day. He did not enjoy any pleasures. He did not relish bath and toilet. He did not like make-up.

His pleasure did not grow due to musical instruments, scents, songs, colour, elephants in their rut, horses, lapis lazuli, sapphire, ruby, gold, silver, diamonds and crystals. He did not feel pleasure in anything that money could buy or mind could desire. He did not feel glad due to the animals of the forest or by moving about in the firmament.

Rock, clay and wood are the three substances used for making the idols of Viṣṇu. Of these three, which is the most preferable ? How can an idol marked by all traits could be made ?

If the idol is made of one of these three and is installed it shall be liked by the lord. It will be worshipped by devas". Thus the king became worried and he thought thus.

After worshipping the lord in accordance with the injunctions laid down in the Scriptural text Pañcarātra,[1] the king began to eulogise.

O Vāsudeva, obeisance be to you. O cause of liberation, obeisance to you. O lord of the world, protect me from the ocean of worldly existence of birth and death.

O lord, resembling the firmament, devoid of impurities, obeisance to you. O Saṅkarṣaṇa, obeisance to you. O holder of the earth, protect me.

Obeisance to you, the deity having the lustre of gold-wombed Brahma, obeisance to you, O shark-emblemed one. Obeisance to you. O lover of Rati, O enveloper and annihilator, protect me.

Obeisance to you, O deity resembling collyrium. Obeisance to you, O deity favourably disposed towards your devotees. O Aniruddha, obeisance to you. Protect me. Be the bestower of boons.

O abode of the learned, obeisance to you; obeisance to you O deity fond of the learned. Obeisance to you O Nārāyaṇa. Protect me who have sought refuge in you.

Obeisance to you, O most excellent one among the strong. Obeisance to you, O ploughshare-armed deity. O great grandfather, the four-faced lord, the abode of the universe, protect me.

Obeisance to you, the deity having the lustre of blue clouds. Obeisance to you, the deity worshipped by Devas.]

---

1. *Pañcarātra*—a system of spiritual doctrines, by following which one attains the position of Uparicara.

The Prayer for Welfare

Brahmā said :

1-2. Thus the king concluded the great Horse sacrifice in accordance with the injunctions laid down in the Vedas.

He was afraid of the ocean of worldly existence. For the purity of his mind and for attaining the highest region of Viṣṇu, he sat in an isolated place and eulogised the lord, the bestower of bliss on the universe.

The king said :

3-4. O support of the universe, O lord of the universe who enable us to fulfil our desires. O lover of Lakṣmī, O ocean of mercy, favourably disposed to your devotees, and fond of the good, O Viṣṇu, O great lord, save me who have been immersed in the ocean of worldly existence. O deity resembling the fire of dissolution. Obeisance to you the annihilator of the sons of Diti, O Narasiṁha of great vigour and bright eyes, save me.

5. O great Boar[1] just as the earth had been formerly lifted up by you by your curved fangs, from the nether worlds so also save me from the ocean of misery.

6. O lord Kṛṣṇa, these idols of yours, the bestowers of boons, have been eulogised by me. You, Baladeva and others, are stationed in separate forms.

7-9. O lord, O lord of Devas, Garuḍa and others are the parts of your body. O lord, the guardians of quarters[2] with their

1. This refers to the Boar incarnation of Viṣṇu. The boar entered the sea and found out the earth that had sunk. The boar lifted the earth at his tusks, came out of the ocean and set the earth firm over the water. On the way, the fierce and wicked Hiraṇyākṣa hindered him. The Boar killed Hiraṇyākṣa and disappeared.

2. *Guardians of quarters*—lokapālas. They are sometimes regarded as the guardian deities of different orders of beings, but more commonly of the four cardinal and four intermediate points of the world. They are 1 Indra, of East; 2 Agni of South-east; 3 Yama of South; 4 Sūrya of South-west; 5 Varuṇa of West; 6 Vāyu of North-west; 7 Kubera of North; 8 Īśāna of North-east. Others substitute Nirṛti for Sūrya and Īśāni or Pṛthivī for Īśāna. According to Dharma-saṅgraha, the Buddhists enumerate 14 lokapālas.

weapons and Keśava and others are the parts of your body. O lord of the Universe, O lord of all worlds, of large and delighted eyes, your different forms mentioned by the learned have been worshipped and eulogised by me. O lord, you who have been bowed by me are the bestower of virtue, love and wealth. Grant boons and confer your blessings upon me, O lord.

10. Hara, Saṅkarṣaṇa and others who have been glorified as your variant forms, have been evolved for your worship. They are dependent on you, they resort to you for support.

11. O lord of Devas, in fact, you have no other form separate from you. The various forms of yours are only for your worship by the devotees.

12. O lord, how can man mention you as twofold, you who are one and only one. You are all-pervading Consciousness by nature and you are unsullied.

13-14. Your supreme form is devoid of positive and negative aspects. It is unsmeared. It is devoid of impurities. It is subtle, steady, unmoving and firm. It is rid of all sins. It is stationed as mere existence. O lord, even Devas do not know that. How can I know it ?

15-16. The learned worship that other form of yours which is clad in yellow robes, has four arms, holds conch, discus and iron club in hands, wears a crown, shoulder-lets etc, has the scar Śrīvatsa in the chest and is adorned by garlands of sylvan flowers. Others also who resort to you for support worship that form.

17. O lord of Devas, most excellent one among Devas, O bestower of freedom from fear on devotees, O deity with eyes like the petals of lotus, save me. I am immersed in the ocean of sexual objects.

18. Excepting you, O lord of worlds, O husband of Lakṣmī, I do not see any one in whom I can seek refuge. O slayer of Madhu,[1] be pleased.

---

1. *O slayer of Madhu.* Madhu and Kaiṭabha sprang from the ears of Viṣṇu. They were about to kill Brahmā who was lying on the lotus springing from Viṣṇu's navel. Viṣṇu killed them and obtained the names ; Kaiṭabhāri and Madhusūdana.

19-22. I have hundreds of ailments due to old age. I am afflicted by miseries. I am deluded. I experience pleasure and pain, happiness and sorrow. I have been bound and fettered by nooses of activities. I have fallen into the very terrible and awful ocean of worldly existence. Having sensual objects for its waters it is very difficult to cross. Passionate attachment and invidious hatred make it agitated like the fishes. It is majestic with the sense-organs acting as whirlpools. Greed and sorrow constitute its turbid waves. There is no one to cling to or to resort to as support. The ocean of worldly existence is very fickle but without any essential significance. O lord, deluded by Māyā I am wandering in it for a pretty long time. I am born again and again into thousands of species of living beings.

23. O lord, I have passed through births, thousands and ten thousands of them of diverse kinds, in this world.

24-25. The Vedas have been studied by me together with their ancillaries. Different scriptural texts, Itihāsas and Purāṇas and many fine arts have been learnt and understood by me. Satisfaction and dissatisfaction, hoarding and dwindling, income and expense, victory and defeat, prosperity and adversity, rise and fall have been experienced by me.

26. Separations from and union with wives, enemies, friends and kinsmen have been faced by me. Many and many kinds of fathers have been seen by me.

27. Many miseries have been experienced by me. Many miseries have been misunderstood and enjoyed as pleasures by me. I have had cousins and kinsmen, sons and brothers, in plenty.

28. I have lived within the belly of women that abounds in urine and floating masses of faeces. O lord, great misery has been experienced by me while staying in womb.

29. O lord, all those miseries that are usual in childhood, youth and old age have been suffered by me.

30. The miseries at death, in the path and the abode of Yama as also the tortures in hell have been experienced by me.

31-33. Again and again, I have been born amongst worms, insects, trees, elephants, horses, deer, birds, buffaloes, camels, cows and monkeys, among the twice-born people and Śūdras, in the wombs of rich Kṣatriyas and impoverished ascetics, of kings and their servants and other embodied souls. O lord, I have taken birth in their houses again and again.

34. O lord, many times I have been the slave of glorious prosperous men. From the impoverished state I had attained the state of a lord and master.

35. Many were killed by me. I have been killed by many. I have caused death to many and my death has been caused by many. Much had been given to me by others and many times gifts have been distributed by me.

36. For and on behalf of my parents, friends, brothers and wives, among rich and learned brahmins well-versed in the vedas and poor ascetics.

37-42. Setting shame and bashfulness aside, O lord, many piteous words have been uttered by me. O lord, I do not see that abode amongst mobile and immobile beings of divine, animal or human origin, where I have not been.

O lord of the universe, sometimes I had my stay in hell. Sometimes I stayed in heaven. Sometimes my stay was confined to the limits of human world and sometimes in the sacred waters of holy centres. Just as the bucket in the contrivance to raise water, goes up or down or stays in the middle, bound always with the rope, so also, O excellent Deva, I have been fettered by the rope of Karman. I whirl up and down and in the middle due to the influence of Karman. Thus, in the wheel[1] of worldly existence, which is very awful and which causes hairs to stand, I have been revolving for a pretty long time. I do not know what I do. All my sense organs are in utter confusion.

43. A fugitive (terrified of life) attacked by grief and greed I have become senseless. Now, O lord, utterly helpless and confused, I seek refuge in you.

44. O lord, save me who have become miserable and immersed in the ocean of worldly existence. O lord of the universe, if you consider me your devotee have pity on me.

45. Excepting you I have no other kinsmen who may have some consideration for me. O lord, after resorting to you, my lord, I cease to have any fear from any quarter or direction.

---

1. The idea often occurs in Sanskrit poetry.

नीचैर्गच्छत्युपरि च दशा चक्रनेमिक्रमेण ।

46-49. O lord, I have no fear at all in regard to life or death or acquisition and preservation of good things.

O lord, those base persons who do not worship you duly cannot have redemption from the fetters of worldly existence.

If they have no devotion to Viṣṇu the creator of the universe, of what avail is their mobility of birth, good conduct, learning, or even life itself?

Those who are deluded and are under the influence of Tāmasika nature censure you. They fall into hell. They are born again and again. They have no redemption from the ocean of hell.

50-55. Those men of evil nature, O lord, who slender you, are the basest of men.

O Viṣṇu, wherever I am born as a result of my activities, may my devotion unto you be always steady. It is by propitiating you that Devas, Daityas and other persons of self restraint have attained the greatest realization. Who will not worship you, O Lord?

O Lord, even Brahmā and other Devas are not competent to eulogise you adequately. How can I then, with the limited human intellect eulogise you who are beyond and greater than nature.

O lord, due to my ignorance you have been eulogised in a haphazard manner by me. If you have mercy on me forgive my fault.

O lord, good men have forbearance in regard even to one who has committed a crime. Hence, O lord of Devas, be pleased to retain affection for your devotees. O lord, you have been eulogised by me with the mind full of devotion. Vāsudeva, may all that be true. Obeisance to you, O lord.

Brahmā said :

56. O excellent sages, the Garuḍa-emblemed deity who was eulogised thus by him became pleased with him and granted him the boon of his choice.

57. He who worships the lord of the universe every day and eulogises him by this hymn, shall become intelligent. He shall certainly obtain liberation.

58. The pure man who repeats this excellent hymn during the three Sandhyās every day shall attain virtue, wealth, love and liberation. He shall surely become a scholar.

59. He who reads, listens to and narrates this with great concentration shall shake off his sins and obtain the divine world.

60. This hymn is conducive to wealth. It dispels sins. It is auspicious. It bestows worldly pleasures and salvation. It is a rare esoteric secret. It is sacred. It should not be imparted to any one and everyone.

61. It should not be imparted to an atheist, a fool, an ungrateful person, an arrogant or to one of wicked intellect. It should never be handed over to a knave.

62. It should be imparted to one endowed with devotion, good qualities and good conduct, to a devotee of Viṣṇu, to a calm person habituated to perform his duty with faith.

63. This hymn Kāruṇyastava (a hymn of mercy) causes destruction of sins. It bestows happiness and salvation, and grants desires. This hymn of the lord mentioned by me is the most excellent of all.

64. Those pure men who meditate continuously on the slayer of Mura,[1] the subtle deity, the ancient Puruṣa attain liberation and enter Viṣṇu as do the butter-offering consigned to the fire of sacrifice by reciting the Mantras.

65. Viṣṇu is the only lord who dispels sorrows of worldly existence. He is greater than the greatest being. There is no one greater than that lord. He is the creator, protector and annihilator. He is the essence of all material objects.

66. Of what avail is their learning? Of what avail are the good qualities they possess? Of what avail are their sacrifices, charitable gifts and severe penance? All these are useless if they do not have devotion to lord Kṛṣṇa who is the preceptor of the universe and who is the bestower of happiness and salvation.

67. He who has devotion to the deity known as the best of all Puruṣas is the most blessed in the world. He is pure. He is a

1. *The slayer of Mura*: Lord Kṛṣṇa slew the two powerful asuras: Mura and Naraka when he attacked Prāgjyotiṣa, the capital city of Naraka.

great scholar, the most excellent by virtue of sacrifices, austerities and noble traits. He is the wise knower, liberal donor and speaker of truth.

CHAPTER FORTYSEVEN

The Origin of Idols

Brahmā said :

1-2. O leading sages, after eulogising and bowing thus to the eternal lord of the universe, Vāsudeva the bestower of all desired benefits, the worried king spread Kuśa grass on the ground and a single cloth over Kuśa grass. Keeping his mind concentrated on him he restrained his sense-organs and went to sleep.

3. At the time of going to bed his thought was—"How does Vāsudeva, the lord of Devas become visible ? How is that lord going to dispel my agony ?

4. Vāsudeva, the preceptor of the universe revealed himself to the sleeping king as one who held conch, discus and iron club.

5-8. He saw the lord of Devas, the preceptor of the universe, in the course of a dream. The lord was holding conch and discus. His fierce hands held iron club and discus. He had the bow Śārṅga, arrow and sword. There was a halo of shining refulgence. He had the colour and lustre of the sun at the end of Yugas. He resembled the blue lapis lazuli. He was seated on the shoulders of Garuḍa. The splendid deity had eight arms. O self-possessed sages, the lord spoke to the king :—"Well done, O king, of great intellect".

O king, I am satisfied on account of this great sacrifice and your devotion and faith Why do you bewail in vain ?

9. O king, the idol here is eternal and worthy of being worshipped. I shall tell you the means whereby you will obtain that idol.

10-12. When this night dawns, at the rise of the sun devoid of impurities, (you shall go) to the place where the sea water comes to an end. It is adorned by different trees. O king, even within the shore line much water is seen. It is the water that has rushed in there in a flood from the waves of the briny sea. There is a great tree on the shore standing both on land and in the water. Though the billows strike at it, the tree does not shake.

13. O king, go there alone in a sportful mood. Take an axe with you and wade through the waves. You will reach the tree.

14-15. On reaching the holy fig tree chop it off unhesitatingly. Chop, pear and chisel that tree of wonderful appearance. O king, evolve my divine idol after full consideration. Leave off worries that delude you.

Brahmā said :

16. After saying this, Lord Viṣṇu, the highly blessed deity, vanished from sight. On account of this vision in his dream the king was extremely surprised.

17. The king spent that night eagerly expecting (what had been foretold). His mind dwelt on it alone. He repeated the Mantras and hymns pertaining to Viṣṇu.

18-19. When the night dawned into day the king got up. He took a holy dip in the ocean in accordance with the injunctions. He gave charitable gifts to the brahmins, offering villages and cities. After performing the routine rites of the forenoon, the king went ahead.

20. Neither a chariot nor a charioteer, neither an elephant nor a foot-soldier accompanied him. The highly intelligent king entered the great shore alone.

21-22. There he saw the huge tree, the refulgent tall tree. It was very terrible, fierce, holy and extensive. Its height was great and the size very large. It stood well protected near the seashore. It had the colour and lustre of dense red madder. The tree had neither a name nor a species.

23. O brahmins, on seeing that tree the king was joyous. He chopped it off with his sharp and steady axe.

24. He was desirous of splitting it unto two. When the log was being examined a wonderful event was seen.

25-28. Viśvakarmā[1] and Viṣṇu assumed the forms of two brahmins and came there. Both these brahmins were equally highly blessed. They shone with their refulgence. They had divine garlands and unguents. They approached king Indradyumna and said : "O great king what is it that you are going to do here ? O king of powerful arms, why was this tree ehopped off ? O king of powerful arms, this tree had been standing isolated on the shore of the great sea (away) from the desolate thick forest. Why has it been cut down ?

Brahmā said :

29-30. O brahmins, on hearing their words the king became glad. On seeing them arrive there like the moon and the sun endowed with forms the king bowed to these lords of Universe. He spoke to them sweet and soft words as he stood with his head lowered in reverence.

The king said :

31. It is my desire to propitiate the lord of Devas, the lord of the worlds devoid of beginning and devoid of end. For that I shall make the idol.

32. In the course of a dream I have been directed by the lord of Devas the noblest and the greatest Soul. It has thus been narrated to you two.

33. On hearing the words of the king who was on par with lord Indra, the lord Viṣṇu, the lord of the Universe laughed with satisfaction and spoke thus.

Viṣṇu said :

34-38. Well done, well done, O highly blessed one. Your inclination is excellent. The ocean of worldly existence is terrible. It is as restless as the leaves of the plantain tree. It is insignificant and more or less full of misery. Enjoyment of pleasures is like the crocodile. It makes it excited. The sense-organs act like foams and whirlpool. It is very difficult to cross. It causes hairs to stand on end. Hundreds of different ailments

1. *Viśvakarmā*, the architect of gods.

act like eddies. The ocean of worldly existence is like a water bubble. Since in such an atmosphere your mind is inclined to propitiate Viṣṇu, you are really blessed. O leading king, you are adorned by all good qualities. The entire Earth with all subjects, mountains, parks and forests, towns and villages, and adorned by the four castes, is blessed, since you, O leading king, are the lord and protector of subjects.

39. Come on, O highly blessed one, this tree is comfortably cool. Sit here alongwith us both. We shall discuss pious topics.

40. This is my associate who has come here to help me. He is the most excellent among the artisans. He is equal to Viśvakarmā himself. He is an expert in all activities. He will make the idol thought of by you. Leave the shore now.

41-47. On hearing these words of the brahmin, the most excellent king left the shore and stood in the cool shade of the tree. Then the soul of the universe, the deity who had assumed the form of a brahmin, O leading brahmins, gave this order to the chief of Artisans—"Make the idol. The first one shall be in the form of Kṛṣṇa. It should be extremely calm. The eyes should be as large as the petals of the lotus. He should have the scar Śrīvatsa and Kaustubha[1] jewel. He should hold conch, discus Sudarśana[2] and iron club.

The second idol should have the colour and lustre of the moon and cow's milk. It should be marked by the Svastika sign. He should hold the ploughshare as his weapon. He is the lord of great strength named Ananta.[3] His end has never been seen and understood by Devas, Dānavas, Gandharvas, Yakṣas, Vidyādharas and serpents. Hence he is known as Ananta.

---

1. *Kaustubha*: —a celebrated jewel, obtained with thirteen precious things at the churning of milky ocean and suspended on the breast of Kṛṣṇa.

2. *Sudarśana*: —The discus of lord Kṛṣṇa which he received from the fire-god to fight with Indra when the latter showered rain to protect the forest Khāṇḍava from burning. According to another version, Viśvakarmā, the divine architect put the sun in a turning machine, turned him and decreased his radiance. Out of the dust of the sun, produced by this process, Viśvakarmā made the discus-weapon, the aerial chariot, Puṣpaka, the Trident of Śiva and the Śakti (lance) of Subrahmaṇya. Of these weapons, the discus Sudarśana was given to Mahāviṣṇu.

3. *Ananta*, the Nāga chief Śeṣa. Balarāma, the eldest brother of Śrīkṛṣṇa is said to be part incarnation (aṁśāvatāra) of Śeṣa

The third idol should be of Subhadrā[1] the sister of Vasudeva. It shall be splendid and gold-coloured. It should be marked with all characteristics.

Brahmā said :

48. On hearing his words, Viśvakarmā did all efficiently, instantaneously. He made the idols of auspicious traits.

49. The ear-rings were of wonderful design and shone in the ears. The hands were kept on the discus and ploughshare, Kṛṣṇa holding the discus and Balarāma the ploughshare. The idols were approved of by the pious people.

50-51. The first idol had white lustre and colour. It was as refulgent as the autumnal moon. The eyes were reddish. The body was huge and the head looked savagely fierce due to the hoods. It was the fierce Balarāma who was clad in blue robes, He was haughty and intoxicated due to his inordinate strength. He wore a single ear-ring. He had a divine form. He held the iron club and the threshing rod.

52-53. The second idol was Viṣṇu's. His eyes resembled the lotus; his body the blue cloud. He shone like the Atasi flower. His eyes were as large as the petals of the lotus. He had yellow garments. He was very fierce and auspicious. He was marked by the characteristic sign of Śrīvatsa. The discus filled one of his hands. He had a divine form that dispelled sins.

54-55. The third idol made by Viśvakarmā was that of Subhadrā. She had the colour and lustre of gold. Her eyes were large like the petals of a lotus. She was clad in robes of various and wonderful colours. She was bedecked in necklaces and shoulderlets. She was adorned by wonderful ornaments. Gem-studded necklaces dangled round her neck. Viśvakarmā made her very beautiful with plump and elevated breasts.

56-57. On seeing this wonderful deed of making the idols in a trice, on seeing that the beautiful idols richly endowed with all characteristic signs, clad in a pair of divine clothes and adorned by different jewels were made quickly, the king was excessively surprised and he spoke thus.

---

1. *Subhadrā*—sister of Śrīkṛṣṇa was married to Arjuna. Abhimanyu was her son. She is deified.

Indradyumna said :

58-60. Are you two Devas who have come here in the guise of brahmins ? Both of you have wonderful activities. You are of divine conduct, not human.

If you are not Devas or human beings, are you Yakṣas or Vidyādharas ? Are you Brahmā and Hṛṣīkeśa ? Are you Vasus or Aśvins ? I do not know whether you are really present here or merely stationed in Māyā form (whatever it may be). I seek refuge in you two. May your real self be revealed to me.

CHAPTER FORTYEIGHT

Description of Puruṣottama

Śrī Bhagavān said :

1-2. I am neither a Deva nor Yakṣa neither a Daitya nor the king of Devas. I am neither Brahmā nor Rudra. Understand me to be Parameśvara (The Supreme Lord). I dispel the agony of all worlds. My strength and manliness are in perfect state. I have no end. I am to be propitiated by all living beings.

3. The deity whom the Yogins call Vāsudeva can be comprehended only through perfect knowledge. It is mentioned in all scriptures. The lord is mentioned (as Brahma) in Vedānta texts.

4. I am Brahmā, Viṣṇu and Śiva. I am Indra, the king of Devas I am Yama who restrains the universe.

5. I am the earth and other elements. I am the threefold sacrificial fire.[1] O king, I am also the firegod swallowing what is consigned into him. I am Varuṇa, lord of Waters. I am earth and the supporter of the Earth.

6. Whatever there is in the world that can be expressed by a word, whether mobile or immobile, I am that.

1. *Three fires*—Gārhapatya, Āhavanīya and Dakṣiṇa.

The whole universe consisting of mobile and immobile beings is nothing other than what I am.[1]

7. O excellent king of good holy rites ! I am pleased with you. Choose any boon that you wish. Whatever is desired by you, whatever is cherished in the heart by you, I shall give you immediately.

8. Persons without merit do not have my vision even in a dream. Due to your steadfast devotion you have seen me directly.

Brahmā said :

9. O brahmins, on hearing these words of Vasudeva the king experienced horripilation all over his body and he recited the following prayer :

The king prayed :

10-16. O lover of Śrī, obeisance be to you. O consort of Śrī, obeisance to the yellow-robed one. O bestower of glory, O lord of Śrī, O abode of glory and prosperity, obeisance to you. O home of Glory, I bow down to the primordial Puruṣa. Īśāna the lord of all, having faces all round. I bow down to you who are eternal and unsullied.

I make obeisance to one who is beyond sound, beyond attributes, devoid of positive and negative aspects, unsmeared, attributeless, subtle and omniscient and who conceives and creates all.

I bow down to one who resembles the colour in the rainy season; who is engaged in activities conducive to the welfare of cows and brahmins, who protects all, who pervades all and who purifies all.

I bow down to the lord who holds conch and discus, who holds iron club and the threshing rod; I bow down to the lord who grants boon and who has the lustre of the petals of the blue lotus.

I bow down to Hari who lies down on the serpent couch

---

1. This tendency towards monotheism is due to the influence of Vedantic advaitavāda, but generally the Purāṇas represent polytheistic creed.

in the milky ocean. I bow down to Hṛṣīkeśa who dispels all sins.

I bow down to you, the lord of the chiefs of Devas, who bestows boons and pervades all.

Brahmā said :

17. After eulogising thus, he bowed to the lord with palms joined in reverence. After bowing down and falling down on the ground he said.

The king said :

18-21. O lord, if you are pleased with me, I choose this excellent boon. The following persons shall meditate on the greatest region :—Devas, Asuras, Gandharvas, Yakṣas, Rākṣasas, Nāgas, Siddhas, Vidyādharas, Sādhyas, Kinnaras, Guhyakas, the sages who are highly blessed and experts in the different texts of scriptures, recluses, interpreting Yogins, Vedic scholars, and those others who are conversant with the scriptures on liberation. The region that is devoid of attributes, free from impurities, peaceful, highly sanctifying and worthy of being hidden as a secret. Due to your favour I wish to go to that region which is very difficult of access.

The Lord said :

22. May everything be to your welfare. Obtain everything desired by you. Everything will happen as you wish by my favour. There is no doubt about it.

23. O excellent king, rule over the great kingdom continuously for ten thousand nine hundred years.

24-26. You will then go to the divine region which is difficult of access even to Devas and Asuras. Your desire shall be fulfilled. I shall show you the calm and peaceful region worthy to be known. It is the unchanging, unmanifest secret region, greater than the greatest, subtle, unsmeared, motionless and steady. It is devoid of old age and grief, devoid of activities and cause. I shall show you that region by attaining which you will derive the highest bliss and realize the greatest goal.

27-28. O leading king, may your fame stay here on the Earth as long as there are clouds, as long as the sky exists, as long as the moon, sun and stars last, as long as the seven oceans exist; as long as Meru and other mountains stand and Devas stand in heaven. So long your fame will remain undiminished.

29. This sacred water-reservoir named Indradyumnasaras is born as a part of sacrifice. By taking bath in it even for once, people attain the world of Indra.

30. He who offers rice balls on the splendid bank of the lake shall redeem twentyone generations and go to the world of Indra.

31. He will go there in aerial chariot honoured by celestial damsels and the divine musicians singing in loud voice. He shall stay there for the duration of fourteen Indras.

32-36. To the South of the lake, in the South West corner there is a holy fig tree. There is a raised platform close by. It is covered by a bushy growth of Ketaki plants. The place is full of different trees with innumerable coconut palms, Campakas, Bakulas, Aśokas, Karṇikāras, Punnāgas, Nāgakesaras, Pāṭalas, Āmrātas, Saralas, sandal trees, Deodars, Nyagrodhas, Aśvatthas, Khadiras, Pārijātas, Arjunas, Hintālas, Tālas, Śiṁśapas, Badaras, Karañjas, Lakucas, Plakṣas, Jack, Bilva and many other trees. All of them adorn the place.

37-41. On the fifth day in the bright half of the month of Āṣādha when the constellation is Maghā, devotees will keep us there for seven days. Good-featured Courtesans clad in splendid dress will install the idols. Sweet and pleasing songs as well as dances coupled with sports (will entertain them). Fanning with chowries having golden handles and fans decorated with jewels, the auspicious ladies will instal us there. There will be religious students, recluses, excellent brahmins, householders, forest-dwellers. Siddhas, and others will assemble there and eulogise Rāma and Keśava by reciting hymns of excellent words and letters and the Mantras of Ṛk, Yajus and Sāman.

42. By eulogising, visiting and devoutly bowing to the idols men shall stay in the prosperous city of Hari for ten thousand years in accordance with the divine reckoning.

43-45. He will be honoured and worshipped by heavenly nymphs and Gandharvas singing sweetly. He shall sport about there as a follower of Hari, Keśava. He will go to the excellent world on an aerial chariot that has the colour of the sun wearing a shining necklace of precious gems. He will enjoy all desired pleasures in that excellent world. When the power of penance dwindles he will return to the earth as a man and be born as a brahmin. He will have crores of coins and wealth. He will certainly be a master of four Vedas.

Brahmā said :

46. After granting him the boons thus and giving him the time-limit O brahmins, Hari vanished along with Viśvakarmā.

47. The king was delighted. The hairs over his body stood up. He considered himself blessed due to the vision of Hari.

48-53. The idols of Kṛṣṇa, Balarāma, Subhadrā the bestower of boons, were brought on the divine chariots. They were rendered beautiful and wonderful by the adornment of jewels and gold coverings. With shouts of victory and auspicious slogans the intelligent king accompanied by his ministers and priests brought the images there.

With the accompaniment of sounds of different musical instruments and auspicious chanting of vedic Mantras, he installed them in a holy, beautiful auspicious place. He got them installed through brahmins in an auspicious time when the constellation was auspicious and the (lunar day) was splendid, in accordance with the injunctions and regulations laid down in the śāstras. The king did every thing with the permission of his preceptor. After offering monetary gifts duly to the preceptor he distributed money among the Ṛtviks and others in accordance with the injunctions of the Śāstras.

54-58. After duly performing the rites of installation in the palace, the most excellent abode, he established all of them duly by holy rites. He worshipped them with fragrant flowers of all sorts. He offered gold, jewels, pearls and splendid clothes. Gems of various kinds, divine chairs, villages, towns, cities, lands and territories were gifted by him. After giving away such gifts, after performing different sacrifices and after ruling over the kingdom in the most fitting manner the king became contented. He abandoned every thing he possessed.

Then he attained the highest abode, the greatest region of Viṣṇu.

59-60. Thus excellent sages, the pious king has been recounted by me. The greatness of the holy centre has also been mentioned. What else do you wish to hear? On hearing the words of Brahmā born of the unmanifest, the Brahmins thought it wonderful and gladly asked him again.

The sages said :

61-62. O most excellent Deva, at what time is one to go to Puruṣottama shrine ? O lord, what is the mode whereby the Pañcatīrtha pilgrimage is to be performed ? Tell us the respective merits and benefits of taking holy dip and offering charitable gifts in each of these Tīrthas as well as of visiting the deity. Mention them separately.

Brahmā said :

63-71. If any one observes fast and performs penance in the holy centre of Kurukṣetra, standing on one leg, conquering anger and sense-organs and continues it for seventy thousand years he may derive some benefit thereof. But, O excellent Brahmins, if he observes fast and visits Puruṣottama but once he obtains a greater benefit than that. Hence, O excellent sages, Puruṣottama is to be visited in the month of Jyeṣṭha assiduously by brahmins and other castes who desire to attain heavenly world and who have perfect restraint. After performing pilgrimages to the five Tīrthas duly, the excellent man should visit Puruṣottama on the twelfth day in the bright half of the month of Jyeṣṭha. Those who visit the undiminishing lord Puruṣottama on the twelfth day, reach the world of Viṣṇu from where they never fall off. Hence, O excellent brahmins, one must assiduouly go there in the month of Jyeṣṭha. After taking the holy dip in the five Tīrthas, Puruṣottama should be visited. Even that person who is far off but who devoutly glorifies Puruṣottama everyday with a pure mind shall go to the city of Viṣṇu. The man who undertakes pilgrimage with faith and concentration to Kṛṣṇa (shrine) shall be liberated from all sins. He shall go to the world of Viṣṇu. By visiting the wheel of Hari, that is kept above the palace even from a distance and by bowing to it devoutly, the man is immediately liberated from sins.

CHAPTER FORTYNINE

A Visit to the Holy Banyan Tree by Mārkaṇḍeya

Brahmā said :

1-4. At the close of the Kalpa, O excellent sages, when the great annihilation began to function, when the sun, moon and wind perished, when the mobile and immobile beings were destroyed, when the sun of dissolution rose up, when the fierce rumbling sound of the clouds of dissolution was heard when the trees and mountains crumbled due to the calamitous mass of lightning and thunder, when the whole world was crushed, when the great comets portended distinction, when the waters in the lakes and rivers were dried up, O brahmins, the fire of utter annihilation accompanied by the wind entered the worlds, brightly illuminated by the twelve Ādityas.

5. It pierced the Earth, entered the nether worlds and caused consternation among Devas, Dānavas and Yakṣas.

6. O leading sages, burning from below, the fire destroyed everything in a trice, the world of Nāgas and whatever there was on the earth.

7-8. The Doomsday fire blazed up hundreds and thousands of Yojanas. The wind blew quickly. The entire universe including Devas, Asuras, Gandharvas, Yakṣas, Nāgas and Rākṣasas was burned by the blazing lordly fire.

9-10 When blazing brightly, it was very terrible. Known as Kalpa fire it had great flames and excessive refulgence. It shone and produced a loud report. Burning with its own brilliance it resembled ten million suns. Immediately it burned the three worlds, the abodes of Devas, Asuras and mortals.

11. In the middle of this terrible dissolution of such a

devastating nature an extremely virtuous sage was engaged in the path of meditation.

12. O Brahmins, he stood there alone. He was known as Mārkaṇḍeya. He was bound by the noose of delusion. His sense-organs were agitated by hunger and thirst.

13-14. O brahmins, his throat, lips and palate were parched. On seeing the great fire he became extremely terrified. Oppressed by thirst and faltering at every step, he wondered over the earth like a senseless fugitive. Unable to find a saviour he ran about here and there.

15-19. He did not derive any pleasure. O brahmins, he did not find any place of rest. He thought within himself :— "I do not know in whom I shall take refuge. How can I see that lord, the eternal Puruṣeśa" Thinking thus with his mind in concentration on the eternal lord the cause of the great dissolution he reached that divine region of the eternal lordly Banyan tree well known as Puruṣeśa. O excellent sages, he hastened near the tree. After reaching it he sat under its root. There was no fear from the black fire there. There was no showering of burning sparks of fire. The Doomsday fire did not come there. There was no thunderbolt either.

CHAPTER FIFTY

Mārkaṇḍeya views annihilation

Brahmā said :

1. Then great clouds rose up in the sky presenting a wonderful sight. They were like herds of elephants bedecked in necklaces of lightning streaks.

2-5. Some of them were dark-complexioned like the blue lotus. Some resembled the lilies. Some the filaments. Some were yellow. Some had the green shining colour. Some resembled the Eggs of the crow. Some had the lustre of lotus petals. Some were of vermillion hue. Some had the huge size of excellent cities. Some were comparable to excellent mountains.

Some shone like collyrium. Some had the lustre of emerald. Great clouds bound by clusters of lightning and streaks rose up, O highly blessed ones. They had terrible forms and they roared with a terrible rumbling noise.

6-10. The clouds then covered the sky. The entire earth including the mountains, forests and mines, and the quarters were filled by them. They were showering jets and columns of water, O excellent sages. Thereafter, urged by lord Brahmā the terrible clouds flooded the entire earth with water. Showering water they filled up earth. They extinguished the awful, terrible and inauspicious fire. Urged by lord Brahmā, they rained for twelve years filling everything with currents of water. Then, O brahmins, the oceans transgressed their own shore-lines.

11-15. The mountains crumbled. The earth sank. At the extremities of the sky the clouds whirled and revolved. They enveloped the sky. Struck by the forceful gust of wind they perished. O excellent sages, Viṣṇu the primordial lord residing in a lotus drank up the terrible wind. O brahmins, he then slept in that terrible vast sheet of water without any support and enveloped in darkness. When Devas, Asuras and men perished, when the earth was rid of Yakṣas and Rākṣasas, the tired sages meditated on the Lord. On opening up his eyes he saw the earth filled with water. He did not see the Banyan tree, earth, quarters and the sun.

16-18. He did not see the moon, wind, Devas, Asuras or Nāgas, in that terrible vast sheet of water when mobile and immobile beings had perished. Getting immersed therein, O brahmins, the sage began to swim. In great agony he swam about here and there. O brahmins, he was about to be drowned. He could not see any saviour. On seeing him perplexed and bewildered the lord who had been delighted at his meditation, spoke to him in sympathy.

The Lord said :

19-20. O dear, O Mārkaṇḍeya of holy rites, you are tired like a boy. You are my devotee, hence, come to me quickly. O dear one, O excellent sage, do not be afraid. You have come to my presence. O Mārkaṇḍeya of great courage, I find that you are like a boy afflicted by fatigue.

Brahmā said :

21. O brahmins, on hearing his words, the sage was extremely infuriated and surprised too. He said.

Mārkaṇḍeya said :

22-24. Who is calling me by name as though slighting my penance ? Who is thwarting, as it were, my body, many thousand years old ? This looks quite unmannerly. I have been honoured by Devas, too. Brahmā, the lord of Devas addresses me "O Long-lived one". My head is hardened due to extreme penance. Who is that short-lived rogue who wishes to hasten his death by calling me Mārkaṇḍeya ?

Brahmā said :

25-26. O brahmins, after saying thus, the sage became worried and anxious—"Is this a dream that I have seen ? Or is this a delusion ?"

After thinking thus he decided thus dispelling his misery "I shall seek refuge in lord Viṣṇu with devotion".

27. The sage then sought refuge in Viṣṇu. His mind solely dwelt on him alone. Once again he looked at the Banyan tree towering above the water.

28-34. On one of its wide branches there was a beautiful golden and divine palanquin made by Viśvakarman. It was studded with diamonds and lapis lazuli. It was decorated with crystals and corals. Rubies too were put in precious stones, covered with various sheets and beautified by valuable gems. It looked miraculous in many ways. It was adorned by a halo zone. He saw lord Kṛṣṇa who had assumed the form of a boy stationed on it. He had the refulgence of a crore of suns. He shone in his brilliance. He had four arms and beautiful limbs. His eyes were large like the petals of a lotus. He had the scar Śrīvatsa on his chest. He held a conch, a discus and an iron club. His chest was covered with garlands of sylvan flowers. He wore divine ear-rings, weighty necklaces round his neck. He was bedecked in divine gems and jewels. On seeing him the eyes of the sage bloomed in wonderment. His hairs stood up all over his body. He bowed to the lord and said this :

Mārkaṇḍeya said :

35. How is it that this boy stays here alone and fearless in this terrible vast sheet of water where all mobile and immobile beings have perished ?

Brahmā said :

36. Although the sage was aware of the past, present and future, he did not understand the lord as he was deluded by his Māyā. When he did not understand him he said with dejection :

Mārkaṇḍeya said :

37-43. In vain is the vigour of my penance; futile is my perfect knowledge, futile are my rites, my long life is in vain. My human birth itself is in vain, since I do not know the divine lord sleeping in the palanquin.

Brahmā said :

That brahmin who pondered thus, who senselessly floated about for a saviour and who was completely bewildered became extremely dejected and dispirited. O brahmins he could not look at the brilliance of the boy as he stayed there resembling the rising sun and supported by his own greatness. O leading sages, on seeing the sage coming towards him the boy said to him laughingly in a voice that resembled the rumbling sound of the cluster of clouds.

The Lord said :

O dear one, I know that you are tired and you have approached me for protection. Enter my body quickly. This is the plan devised by me for you.

Brahmā said :

On hearing his words the deluded sage did not utter anything. The helpless sage entered his wide open mouth.

CHAPTER FIFTYONE

Mārkaṇḍeya wanders in the belly of the Lord

Brahmā said :

1. After entering the belly of the boy the sage saw the entire earth consisting of different realms and countries.

2-4. He saw seven oceans[1] :—Of salt water, sugarcane juice, wine, ghee, curds, milk and fresh water. He saw seven continents—Jambū, Plakṣa, Śālmala, Kuśa, Krauñca, Śaka and Puṣkara. He saw Bhārata and other Varṣas (sub-continents). He saw the golden mountain Meru, its peaks shining with gems and jewels. It had many caves.

5. He saw four castes,[2] first to last in his belly. He saw deer, monkeys, lions, boars, Sṛmara variety of deer, rabbits, elephants and other animals.

6-9. Whatever holy centre, village or city there was on the earth, he saw everyone of them therein. He saw agricultural operations, breeding of cows and cattle and business activities of buying and selling. He saw therein Indra, Devas and other heaven-dwellers, Gandharvas, Apsaras, Yakṣas, eternal sages, Daityas, Dānavas, Serpents and snakes. O excellent sages. He saw Rāhu the son of Siṁhikā, and other enemies of Devas. O excellent brahmins, in his belly he saw those mobile and immobile beings which had been formerly seen by him on the face of the earth.

10-12. Or of what avail is much talk or the same thing repeated over and over again ? He saw the entire mobile and immobile beings beginning with Brahmā and ending with a blade of grass. He saw the Bhurloka, Bhuvarloka, Svarloka, Mahar, Jana, Tapas, Satya, Atala, Vitala, Pātāla, Bhūtala, Vitala, Rasātala and Mahātala. In fact, he saw the entire cosmic egg in his belly.

---

1. *Seven oceans* : Sea of Lavaṇa (salt water), of Ikṣu (sugarcane juice), of Surā (liquor), of Ghṛta (clarified butter), of Dadhi (curd), of Dugdha (milk) and of Fresh Water. Each of these surrounds a particular island.

2. *Four Castes* : Brāhmaṇa, Kṣatriya, Vaiśya, Śūdra. These castes exist even today, though they are dwindling fast.

13-16. O excellent brahmins, by the favour of that lord his movement was unimpeded. His memory was unimpaired. O brahmins, wandering thus over the entire universe in his belly he could never reach the end of the body of Viṣṇu.

O brahmins, when he could not reach the end of his body, the sage sought refuge in the lord the bestower of boons.

Then, O brahmins, he suddenly came out of the open mouth of the noble-souled Puruṣa with the speed of the wind.

Extra eight verses according to another reading occur between the 4th and 5th verses of Chapter 51

He saw the Meru mountain inhabited by sages and abounding in trees. It was full of animals and mysterious and wonderful objects. It was beautified by tigers, lions, boars, Camara, deer, buffaloes, elephants, monkeys and other animals. It was peopled by Lord Indra and other Devas, Siddhas, Cāraṇas, Nāgas, and those others who lived in the abode of Devas.

Brahmā said :

Thus the excellent sage, the brahmin, who wondered about in the belly of that boy, saw the glorious Sumeru, Himavān, Hemakūṭa, Niṣadha, Gandhamādana, Śveta, Durdhara, Nīla, Kailāsa, Malaya, Vindhya, Pāriyātra, Arbuda, Sahya, Śuktimān, Maināka, and the mountain Ṛkṣa. He saw these and other mountains that were there. O excellent sage, he saw them bedecked in gems and jewels. He saw Kurukṣetra, Pañcāla, Matsya, Madras, Kekayas, Bāhlīkas, Śūrasenas, Kāśmīras, Taṅgaṇas, Khasas, Kirātas, Karṇapravaraṇas and Marus.

CHAPTER FIFTYTWO

The Review of the Prayer to the Lord

Brahmā said :

1. O excellent sages, after coming out of the belly of that boy, he once again saw the earth turned into a vast sheet of water. It was devoid of people.

2. He saw that same lord in the form of the infant boy whom he had seen before. He was stationed on the branch of banyan tree in a palanquin.

3. That lord had the scar Śrīvatsa on his chest. He was clad in yellow robes and had four arms. His wide eyes resembled the large petals of the lotus and he stayed there taking up the universe.

4. On seeing the sage floating and swimming like a senseless person and approaching him after coming out of his mouth, the lord spoke with laugh.

The Lord said :

5. O dear one, I hope you stayed in my belly comfortably and have had your rest. While wandering about what wonderful thing did you observe there ?

6. O excellent sage, you are my devotee and have resorted completely to me. But you are tired. Hence, to help you I speak to you. See me again.

Brahmā said :

7-10. On hearing his words he experienced horripilation due to delight. He looked at the deity who was bedecked with lustrous gems and jewels and who was too dazzling to be seen. In a Muhūrta, O brahmins, by the favour of that lord he had a new pair of eyes delighted and devoid of impurities. O brahmins, the sage bowed his head at his feet that are worshipped by Devas and which had red toes and sole. With a voice chocked with delight he began to eulogise him. The delighted sage looked at the Supreme being again and again with palms joined in reverence and began to eulogise :

Mārkaṇḍeya said :

11. O lord of Devas, O lord of Universe, you have assumed the form of a boy by your Māyā, O beautiful lotus-eyed one, save me, I am miserable and I have sought refuge in you.

12. O most excellent one among Devas, I am scorched by the fire called Saṁvarta. O lord, save me. I am afraid of the rising of sparks of fire in flames.

13. I am dried up by the fierce wind that is the life-giving breath of the universe. I am perplexed and bewildered as well as tired. Save me, O lord, save me.

14. Scorched by the Ādityas, Pralayāvartaka and others, I do not derive peace. Save me, O lord.

15. I am thirsty and afflicted by hunger. O lord of universe, I am miserable too. I do not see any saviour. Save me, O lord.

16. In this terrible vast sheet of water, as the mobile and immobile beings have perished I do find no resort, save me, O lord.

17. O lord of Devas, the mobile and immobile beings were seen by me in your belly. I am surprised and bewildered. Save me, O lord.

18. In this worldly existence that has no basic support, be pleased O Lord, O most excellent one among Devas, be pleased. O deity fond of the learned and Devas, be pleased.

19. Be pleased, O Lord of the learned. Be pleased, O support of the learned. Be pleased, O lord of the worlds, O cause of the cause of the Universe.

20. Be pleased, O lord of Devas. Be pleased with me, O deity that bear the burden of the earth. Be pleased, O deity residing in waters. Be pleased, O slayer of Madhu demon.

21. Be pleased, O lover of Lakṣmī, be pleased, O lord of Devas. Be pleased, O slayer of Kaṁsa and Keśin. Be pleased O destroyer of Ariṣṭa.[1]

22. Be pleased, O Kṛṣṇa, O destroyer of Daityas. Be pleased, O slayer of Danu's sons. Be pleased, O resident of Mathurā. Be pleased, O scion of the family of Yadus.

23-24. Be pleased, O younger brother of Indra, be pleased O bestower of boons, O unchanging one, You are the earth, water, fire, wind and firmament. You are the mind, Ego, and

---

1. *Ariṣṭa* : An asura, a servant of Kaṁsa. Once, at the instance of Kaṁsa he went to Gokula disguised as an ox to kill Śrīkṛṣṇa. The ox instilled terror in people by crushing hills and mountains, with its horns and bellowing like a bull. But Śrikṛṣṇa faced the beast with courage and rained blows on him so that it was thrown hundred yojanas away and it cried. At the time of death it regained its former form and was recognized as asura

cosmic intellect. You are the Primordial Nature. O lord of the universe, you are Sattva and other things.

25. You are the Puruṣa, the seed of the Universe. You are more excellent than others. You are the sense-organs. O lord, you are the objects, and subtle primary elements.

26. You are the guardian of the quarters. You are Devas, Yajñas and sacrificial gifts. You are Indra, Śiva, offering and the sacrificial fire.

27. You are Yama, the lord of manes; O lord, you are the lord of Rākṣasas (Nirṛti) himself. You are Varuṇa, lord of waters; you are wind and the lord of wealth (Kubera).

28. You are Īśāna, Ananta, Gaṇeśa, Ṣaṇmukha, Vasus, Rudras, Ādityas and Khecaras (Planets).

29-30. You are Dānavas, Yakṣas, Daityas, Maruts, Siddhas, Apsaras, Nāgas, Gandharvas, Cāraṇas, manes, Vālakhilyas, and Prajāpatis. O Acyuta, you are sages, ascetics, Aśvins and demons.

31-33. You are other species too, whatever can be termed a living being. Of what avail is much talk ? You are everything beginning with Brahmā and ending with the blade of grass. You are the whole universe consisting of mobile and immobile beings, all things of the past, present and future. Your greatest form, O lord, is steady, motionless and fixed. Even Brahmā and others do not know that. Then what about others of deficient intellect. O lord, you are intrinsically pure. You are perpetual and greater than Prakṛti.

34-35. You are unmanifest, permanent, infinite, all-pervasive, supreme lord. You are the firmament, the greatest being, the calm one, the unborn and unchanging.

36. Who is competent to eulogise you adequately, you who are devoid of attributes and unsullied. O lord, you have been eulogised by me the deficient one of insignificant mind. O lord of the chiefs of Devas, it behoves you to forgive that, O eternal one.

CHAPTER FIFTYTHREE

Mārkaṇḍeya's Vision of the Holy Lord

Brahmā said :

1. Thus eulogised by Mārkaṇḍeya, O brahmins, the lord became pleased. He said in a voice as majestic as the rumbling sound of clouds.

The Lord said :

2. O excellent sage, tell me freely what you have in your mind. O brahmanical sage, I shall give you everything, whatever you may desire from me.

Brahmā said :

3. O brahmins, on hearing the words of that noble infant, the sage became extremely delighted. With his mind dwelling on him he said :

Mārkaṇḍeya said :

4. O lord, I wish to know you. O bestower of salvation, I wish to know your Māyā (Illusion). O lord of Devas, by your favour, my power of memory is not impaired.

5. I have hurriedly wandered through your body. O lord, I entered your body through your mouth. O lord, I saw all worlds in your belly.

Extra verses

[O lord, the following are stationed within your body viz.—Devas, Dānavas, Rākṣasas, Yakṣas, Gandharvas and Nāgas. Indeed, I saw the whole universe consisting of mobile and immobile beings. I saw the border lands of the mountain Sumeru thronged by sages and beautified by minerals. The place was full of trees and creepers of all kinds; fountains and springs there were many, it was full of animals of all kinds; it was wonderfully charming and beautified by animals such as tigers, lions, boars, Samara deer, buffaloes, elephants, antelopes, monkeys, and other animals. It was occupied by Indra and other Devas, Siddhas, Cāraṇas, Nāgas, Sages, Yakṣas, Apsaras and other dwellers of heaven. Such was the borderland of the mountain Sumeru. I, an excellent sage and a brahmin, wandered further on in your belly, as a boy.

I saw the Himavān, Hemakūṭa, Niṣadha, Gandhamādana, Śveta, Kaṅkanīla, Kailāsa, Dardura, Mahendra, Malaya, Vindhya, Pāriyātra, Arbuda, Sahya, Śuktimān, Maināka, Cakra and many other mountains. O lord, I, the excellent sage, saw all those mountains adorned by gems and jewels.

I saw Kurukṣetra, Pañcāla, Matsya, Madras, Kaikayas, Bāhlīkas, Śūrasenas, Kāsmīras, Kirātas, Karṇaprāvaraṇas, Ekapādas, Dvipādas, Tripādas, Bahunetrakas, Aindras, Prāgjyotiṣas, Kambojas, Tāmraliptakas, Aṅgas, Vaṅgas, Suhmas, Kalāpas, Utkalas, Mahoragas, Nāgas, Kaliṅgas, Koṅkaṇas, Arbudas, Mālavas, Draviḍas, Saurāṣṭras, Navanas and many other lands. Wandering through your body I saw these and many other lands, O noble-souled one.

I saw the following holy centres :—Prayāga, Kurukṣetra, Puṣkara, Naimiṣa, Gayā, Gaṅgādvāra, Kubjāmra, Badarī, Sindhusāgara, Kokāmukha, Śuddhatīrtha, Brahmāvarta, Kuśasthalī, Lauhajaṅgha, Aśvatīrtha that rids one of all sins, Kardamāla, Agnitīrtha, Amarakaṇṭaka, Lohārgala, Jambūmārga, Bhogatīrtha of much holy water, Utpalāvartaka, the holy centre Śrīpuruṣottama, Ekamukha, Kedāra, Kāśī, Viraja, Kālañjara, Gokarṇa, Śrīśaila and Gandhamādana. O Lord I saw these and other holy centres, shrines and temples in your body, as a boy.

I saw the following holy rivers :— Gaṅgā, Śatadrū, Yamunā, Kauśikī, Carmaṇvatī, Vetravatī, Candrabhāgā, Sarasvatī, Vipāśā, Vitastā, Sindhu, Godāvarī, Vasvokasāra, Nalinī, Payoṣṇī, Narmadā, Aparṇā, Tuṅgabhadrā, Karatoyā, Mahānadī, Suvarṇā, Kṛṣṇā, Śibirā the great river, Vaitaraṇī, Kāverī, Śoṇa, Bhīmarathī, Viśālā, Śiprā and Vetravatī. These and other rivers I saw while wandering through your belly entirely, the belly of a noble soul. I saw the sky beautified by the moon and sun. It was shining with its own refulgence similar to that of fire and sun. O boy, I saw the earth too, rendered splendid by the forests. There the brahmins performed various sacrifices. The Kṣatriyas were engaged in the activities of pleasing and humouring the people of all castes. The Vaiśyas performed the agricultural operations. O Puruṣottama, all these and many other things were seen.]

6. O lotus-eyed one, I wish to know you, the unchanging one. Why have you swallowed this universe and why do you stay here in the form of an infant ? It behoves you to expound all this to me.

7. O sinless one, what for is the entire universe stationed in your body ? O suppressor of enemies, how long have you to stay here ? O lord of Devas, I wish to know. Tell me everything in detail.

8. O lotus-eyed one, I wish to hear everything in detail and in the precise manner. O lord, what I have seen is immense and inconceivable.

Brahmā said :

9. Thus requested by him, the lord of Devas of great refulgence, the foremost among the eloquent ones spoke the following words to Mārkaṇḍeya.

The Lord said :

10. Admittedly, O brahmin, Devas do not know me in reality. Out of affection for you I shall tell you how I create this universe and discharge it.

11. O brahminical sage, you are one with great filial affection. You have sought refuge in me alone. Your celebacy is great. Hence, I have seen directly.

12. Formerly, the term 'Nāra' was given by me to the waters. They are my perpetual resort. Hence, I am called Nārāyaṇa.

13. I am Nārāyaṇa; I am the permanent unchanging, source of origin, the dispenser of destiny and the annihilator of all living beings.

14. O excellent brahmins, I am Viṣṇu, I am Brahmā, I am Indra too. I am king Vaiśravaṇa[1] and Yama the Lord of ghosts.

15. O excellent brahmin, I am Śiva, Soma and patriarch Kaśyapa. I am creator and dispenser of destiny and I am sacrifice too.

---

1. *Vaiśravaṇa* : Kubera, king of Yakṣas.

16-17. The fire god is my mouth, the earth is my foot, the moon and sun constitute my eyes; heaven is my head. The hollow space and quarters are my ears, the waters originate from my sweat, the firmament constitutes my body, the wind is stationed in my mind. I have performed hundreds of sacrifices with the requisite monetary gifts.

18-21. Those who have learned the Vedas worship me at the sacrificial altar. The leading Kṣatriyas and the rulers of the earth, desirous of attaining heaven also worship me. Similarly, the Vaiśyas desirous of conquering upper regions, worship me.

It is I who assume the form of Śeṣa and hold aloft the earth having the mountains Meru and Mandara as its ornaments and extending as far as the four oceans.

O brahmin, formerly, this earth was about to sink under water. Assuming the form of boar, it was lifted up by me with my strength.

O excellent brahmin, I have become the submarine fire Vaḍavā[1] and entering the ocean I drink up waters and let them out as well.

22-27. The brahmins form my face, Kṣatriyas my arms, Vaiśyas my thighs and Śūdras my feet. They become thus by their exploits gradually. The Ṛgveda, Sāmaveda, Yajurveda and Atharvaveda spring up from me and re-enter me alone.

It is me alone that the brahmins, ascetics, those who value peace very much, those who have restrained themselves, those who are desirous of gaining perfect knowledge, those who are devoid of lust and wrath, those who are unattached, those who are bereft of sins, those who adhere to Sattva quality, those who have no arrogance or egotism and those who are experts in spiritual matters for ever worship and meditate upon.

I am the luminary named Saṁvartaka. I am the fire called Saṁvartaka. I am the sun called Saṁvartaka. I am the wind called Saṁvartaka.

---

1. *Baḍavā* : the fire of sage Aurva's penance which started to burn the world but which, at the request of pitṛs he threw down into the sea where it took the shape of a horse-head and living beneath the sea continued vomiting heat at all times.

O excellent brahmin, what appear like the forms of stars in the firmament are the pores of my hairs. Understand this.

28-33. Understand that all oceans, the storehouses of gems and jewels, and the four quarters are my robes, bedsheets, and abode. Lust, fury, delight, fear and delusion, O excellent one, understand that all these constitute my forms.

O brahmin, by performing splendid actions men attain me. Adhering to truthfulness, charitable gifts, severe penance and nonviolence towards all creatures, performing holy rites laid down in accordance with my injunctions (people attain me). Those who ponder over my body are active, only because I prompt their knowledge and conscience and not in accordance with their love.

The twice-born, those who learn the Vedas well, those who worship by holding different sacrifices, those who have restrained themselves and those who have conquered anger—attain me. I cannot be attained at all by men of evil actions.

34-39. (I cannot be attained) by persons overwhelmed by greed, by miserly persons, by ignoble persons and those who have not regulated their life actions too.

Know that this is the benefit of men who have purified their souls inasmuch as I am inaccessible to those of confused state or deluded mind, who have recourse to deceptive Yogic path.

O excellent one, whenever virtue is afflicted or fades away and evil rises up, I create myself then.

When the terrible Daityas and Rākṣasas who are fond of violence and who cannot be killed by excellent Devas come to be born in this world, I take birth in the houses of meritorious persons entering human bodies and suppress every evil. I create Devas, human beings, Gandharvas, Nāgas, Rākṣasas, the mobile and immobile beings and then I annihilate them by my own Māyā. At the time of Karman or realization of their fruits, I think about proper bodies and create them.

Additional verses

[I create them by permeating into human bodies for fixing up the bounds of decency.

My virtue is white in colour in Kṛta age, it is dark in Tretā, red in Dvāpara and black in Kali age. At that time (i.e. in Kali age) there will be three parts of evil.

When the hour of destruction arrives I adopt the extremely terrible form of Kāla (God of Death) and destroy the set of three worlds. Alone, I destroy everything mobile and immobile. I have three duties, viz., creation, sustenance and dissolution. I am the soul of Universe. I am conducive to the happiness of all worlds. I am unbroken (i.e. not divisible). I am all-pervasive, infinite, Hṛṣīkeśa of great strides. Alone I lead the wheel of time (I make it move and whirl). That is my form as Brahman. It suppresses all living beings and it endeavours for all living beings.]

40. Thus, O excellent sage, my soul is well embedded in all living beings. O leading brahmin, still no one knows me.

41-44. All devotees in the whole of the universe worship me in every way.

O sinless brahmin, whatever of painful nature has been experienced by you in me, is entirely for the rise of happiness and welfare.

All mobile and immobile beings seen by you in the world have been evolved by me. My soul is the conceiver and creator of all living beings.

I am named Nārāyaṇa. I hold conch, discus and iron-club. I am the soul of the universe. Fascinating all the worlds, I sleep, O brahminical sage, till a thousand sets of four Yugas pass off completely.

45. Thus, O excellent sage, for the duration of the period till Brahmā rises up I remain in the form of an infant though I am not an infant.

46. O leading brahmin, honoured and worshipped by brahminical sages, boon has been granted to you by me in the form of Brahmā. I have been propitiated many times.

47. When the mobile and immobile beings had perished you set out. Seeing everything in a vast sheet of water you were bewildered. It was observed by me and hence you were shown the universe.

48-52 When you entered my body you saw the universe and were surprised. You could not understand the real nature behind it. Then, O brahminical sage, you have been disgorged through the mouth immediately by me. My own soul incomprehensible to Devas and Asuras was revealed to you by me.

O brahminical sage, till Brahmā of great penance wakes up, move about here comfortably and confidently.

O excellent brahmin, after the grand-father of the universe has woken up, I shall singly create elements, physical bodies—viz. ether, earth, fire, wind, and water. Indeed, I shall create mobile and immobile creatures.

Brahmā said:

53. O brahmins, after saying this, when the period of a thousand sets of four Yugas was completed the lord again spoke to him in a voice as majestic as the sound of rumbling cloud.

The Lord said :

54-55. O sage, tell me the real truth. What did you eulogise me for ? Choose the most excellent boon. Ere long, I shall give it to you. You are more long-lived than Devas. You are my devotee of steady holy rites thereby, O leading brahmin. Now obtain a still longer life.

Brahmā said :

56. On hearing that splendid speech of the lord and glancing at him, the sage bent down his head, made obeisance and spoke thus again :

Mārkaṇḍeya said :

57-60. O lord of Devas, O most excellent of the twice-born, since your form has been seen, O Hari, when you are seen, my delusion has gone away. It is the truth. Similarly, O lord of the Universe, I wish for the welfare of all worlds. I wish for the toning down of diversity by your favour. In this holy and pure shrine of Puruṣottama, O lord, I shall build a big temple for Śiva. It shall resolve the dispute between the devotees of Śiva and the devotees of Viṣṇu. In your place, let me instal Śaṅkara.

61. Thereby the people in the world will know Lord Viṣṇu and Lord Śiva as the same form.

Then the lord of the universe replied to the great sage.

The Lord said :

62-63. This Liṅga is the greatest cause, the lord of the worlds. It is for the sake of propitiation and for toning down the rigour of diversity.

O leading brahmin, at my behest, build the Śiva temple instantaneously. By virtue of power stay in the world of Śiva.

64. O brahmin, when Śiva is installed it is I who am installed. There is no difference between us two. We are one in (emotional fervour) but split into two forms externally.

65. He who is Rudra is himself Viṣṇu. He who is Viṣṇu is himself Rudra. There is no difference between the two as in regard to the Wind and Ether.

66-69. Only childish men do not know that he who is Garuḍa-emblemed is the full-emblemed three-eyed lord who slew the Tripuras. Hence, O brahmins, build a temple of Śiva, named after you. To the north of the lord of Devas make the holy reservoir very splendid. It will be well known in the mortal worlds by the name Mārkaṇḍeya Hrada. O excellent brahmin, he will dispel all sins.

Brahmā said :

O excellent sages, after saying this to Mārkaṇḍeya the all-pervading lord Janārdana vanished there itself.

CHAPTER FIFTYFOUR

Visit to Kṛṣṇa Shrine

Brahmā said :

1. O brahmins, henceforth, I shall recount the mode of visiting the five Tīrthas (holy centres) and the benefit derived from holy dips, charitable gifts and visits to the deities.

2. The pure man should go to the eddy called Mārkaṇḍeya Hrada and dive therein facing the north. He should take the holy dips thrice and repeat this Mantra.

3-4. "O Enemy of Tripuras, O destroyer of the eyes of Bhaga, save me. I am immersed in the ocean of worldly existence. I have been seized by sins and rendered unconscious.

Obeisance to Śiva, the calm one, the dispeller of sins. O lord of Devas, I am having my holy ablution. May my sins perish".

5. After taking the holy dip in the water of depth upto the umbilicus, the intelligent devotee should duly perform Tarpaṇa of Devas, sages, manes, and others by means of water mixed with gingelly seeds.

6-7. After bath and Ācamana, the devotee shall go to the temple of Śiva. He shall enter the shrine of deity and circumambulate thrice. After worshipping the lord by the root Mantra, O Brahmins, he shall bow down and propitiate the lord by the Aghora Mantra.

8. O three-eyed lord, obeisance be to you. O Moon-ornamented lord, obeisance to you; O Virūpākṣa, save me. O Mahādeva, obeisance be to you.

9. By taking the holy dip in the eddy of Mārkaṇḍeya Hrada, thus, and by visiting Śaṅkara, the man obtains the benefit of ten horse-sacrifices.

10-11. Liberated from all sins, he goes to the world of lord Śiva. There he enjoys excellent pleasures till the ultimate dissolution of all living beings. He then returns to this world and is born as a brahmin of vast learning and renown. He adopts Yoga pertaining to Śaṅkara and attains salvation.

12. Thereafter, the devotee should go to the holy fig tree on a par with the Kalpa tree, circumambulate it thrice and worship the banyan tree with great devotion, repeating the following Mantra :—

13-14. "Oṁ obeisance be to the holy banyan tree of unmanifest form, cause of the great dissolution, permeated by the great tasty juice.

O banyan tree, you are immortal, surviving all through the Kalpa. You are the abode of Viṣṇu. O banyan tree, dispel my sin. O Kalpa tree ! obeisance to you".

15. By devoutly circumambulating and bowing down to the Banyan tree resembling the Kalpa tree the man is immediately liberated from sins like the serpent that is rid of its old and decaying slough.

16. O brahmins, even by passing through the shadow of this Kalpa tree, a man eschews the sin of brahmin slaughter. What doubt is there in regard to other sins ?

17-18. By visiting Viṣṇu in the form of the banyan tree that has originated from the body of Kṛṣṇa and that is a great being consisting of splendour of the Brahman and by bowing to it, O brahmins, the devotee derives a benefit that is superior to the benefit of Rājasūya and horse-sacrifice. Redeeming the members of his family he goes to the world of Viṣṇu.

19. By making obeisance to Vainateya, Garuḍa son of Vinatā who is stationed in front of Kṛṣṇa, the devotee shall become liberated from all sins. He shall then go to the city of Viṣṇu.

20. He who visits Puruṣottama, Saṁkarṣaṇa and Subhadrā after visiting the banyan tree and Vainateya, attains the greatest goal.

21. After entering the shrine of Viṣṇu and circumambulating the lord thrice he should worship and propitiate Saṅkarṣaṇa and Subhadrā, repeating their own Mantra :—

22-23. Obeisance to you, O Rāma holding the ploughshare. Obeisance to you, O deity with the iron club as the weapon. Obeisance to you, O lover of Revatī.[1] Obeisance to you, (O deity) favourably disposed towards devotees. Obeisance to you, O excellent one among strong persons. Obeisance to you, the holder of the earth. O enemy of Pralamba, Obeisance be to you. Save me, O elder brother of Kṛṣṇa.

24-26. By propitiating lord Balarāma thus, the man will derive the desired benefit. The lord is worshipped by Devas. He is invincible. He has the size and shape of the peak of the mountain Kailāsa. His face is lovelier than the moon. The lord wears blue robes; his head is hideous on account of hoods. He holds the plough. He has great strength. He is bedecked with single ear-ring. He who devoutly propitiates

1. *Revatī*—Wife of Balabhadra or Balarāma.

the son of Rohiṇī[1] is liberated from all sins. He goes to the world of lord Viṣṇu.

27-28. The man enjoys happiness there until the dissolution of all living beings. When the merit dwindles down he returns to the earth, here in the excellent family of Yogins. He becomes an excellent brahmin, the master of all scriptures. He derives perfect knowledge and attains salvation that is difficult of access to others.

29. After worshipping the ploughshare-bearing lord thus, the clever devotee shall worship Kṛṣṇa with great concentration uttering the twelve-syllabled Mantra.

30. The self-possessed bold persons who devoutly worship Puruṣottama by reciting the twelve-syllabled Mantra attain Salvation.

31. O brahmins, neither Devas nor Yogins, nor the Chanters of Sāman hymns attain that goal which those who are devoted to the twelve-syllabled Mantra attain.

32. Hence, one should devoutly worship Kṛṣṇa, the preceptor of the universe, by reciting that Mantra alone. After worshipping with scents, fragrant flowers, etc. he should bow to the deity and propitiate him.

33-37. Be victorious O Kṛṣṇa, O lord of the universe. Be victorious O destroyer of all sins. Be victorious O slayer of Cāṇūra and Keśin. Be victorious O slayer of Kaṁsa.

Be victorious O lotus-petal-eyed lord. Be victorious O holder of discus and iron club. Be victorious O deity dark in complexion like the blue cloud. Be victorious O bestower of happiness on all.

Be victorious O lord worthy of being worshipped by the universe. Be victorious O destroyer of the world. Be victorious O Viṣṇu worthy of being worshipped by the worlds. Be victorious, O bestower of desired benefit.

O excellent lord, O Puruṣottama, I am immersed in the terrible ocean of worldly existence. It is significant. Miseries are like foams therein. It is terrible with wrath making it agitated as if through crocodiles. The objects of sense-organs,

1. *Rohiṇī* : mother of Balabhadra. She was the second wife of Vasudeva, the other being Devakī, mother of Śrīkṛṣṇa.

constitute the flooding waters therein. The different ailments are like its waves and foams. It is impassable due to the whirlpools of delusion. O lord, save me.

38-41. O brahmins, by worshipping Kṛṣṇa thus the devotee attains the benefit of thousands of horse-sacrifices. Kṛṣṇa is the lord of Devas. He is the bestower of boons. He is favourably disposed towards his devotees. He is the bestower of all benefits. He has two arms and stout shoulders. His eyes are large as the petals of the lotus. His chest and arms are large. His face is splendid. He is clad in yellow robes. He holds conch, discus and ironclub in his hands. He has a coronet and shoulderlets as ornaments. He is endowed with all noble characteristics. He is adorned by the garlands of sylvan flowers. After visiting him the man shall join his palms in reverence and prostrate in front of him like a rod. He derives the benefit of thousands of horse-sacrifices.

42. By visiting and bowing to Kṛṣṇa the man obtains that benefit which has been glorified as the result of holy dip and charitable gifts in the holy centres.

43. By visiting and bowing to Kṛṣṇa a man obtains that benefit which results from a sacrifice where much gold is distributed together with precious stones and other valuables.

44. By making obeisance to Kṛṣṇa a man obtains that benefit which has been glorified as the result of sacrifices and the Vedas.

45. By visiting and bowing to Kṛṣṇa a man obtains that benefit which is attained by all charitable gifts, holy rites and observances.

46. By visiting and bowing to Kṛṣṇa a man obtains that benefit which has been cited as the benefit accruing from different sorts of severe austerities.

47. By visiting and bowing to Kṛṣṇa a man obtains that benefit which is glorified as the result of the vow of celibacy perfectly practised.

48. By visiting and bowing to Kṛṣṇa a man obtains the benefit of a householder who strictly adheres to the disciplined conduct of life.

49. By visiting and bowing to Kṛṣṇa a man obtains the

benefit glorified as the result of life in the forest led by (forest-dweller).

50. By visiting and bowing to Kṛṣṇa, a man obtains the benefit cited as the result of renunciation as mentioned before.

51. O brahmins, of what avail is much talk in regard to the greatness of that lord. By devoutly visiting Kṛṣṇa a man obtains salvation which is most difficult to obtain.

52-53. The man will be liberated from sins accumulated in the course of crores of Kalpas. He will be endowed with the greatest glory. He will be endued with good qualities. He will redeem twentyone generations of his family. He will go to the city of Viṣṇu on a very brilliant aerial chariot flourishingly endowed with all desirable things.

54-55. For a period of hundred Kalpas he will enjoy pleasures pleasant to the mind along with Gandharvas and Apsaras like the four-armed Viṣṇu.

Falling off from that world he comes here to the earth and is born as one conversant with Dharma, master of Vedas and devoid of malice in the excellent family of brahmins.

56. He will be engaged in the performance of his own duty. He will be quietly controlling his sense organs. He will be engaged in the welfare of all living beings. Attaining perfect knowledge pertaining to Viṣṇu, he will attain salvation.

57. Thereafter, O brahmin, he shall worship Subhadrā, favourably disposed towards her devotees by reciting the requisite Mantra. He shall then propitiate her by bowing to her with palms joined in reverence.

58. Obeisance to you O omnipresent Goddess. Obeisance to you the bestower of auspicious happiness. Save me, O Goddess with eyes like the petals of a lotus. O Kātyāyanī, obeisance be to you, Subhadrā.

59-61. By thus propitiating that Goddess, who creates the universe, who is beneficial to the universe, who was the sister of lord Baladeva, who is the bestower of boons and who is auspicious, the man goes to the abode of Viṣṇu, on an aerial chariot that can go at one's own sweet will. Till the dissolution of the world he sports there like a Deva. Then he comes here and attains the state of a human being. He shall become a brahmin conversant with the Vedas. After attaining Yoga pertaining to Lord Viṣṇu he attains liberation.

CHAPTER FIFTYFIVE

The Greatness of Narasiṁha

Brahmā said :

1. By thus visiting and bowing to Bala, Kṛṣṇa and Subhadrā, the devotee obtains virtue, wealth, love and liberation.

2. Just as he comes out of the temple of the deity, the man becomes blessed. After bowing to the deity the man returns to his abode with great concentration.

3. He returns to his abode where lord Viṣṇu's idol, made of lapis lazuli, is covered up by sands. By bowing to the lord who vanished there he enters the city of Viṣṇu.

4. O brahmins, that lord who is identical with Devas and who slew the most excellent one among Asuras stays there with half of his body made like that of a lion.

5. By devoutly visiting Narasiṁha lord, and by bowing to him one is liberated from all sins. There is no doubt in this.

6. Those men on the earth who are the devotees of Narasiṁha, incur no sin at all. They will have all desired benefits.

7. Hence, by all means one shall resort to Narasiṁha since he bestows the benefit of virtue, wealth, love and salvation.

The sages said :

8. O lord, since you say that the glory of Narasiṁha is the bestower of happiness and is very difficult of access it has kindled great wonder in us.

9. O lord of the universe, we wish to hear the power of that lord in detail. Our eagerness is very great.

10. O lord, obeisance be to you. For rendering help to devotees, tell us how Narasiṁha, the lord of great strength becomes pleased.

11. Tell us all about those (achievements) which originate by the favour of Narasiṁha. O great grandfather, be pleased with us.

Brahmā said :

12. O brahmins even as I recount listen to the power of that lord who is unconquered and incomprehensible and who bestows worldly pleasures and salvation.

13. O brahmins, who is competent to recount the good qualities of that lord half of whose body is that of a lion ? I shall mention a few succinctly.

14. We hear many human and divine accomplishments which are undoubtedly realized by the favour of that lord.

15. Due to the favour of that lord, one's movement becomes unimpeded in the mortal world, heaven, netherworlds, quarters, water, city as well as mountain.

16. In this world including the mobile and immobile beings O brahmins, there is nothing impossible to achieve for lord Narasiṁha who is always sympathetic to his devotees.

17. I shall mention the mode of procedure for the worship of the lord. This is helpful to his devotees. I shall mention what it is whereby the deity with half the body of a lion is propitiated.

18. O leading sages, listen to the eternal Kalparāja (Royal ritual), the real principle of Narasiṁha which has not been understood by Devas and Asuras.

19. O brahmins, the leading aspirant devotee should subsist on a diet of milk accompanied by greens, roots, barley food, fruits, fried grain powder and oil cake.

20-22. A pure loin cloth alone should constitute his garment. He should conquer his sense-organs and establish himself for meditation in the forest, an isolated place, mountain, confluence of rivers, a barren land, a holy centre of Siddhas or in the hermitage of Narasiṁha. Then he should worship the lord in accordance with the injunctions. O leading sages, on the twelfth day in the bright half of the lunar month he shall observe fast. With his mind and sense organs in perfect restraint he should repeat the mantra for two million times.

23. O brahmins, there is no doubt that the aspirant would be liberated from all sins whether they be subsidiary or major.

24-25. He should circumambulate and worship Narasiṁha with flowers, scents, incenses, etc. After bending the head before the lord the devotee should apply Jāti flowers smeared with camphor and sandal paste on the head of lord Narasiṁha. Thereby Siddhi results.

26-28. The lord is not hindered anywhere in any of his activities. Even Brahmā, Rudra and other Devas are incompetent to bear the refulgence of the lord. What then in regard to Dānavas, Siddhas, Gandharvas, human beings, Vidyādharas, Yakṣas, Kinnaras and Nāgas. There are those who wish for other Mantras, (than those of Narasiṁha). All these perish (on seeing Narasiṁha), like darkness when the refulgence of the sun or fire is revealed.

29. The (Talisman) that is inspired once by the repetition of Mantras bestows steady pleasures. The talisman that is inspired thus twice, becomes a divine amulet. It protects the devotee from Devas as well as Dānavas.

30. It should also protect from all those enemies such as Gandharvas, Kinnaras, Yakṣas, Vidyādharas, Nāgas, goblins, demons as well as similar antagonists.

31-34. The amulet that is inspired (with Mantras) thrice, cannot be broken by Devas and Asuras.

O excellent Brahmins, lord Narasiṁha of great strengths protects the aspirant devotee within a radius of twelve Yojanas.

The devotee should then go near a Crevasse and observe fast for three nights. He should then kindle the holy fire with Palāśa twigs and logs.

O leading brahmins, the aspirant should make two hundred sacrifices with (as many) Palāśa twigs soaked in honey, sugar and ghee repeating Vaṣaṭkāras.

The opening of Crevasse should be visible instantaneously.

35. The learned aspirant shall unhesitatingly enter the Crevasse with the coat of mail on, as he goes ahead, his difficulty, darkness and delusion perish.

36. A wide royal road beautified by humming bees becomes visible. O brahmins, remembering Narasiṁha he enters the nether worlds.

37-40. After going there, the aspirant should repeat the mantra of Narasiṁha the undiminishing mantra.

Thereafter, thousands of women playing on the lute come out to welcome him. O brahmins, after greeting him they take the leading aspirant, holding him by the hand.

O excellent brahmins, they make him drink the divine elixir. Immediately after drinking it he becomes very powerful. His body becomes divine.

He dallies with those girls till the ultimate dissolution of all living beings. When his body is split he becomes merged in Vāsudeva.

41-46. When the residence there, no longer appeals to him he starts therefrom. The leading aspirant takes the following things with him :- A tablet, a trident, a sword, a yellow orpiment, a jewel, a mercury, a pair of elixir sandals, collyrium, the skin of a black antelope, the pleasing pill, waterpot, rosary, staff, Siddhavidyā named Sañjīvanī and the scriptural texts. If the trident, that is enveloped by the wavelike formation of sparks of blazing fire is placed in the heart even for once it burns sins accumulated in crores of births. If it is placed in poison it destroys poison. If it is placed over the body it dispels leprosy. Even after committing the sin of foetus slaughter he becomes purified by this divine remedy. When patients are afflicted by powerful planets, the devotee shall think about the blazing deity. Thereby the terrible planets will perish quickly in the heart.

47. The amulet (inspired with Narasiṁha Mantra) tied round the neck of children affords a permanent protection: It destroys tumour, pustule, boils, as well as spider poison.

48. If afflicted by ailments, the devotee should perform a sacrifice with sacrificial twigs, ghee and milk, thrice a day during the junctions (i.e. dawn, midday and dusk). If this is continued for a month it will dispel all ailments.

49. I do not see anything that cannot be achieved in the three worlds consisting of mobile and immobile beings. Whatever accomplishment he desires, he certainly achieves it.

50-57. Another method: the devotee worships the lion one hundred and eight times. He takes seven lumps of clay from the anthill, cremation ground, four cross-roads. Mixing them with red sandal he pours cow's milk and rolls it into a lump. With this lump he makes the image of a lion six fingers (in length and height). Taking a bark leaf he applies yellow orpiment over it. This he ties round the neck of Narasiṁha. The aspirant then worships the deity with water. He repeats the Mantra innumerable times. With the sense-organs perfectly under restraint he continues the repetition of Mantra for seven days. Within a Muhūrta the entire earth is flooded with water.

Or the devotee shall worship Narasiṁha on the top of a tree. By performing the Japa of the Mantra one hundred and eight times the devotee can prevent a great downpour.

The noble aspirant puts the image of Narasiṁha in a cage and closes it. He should then whirl it. Within a short while a great gust of wind will undoubtedly blow. He can restrain it quickly by means of water inspired with the repetition of Narasiṁha Mantra seven times.

If the aspirant digs the earth and keeps the image concealed at the threshold of anyone, the entire family of that person will be annihilated. If it is taken out, it accords peace.

58. Hence, O leading sages, the devotee should always worship the lord of beasts, of great power, the bestower of all desires.

59-60. Liberated from all sins he goes to the world of Viṣṇu.

By devoutly worshipping the most excellent one among Devas, who has assumed the form of a lion, the Brahmins, Kṣatriyas, Vaiśyas, womenfolk, Śūdras and the lowcaste people are liberated from inauspicious miseries accumulated in the course of crores of births.

61-67. O Brahmins, by worshipping that excellent Deva they attain all desired things such as Deva-hood, lordship of the immortal beings and Gandharva-hood. They attain the status of Yakṣa or Vidyādhara or other types of desired things.

By visiting, eulogising, bowing to and worshipping Narasiṁha, men obtain a kingdom, heavenly pleasure and salvation which is very difficult to attain.

By visiting Narasiṁha a man obtains the desired benefit. Liberated from sins he goes to the world of Viṣṇu.

By devoutly visiting once that lord who has assumed the form of a lion, one is liberated from inauspicious miseries accumulated in crores of births.

On the following occasions the lord should be remembered. At the time of war, or a calamity very difficult to surmount, or at the time when one is afflicted by thieves, tigers etc., or when there is danger to life in a dense forest or when one is likely to be afflicted by poison, fire and water or when one is afflicted by kings and others, oceans, planets, sickness etc. By remembering the lord on these occasions a man is liberated from hosts of calamities.

Just as the desert of darkness is dispelled at sunrise so also all calamities perish by visiting the lord.

68-77. When lord Narasiṁha is pleased, a man obtains the miraculous pill, collyrium, sandals of the nether worlds, elixir as well as other desired things.

There is no doubt that one obtains all those desires for which one worships Narasiṁha with his desires kept in mind.

By visiting the lord of the chiefs of Devas, by devoutly worshipping him and bowing to him, the devotee derives ten times the benefit of ten horse sacrifices. He is liberated from all sins. He is embellishsd with all good qualities. He is richly blessed with the fulfilment of all desires. He is devoid of old age and death. Seated in an aerial chariot the devotee goes to the world of Viṣṇu.

The aerial chariot is golden. It is embellished with clusters of twinkling bells. It has good refulgence. It is richly furnished with all desirable things. It can go to any place one wishes. It has the colour and lustre of the midday sun. Pearl necklaces are suspended from it. Hundreds of celestial damsels are present in it. It is resonant with the divine sound of singing the Gandharvas. He is eulogised by Apsaras. He is as happy and gay as Devas. He redeems twentyone generations of his family. Thus he goes to the world of Viṣṇu. O excellent brahmins, there in the world of Viṣṇu he enjoys excellent pleasures in the company of Gandharvas and Apsaras. He assumes the form with four arms. He enjoys pleasures and happiness till the final dissolution of the world. When his merit dwindles he returns to this world and is born as a brahmin in an excellent family of Yogins. He masters the four Vedas and their ancillaries. He attains Yoga pertaining to Viṣṇu and obtains liberation.

CHAPTER FIFTYSIX

The Greatness of Śveta Mādhava

Brahmā said :

1. By visiting and devoutly bowing to Vāsudeva-Ananta the man is liberated from all sins. He attains the highest region of Viṣṇu.

2. He has been propitiated by me and thereafter by Indra, Vibhīṣaṇa[1] and Rāma. Who does not wish to be propitiated?

3. The man who takes holy dip in the Śvetagaṅgā and visits Śvetamādhava as well as Matsya Mādhava (Lord Viṣṇu in the form of a fish) goes to Śvetadvīpa.

The sages said :

4-5 It behoves you to recount fully the greatness of Śvetamādhava. O Lord of the Universe, recount the installation of Hari in detail. Lord Śvetamādhava is well known in that sacred and excellent holy centre. He is well known in the whole of the universe. Who installed that lord formerly?

Brahmā said:

6. O Brahmins, there was a powerful king named Śveta in the Kṛtayuga. He was intelligent, valorous and truthful. He was conversant with holy rites and he was steadfast in performing them.

7. In his kingdom, men used to live upto ten thousand years without sickness. No body perished or was despondant in that kingdom.

8-9 When this state of affairs continued thus in the kingdom for some time, O brahmins, the son of a very righteous sage named Kapalā Gautama passed away even before he cut his

1. *Vibhīṣaṇa* : brother of Rāvaṇa. Rāvaṇa, Kumbhakarṇa, and Vibhīṣaṇa were born to Viśravas by his wife Mālinī.

teeth. The intelligent sage brought the dead boy to the presence of the king.

10. On seeing the boy in this long slumber without sentience, O brahmins, the king took a vow of resuscitating the infant boy back to life.

The king said:

11. If I do not within seven days bring back this boy who has gone to the abode of Yama, I shall ascend the burning pyre.

Brahmā said :

12. After saying thus, the king worshipped the great lord with one thousand and one hundred blue lotuses. Then he repeated the Mantra.

13. On seeing the surpassing devotion of the king, the Lord of the universe came there together with Yama and said "I am delighted and satisfied".

14-15 On hearing the words of the Lord suddenly and seeing Lord Hara who had smeared his limbs with ashes, who had hideous eyes, who in refulgenee resembled the Kunda flower and the autumnal moon, who was wearing the hide of a tiger and whose tresses were marked by the moon he fell instantaneously on the ground, bowed to him and spoke.

Śveta said :

16-17. If you have mercy upon me, O Lord, if you are pleased on seeing me, may this boy, the dear child of a brahmin, who is under the control of the God of death, come back to life once again. This is the holy rite I have taken upon myself. O Lord Maheśvara, kindly instal a long life in this boy who is dead suddenly. Kindly accord all round welfare.

Brahmā said :

18. On hearing these words of Śveta, lord Maheśvara became joyous. He called the God of death who is terrible to all living beings.

19. O Brahmins, he restrained the unthwartable Kāla, the

obedient servant of Yama; he resuscitated the boy from the jaws of death.

20-21. After bringing back the sage's son to life and according welfare to the entire universe, O brahmins, the Lord vanished there itself together with goddess Umā. Thus the excellent king enlivened the son of the sage.

The sages said :

22. O Lord of Devas, O Lord of the Universe, O unchanging source of origin of the three worlds, tell us now the greatest fact of the deity named Śveta.

Brahmā said :

23. Listen, O leading sages, O sinless ones, for the welfare of all living beings I shall mention factually what you ask of me.

24. The greatness of Mādhava is destructive of all sins. On hearing it the man attains the desired pleasures.

25. O brahmins, I have heard his anecdote formerly from the sages, the divine story of the deity called Mādhava. Listen to that story which dispels fear, grief and agony.

26-28. King Śveta ruled over the kingdom for thousands of years with great concentration. He pondered over various holy rites of secular and Vedic nature and also over the restraints and observances. O Brahmins, he resolved to propitiate Keśava and adopted holy rites for that purpose. He went to the greatest holy centre on the shore of the Southern Sea. In a beautiful auspicious spot on the shore near Kṛṣṇa's shrine· Śveta built a beautiful palace.

29-30 To the south of the Lord of Devas he built the palace of a hundred bows' lengths. O leading Brahmins, with white marble rocks, Lord Mādhava was made to appear like a white man resembling the moon by king Śveta He performed the installation duly as (previously) thought of.

31-33. The king made charitable gifts to the brahmins, ascetics, poor and helpless persons. Thereafter, the king went to the presence of Lord Mahādeva. Repeating the twelve syllabled Mantra alongwith Oṁkāra he prostrated on the ground. Then the blessed king observed the vow of silence and abstaining from food for a month entered into Samādhi (trance). At the end of prayerful observance the king stood at the feet of Viṣṇu and began to eulogise the lord of Devas.

Śveta said :

34. Om obeisance to Vāsudeva, obeisance to Saṁkarṣaṇa, obeisance to Pradyumna, Aniruddha, obeisance to Nārāyaṇa.

35. Obeisance to the omniformed, to the creator of the form of the Universe, to inconceivable deity devoid of attributes, to the pure one, of (splendid) activities.

36. Om obeisance to the deity with the umbilical lotus, to the source of origin of the lotus-born lord; to the lotus-coloured one, to you with the lotus in hand.

37. Om obeisance to the lotus-eyed bountiful lord with a thousand eyes: obeisance to the thousand-footed, thousand-armed and thousand-furied lord.

38. Om obeisance to Varāha (Boar), the bestower of boons, the most excellent, the most praise-worthy deity of good intellect, Acyuta of gold complexion.

39. Om obeisance to the lord in the form of a boy, obeisance to the deity with the lustre of a tender lotus, obeisance to the deity with the rising sun and the moon for the eyes, obeisance to the lord with the tresses resembling Muñja grass.

40. Obeisance to Keśava, obeisance to Nārāyaṇa. Obeisance to Mādhava, obeisance to Govinda.

41. Om obeisance to Viṣṇu, obeisance to the lord endowed with wealth and strength; obeisance to the slayer of Madhu, to one who holds pure rays.

42. Obeisance to the infinite one, the subtle one, to one who bears the Śrīvatsa scar, obeisance to Śrīvikrama and the deity who wears the divine yellow robes.

43. Obeisance to you the cause of creation; obeisance to the protector and the sustainer, to one endowed with attributes, and also to one devoid of attributes.

44. Obeisance to the lord of dwarfish forms, to one of dwarfish activities, to one of small eyes, to one of dwarfish vehicle.

45. Obeisance to the infinite deity worthy of being worshipped, to one of unmanifest forms, to one who cannot be argued about, to the pure and the dispeller of fear.

46-47. Obeisance to the deity who acts as a raft (for crossing) the ocean of worldly existence, to the deity of colour forum, to the deity of auspicious gentle form, to the deity assuming terrible forms, to the deity that breaks worldly existence, the bestower of worldly pleasures, to the deity in the form of universe; obeisance to the creator of worlds.

48. Om obeisance to the deity of divine forms, to the deity whose breath is constituted by the moon and fire. Obeisance to one whose tresses are constituted by solar and lunar rays. Obeisance to the deity conducive to the welfare of cows and brahmins.

49. Om obeisance to the deity on the form of Ṛk; Obeisance to the deity in the forms of Pada and Krama. Obeisance to you, who are eulogised by the Ṛks; obeisance to the deity whose means is Ṛk.

50. Om obeisance to the upholder of Yaju's mantras, to the deity who has assumed the form of Yajus, to one who is worthy of being worshipped through Yajus, to one who is served, to the lord of Yajus Mantras.

51. Om obeisance to you, O lord of Śrī; Obeisance to Śrīdhara; obeisance to the most excellent one; obeisance to the lover of Śrī; obeisance to one of self-control; obeisance to the Yogin worthy of being meditated upon by the Yogins.

52. Om obeisance to the deity in the form of Sāman. Obeisance to the excellent tone of the Sāman. Om obeisance to the gentle one of Sāman. Obeisance to the deity conversant with the Sāmayoga.

53. Obeisance to the Sāman. Obeisance to the deity sung about by the Sāman songs. Om obeisance to the uplifter of the Sāman. Obeisance to the deity conversant with the Sāman. Obeisance to the composer of Sāman songs.

54. Obeisance to the deity whose head is Atharvaveda; obeisance to the deity whose from is Atharvan; obeisance to the deity whose foot is Atharvan; obeisance to the deity whose hand is Atharvan.

55. Om obeisance to the deity with adamantine head; obeisance to the slayer of Madhu and Kaiṭabha; obeisance to

one stationed in the waters of great ocean. Obeisance to one who redeemed the Vedas and brought them out of waters.

56. Obeisance to Hṛṣīkeśa[1] of brightly illuminated form. Obeisance to you, lord Vāsudeva. Obeisance to you Nārāyaṇa.

57. Obeisance to the deity conducive to the welfare of the world. Om obeisance to the destroyer of delusion. Obeisance to one who breaks existence.

58. Obeisance to one who bestows salvation; obeisance to one who dispels bondage; obeisance to the maker of luminaries. Obeisance to the deity of fiery form.

59. Obeisance to the lord of Yogins; obeisance to Rāma who redeems all; obeisance to happiness; obeisance to the happy-eyed; obeisance to the upholder of merits.

60. Obeisance to Vāsudeva worthy of being saluted; obeisance to Vāmadeva; obeisance to one who creates bodies for the embodied souls; obeisance to the breaker of difference.

61. Obeisance to the one whose body is saluted by Devas; obeisance to you of divine crown; obeisance to one who is the abode of fame; obeisance to one who serves as a shelter.

62. Om obeisance to the maker of riches; obeisance to one who bestows riches and residence; obeisance to the deity of the form of sacrifice; obeisance to the lord of sacrifices; obeisance to the Yogin.

63. Obeisance to the lord of ascetics who preach Yoga. Obeisance to one who holds a discus; obeisance to Saṁkarṣaṇa; obeisance to one who slew Pralamba.[2]

64. Obeisance to the holder of ploughshare whose velocity is great and whose sound resembles the sound of clouds. Obeisance to you a perfect knowledge of the wise, O Nārāyaṇa the ultimate resort of all living beings.

65. O Lord excepting you, I have no other kinsmen or guide for redeeming me from hell. Hence, O deity favourably disposed towards those who bow down, I bow to you with emotional fervour,

---

1. *Hṛṣīkeśa* : One who has controlled the sense-organs that is a yogin. Kṛṣṇa is said to be yogeśvara.

2. *Pralamba* : an asura who attacked Śrīkṛṣṇa and Balarāma but was killed by the latter.

66. O Keśava, O Acyuta, excepting you there is none to wash off the impurity of body and mind, O lord of Devas.

67. I have approached you after eschewing all sorts of contacts and unions. O Keśava, may my contact remain with you for attaining self-realization.

68. O Keśava, I know that this worldly existence is full of pain. It is impossible to cross it during adversities. I am afflicted by my threefold scarching tortures. Hence, I seek refuge in you.

69. The entire universe is deluded by enticing desires through your Māyā. It is attracted by covetousness, etc. Hence, I have resorted to you.

70-72. O Viṣṇu, nothing is conducive to happiness for an embodied soul stationed in the world.

O lord of sacrifices, as the mind is gradually turned to you, one may attain the ultimate pleasure, if one is not enamoured of the benefit of actions. "I am doomed. I am devoid of discriminating faculty". The Universe is seen unhappy and dejected thus.

O Govinda, save me from worldly existence. It behoves you to uplift me. I am immersed in the ocean of worldly existence which cannot be crossed, with delusion forming its waters. O Lotus-eyed one, excepting you there is no other saviour unto me.

Brahmā said :

73-74. O Brahmins, thus the lord was eulogised by king Śveta in that divine excellent holy centre known as Puruṣottama. In consideration of his devotion, Hari, the lord of Devas, the preceptor of the universe came in front of the king surrounded by all Devas.

75-77. He resembled the blue cloud. His eyes were large like the petals of lotus. By the tip of his hand the glorious lord held Sudarśana with a bright disc allround. In his left hand he held the splendid conch Pāñcajanya of great lustre. It was devoid of impurities. It resembled the moon and the liquid content of the milky ocean. The emblem of the lord was the king of birds.[1] The glorious lord held the iron club, sword and Śārṅga bow. He said :—"Well done, O king, since this excellent idea rose within you, O sinless one, choose whatever is desired by you and whatever is conducive to my welfare. I am delighted with you".

Brahmā said :

78. On hearing these nectar-like words of the Lord of Devas, Śveta bent down his head with devotion and said with his mind concentrating on the lord.

Śveta said :

79-80. O lord, if I am a devotee, grant me this excellent boon. The unchanging region of Viṣṇu is above everything upto the abode of Brahmā. It is devoid of impurities and Rajas. It is pure. It is rid of the contact with the world. O lord of the universe, I wish to go to that region by your favour.

The Lord said :

81-82. After enjoying the nectar of ruling over the kingdom you will go to that abode which Devas, sages, Siddhas and yogins do not approach. It is the greatest abode devoid of ailments. After passing over the worlds you will attain my world.

83. O leading king, your glory will spread throughout the world. I will always be present here.

84-88. Devas and Dānavas will sing about this as Śveta Gaṅgā, pure and holy Gaṅgā. My devotees who have great concentration will go to heaven even by touching the sacred water of Śveta Gaṅgā, O leading king, by the tip of Kuśa grass.

He who visits this idol of lunar splendour named Mādhava and worships it even once, casts off other worlds. He is honoured in my world. The idol resembles the conch and cow's milk. It is destructive of sins. It has eyes resembling a lotus.

For many Manvantaras he will enjoy as he pleases the extensive pleasures in the company of my followers. He will be surrounded by beautiful celestial virgins. The Siddhas and Gandharvas will sing his praise and serve him.

1. *King of birds*—Garuḍa, the Vehicle of Mahāviṣṇu.

89-91. Falling off from that place he comes here as a man. He shall be born as a brahmin mastering the Vedas and Vedāṅgas. He will be glorious. He will enjoy all pleasures and live for a long time. He will possess elephants, horses, chariots and other vehicles. He will be surrounded by wealṭh and food-grains. He will be pure and endowed with handome features. He will be fortunate and accompanied by sons and grandsons.

He will return to the holy centre Puruṣottama at the root of the Banyan tree on the sea-shore. Remembering Hari and casting off the body he shall go to that calm and quiet place.

CHAPTER FIFTYSEVEN

Mode of Procedure for a Holy Dip in the Ocean

Brahmā said :

1-3. By visiting Śvetamādhava and Matsyamādhava by his side and by bowing to the first incarnation of Mādhava in the form of a Fish, one is liberated from all miseries. Lord Matsya Mādhava had at the outset assumed the form of Rohita fish. He had been thinking of the earth stationed at the bottom of the nether worlds. He established himself there in order to redeem the Vedas.

4. He goes to the greatest abode where Hari himself is present. Returning to this place(earth)in due course of time he shall become a king on the earth.

5. By resorting to Matsyamādhava a man becomes unthwartable. He shall be a donor, enjoyer of pleasures, a worshipper, a devotee of Viṣṇu and truthful in speech.

6. Afterwards he attains Yoga pertaining to Hari and gains salvation. O leading sages, the greatness of Matsyamādhava has been recounted by me. By visiting him the devotee will obtain all cherished desires.

The sages said :

7. O Lord, we wish to hear further. The rites of wiping off,

causing sprinkling of water by means of Kuśa grass, ablution, charitable gifts, etc are performed on the sea-shore. Kindly mention the entire benefits thereof.

Brahmā said :

8-10. Listen, O leading sages, to the benefit of Mārjana rite performed duly. One attains excellent merit due to devotion. Out of devotion one must direct one's mind towards him. The rite of taking holy dip in the eddy called Mārkaṇḍeya Hrada is to be preferably performed in the forenoon. Especially on the fourteenth day of the lunar fortnight this rite is destructive of all sins. Similarly, the rite of ablution in the ocean is equally praise-worthy at any time. Especially on the full moon day (by the holy dip) one attains the benefit of a horse-sacrifice.

11. The Pañcatīrthi (a set of five holy centres and sacred waters) is as follows :—The eddy named after Mārkaṇḍeya, the holy banyan tree, the shrine of Kṛṣṇa, the shrine of Balarāma and the great Indradyumnasaras (Lake of Indradyumna).

12. One should visit the Tīrtharāja (king of holy centres, the holy Banyan tree) on the full moon day in the month of Jyeṣṭha. If the constellation Jyeṣṭha coincides with it, it is especially auspicious.

13-15. The devotee should be pure mentally, verbally and physically. He should not think of anything else. He should be free from all Dvandvas (mutually opposed pairs). He should free from lustful attachment and rivalry. The beautiful banyan tree is the Kalpa tree itself. After taking holy dip near it, the devotee shall circumambulate the lord thrice with great concentration. O Brahmins, by visiting this Lord one is liberated from sins accumulated in the course of seven births. He attains extensive merits and the desired salvation.

16. O brahmins, I shall mention its names and size, in the Yugas Kṛta, etc, in due order.

17. The names of the banyan tree in the Kṛtayuga etc are respectively.—1) Vata, (2) Vaṭeśvara, (3) Puruṣa and (4) Purāṇapuruṣa, O brahmins.

18. The sizes of the Kalpa tree in the four Yugas are 1) one Yojana 2) three fourths of a Yojana (3) half a Yojana and 4) onefourth of a Yojana.

19. After bowing to the banyan tree repeating the mantra mentioned before, the devotee shall go to the South to a distance of three hundred bow's lengths.

20. At this place one can behold Viṣṇu. Here is a pleasing entrance to the heavenly world. A log of wood equipped with good qualities is dragged by the waters of the ocean.

21. By bowing to him and then by worshipping him, the devotee is liberated from all ailments, sins, evils and things of other sorts.

22-24. Through the heavenly door the devotee views the ocean as one with fierce foams. He shall then perform the rite of Ācamana. Remaining pure be should meditate afterwards, fix the eight-syllabled Mantra in the (fingers of the) hand and (limits of) the body that is the Mantra which learned men say thus—Oṁ namo Nārāyaṇāya.

What can be done with many Mantras that cause only mental confusion ? This mantra Oṁ namo Nārāyaṇāya is the means of achieving everything.

25. The waters are glorified as Nāras because they are the sons of Nara (human beings). At the outset the waters had been the abode of Viṣṇu. Hence, he is known as Nārāyaṇa (having Nāra (waters) for abode.

26. The greatest in the world is Nārāyaṇa. The greatest among Devas is Nārāyaṇa. Truthfulness is devoted to Nārāyaṇa.

27-33. The element earth is devoted to Nārāyaṇa, the element water is devoted to Nārāyaṇa, the element fire is devoted to Nārāyaṇa, the element sky is devoted to Nārāyaṇa, the wind is devoted to Nārāyaṇa, the mind is devoted to Nārāyaṇa, the ego and the cosmic intellect are of the nature of Nārāyaṇa. The past, present, future, whatever is called by the name Jīva (living-organism) is of the nature of Nārāyaṇa.

Sound and other objects of sense-organs, ears and other sense-organs the Prakṛti and Puruṣa—these are of the nature of Nārāyaṇa.

Lord Nārāyaṇa occupies water, dryland, nether worlds. heaven, sky and mountains supporting all these visible objects.

Of what avail is much talk ? The whole universe consisting of mobile and immobile beings, from Brahmā to the blade of grass—is identical with Nārāyaṇa.

O Brahmins, I do not see anything greater than Nārāyaṇa. All these visible and invisible things in the world are pervaded by him.

34. The waters are the abode of Viṣṇu. He is the lord of waters. Hence, one should always remember Nārāyaṇa, the dispeller of sins, in the waters.

35. Particularly at the time of bath the pure devotee shall worship and remember Nārāyaṇa in the water. He shall meditate on him and perform the Nyāsa rite in the (fingers of hand and (the limbs of) body.

36-42. He should fix Oṁkāra and Nakāra (syllable *Na*) in the thumbs of his hands. The other syllables he shall fix in the index and other fingers covering the whole palm.

He shall fix Oṁkāra in the left foot and Nakāra (syllable *Na*) in the right foot. He shall fix the syllable *Mo* in the left hip and the syllable *Nā* in the right hip.

He shall fix the syllable *Rā* in the umbilical spot and the syllable *Ya* in the left arm. After fixing the syllable *Ṇā* in the right arm he shall fix the syllable *Ya* on the head. (The mantra is Oṁ namo Nārāyaṇāya.

The learned devotee shall meditate on Nārāyaṇa, in the heart, at the sides, behind, in front, below and above and thereafter begin Kavaca[1] (coat of mail):—

May Govinda protect me in the East, Madhusūdana in the South, lord Śrīdhara in the West and Keśava in the North.

Similarly, may Viṣṇu protect in the South-East; the undwindling Mādhava in the South-West; Hṛṣīkeśa in the North-West and Vāmana in the North-East.

May Varāha (Boar) protect the ground and Trivikrama above. After making Kavaca (the coat of mail) the devotee should think about the soul.

1. *Kavaca*—Protective armour, composed of mystic syllables to be essentially recited at the worship of a deity.

43. I am lord Nārāyaṇa who holds the conch, discus and club. After meditating on the Self he should repeat this mantra.

44-45. "You are the fire, O Lord of bipeds, he who provides (them) with Semen, he who excites their lust. You are Pradhāna (Prakṛti and chief) of all living beings; the unchanging lord of all individual souls. You are the Araṇi (Source of fire) of the nectar. O Lord of waters, you are the source of origin of Devas. O Tīrtharāja, (king of holy centres), remove my sins, obeisance be to you".

46. It is only after uttering this duly that one should perform the rite of ablution. Otherwise, O excellent brahmins, the holy dip there is not valued much.

47. After performing the rites of ablution and cleansing by means of the Mantras with the water as their divinity, the devotee shall thereafter repeat the Aghamarṣaṇa Mantra three times (all the while) standing within water.

48. O brahmins, just as the horse-sacrifice removes sins so also does the hymn Aghamarṣaṇa[1] remove all sins.

49-51. He should come out of water and wear two washed cloths free from impurities. He shall perform the Ācamana rite and the Prāṇāyāma. He shall then pray to the junction as well as the sungod. Thereafter he should offer a handful of water libation alongwith flowers. With his hands lifted up he should pray to the sun-god with the significant hymns pertaining to him. Thereafter, he shall repeat the sacred Gāyatrī Mantra, hundred and eight times. He shall stand there with perfect concentration after repeating other Mantras pertaining to the Sungod.

52. After circumambulating the sungod and bowing down to him he should sit facing the east and perform the rite of (vedic study, then he should perform Tarpaṇa rites to the Gods and sages.

53. He should perform Tarpaṇa rites for sages, manes and others. He the knower of Mantras, should perform Tarpaṇa by repeating their names and Gotras. The water shall be mixed up with gingelly seeds.

---

1. *Aghamarṣaṇa* mantra : RV.X.190.

54. The brahmin shall be authorized in the Tarpaṇa rite to the manes only after performing Tarpaṇa rite to the deities at the outset with due attention.

55. At the time of Śrāddha, when the ball of rice is offered, the devotee shall offer it with a single hand. When performing the rite of Tarpaṇa he shall use both hands. This is the procedure to be followed always.

56. After repeating the name and Gotra (Spiritual lineage) he shall say 'Tṛpyatām' (may be pleased). Otherwise he should not utter anything. The left-hand should be joined to the right hand (and thus the libation should be offered.

57. If out of delusion the devotee performs the rite of Tarpaṇa with the gingelly seeds kept on any of his limbs, it would be as though he had performed the rites of Tarpaṇa to the forefathers by means of skin, flesh, blood and bone.

58. One should not perform the rite of Tarpaṇa to the deities and Pitṛs with the gingelly seeds kept on any of the limbs. That water will turn into blood and he who offers it shall be sinful.

59. O leading sages, if the person who offers libation stands in water and if the libation is offered on the dry ground, that offering is made futile. It does not benefit anyone.

60. If the man stands on the ground and offers libation into the water, that water libation does not approach the manes. It turns futile.

61. One should not stand in water and offer water libation to the manes. He should come out and perform water libation on a pure spot.

62-65. The Tarpaṇa rite shall not be performed in water or in vessels. While performing the rite one shall not be wrathful nor should one perform it with a single hand. The water libation that is not made on the ground does not benefit the manes.

O brahmins, the earth has been given by me to the manes as their everlasting abode. Hence water libation should be offered there alone by one who seeks pleasure for the manes.

They were born on the surface of earth. They died on the surface of earth and merged with it. During life time it was on this earth that they stood. Hence, one should offer water libation on the ground.

He should spread Kuśa grass with their tips to the East in regard to the Gods; to the South in regard of the manes. He should invoke gods and manes by repeating their Mantras separately.

CHAPTER FIFTYEIGHT

Rules of Worship and Mantras

Brahmā said :

1-2. After performing the rites of Tarpaṇa to Devas, Pitṛs and others and having performed the Ācamana rite silently, O Brahmins, the devotee shall draw the mystic diagram of a city on the shore of a great ocean. It should look very splendid with four corners and four gateways. The figure shall extend to a hand in size. In the middle of the city he should draw the mystic diagram of a lotus with eight petals and a pericarp.

3. After drawing the mystic diagram O brahmins, the devotee should worship Nārāyaṇa, the unborn lord by means of injunctions in regard to the eight syllabled Mantra.

4-6. I shall now mention the excellent means of cleaning the body. He should think of the (syllable *A*) in the heart alongwith a circular line. It should have three blazing tufts that burn and destroy sins. He shall think of the syllable *Ra* stationed in the middle of the lunar disc on the head. It should be white in colour, it should shower nectar and blood on the earth. After dispelling sins thus he is endowed with a divine body.

7. Then he should perform the Nyāsa rite with the eight-syllabled Mantra. He shall begin with the left foot and fix in due order.

8. The aspirant should perform the following rites with the basic Mantra viz. the five limbs belonging to lord Viṣṇu;

the four groups or arrays and the purificatory rite of the hand also belong to the lord.

9-12. Each of the Varṇas (colours, syllables) should be fixed in the figures separately. He should fix the syllable *Om* as the white earth in the left foot, the syllable *Na* pertains to lord Śiva. It is dark-coloured and is stationed in the right foot. They call the syllable *Mo* Kāla (time, God of Death). The devotee should fix it in the left hip. The syllable *Nā* is the seed of everything. It is stationed in the right hip. They call the syllable *Rā* Tejas (fire). It is stationed in the umbilical region, The syllable *Ya* pertains to the wind and it resorts to the left shoulder. The syllable *Ṇā* should be known as omnipresent. It is stationed in the right shoulder. The syllable *Ya* is stationed in the head. It is in this that all the worlds are established.

13. Om obeisance to Viṣṇu—thus the head. Om obeisance to Jvalana (the fiery blaze)—thus the tuft. Om obeisance to Viṣṇu—thus the coat of mail. Oṁ obeisance to Viṣṇu—thus the throbbing for the binding of quarters. Oṁ Hum phaṭ—thus the miraculous weapon. Oṁ Vāsudeva is white—in the head thus. Oṁ Am Saṅkarṣaṇa is red—in the forehead. Garuḍa is the fire, the luminary sun thus. Aṁ Pradyumna is yellow—in the neck. He is the wind and cloud. Oṁ Aṁ Aniruddha is black—in the heart. He is endowed with all power. Thus protected by four arrays the devotee shall start reciting Kavaca.

14-17. "Viṣṇu is stationed in front of me; Govinda in the right side; Madhusūdana in the left; Vaikuṇṭha above; Varāha on the surface of the Earth; Mādhava in intermediary spaces. My protection is afforded by Narasiṁha even as I move about or stay still, whatever I am awake or asleep. I am identical with Vāsudeva". Thus the devotee will become identical with the lord. He shall start the holy rite. As in regard to the body so in regard to the lord he should join the principles (tattvas).

18-19. He should perform the rite of sprinkling with water with the mantra Oṁkāra and ending with Phat, dispelling of calamities. The mantra is efficacious in warding off the evil effect of the malefic eye of the sun, moon and fire. He should fix Viṣṇu in the centre of the lotus between wind and ether.

20-21. He should think of Oṁkāra in the form of a luminary, in the heart. The eternal form of the luminary is seated in the pericarp. He should perform the Nyāsa of the eight-syllabled Mātrā in due order. The greatest worship is rendered to the lord by that Mantra analytically and synthetically.

22. He should perform the worship of eternal lord by the twelve-syllabled Mantra; thereafter he should fix it up in the pericarp, at the outside, after retaining it in the heart.

23. He should meditate upon the eternal lord with four arms and possessed of great strength. He should think upon the lord with lustre of a crore suns. He should invoke the lord after duly thinking about him in his mind.

24. (The invocation is as follows) :—

May the Lord Nārāyaṇa, the bestower of boons come in front of me in the form of a Fish, Boar, Man-lion and a Dwarf. Om namo Nārāyaṇāya—thus is the mantra for invoking the lord (obeisance to Nārāyaṇa).

25. The establishment of the seat is as follows :—

At the extremity of foot-hills of the mountain Sumeru the seat is conceived of in the mystic lotus. "O Slayer of Madhu, stay here for the welfare of all animals. Oṁ namo Nārāyaṇāya (Obeisance to Nārāyaṇa)—thus the establishment of the seat".

26. The Arghya is offered with the following mantra :—

"Oṁ obeisance to Lord Viṣṇu, Hṛṣīkeśa, the lord of Devas, of rulers of the three worlds. Om namo Nārāyaṇāya (obeissance to Nārāyaṇa), thus the Arghya.

27. Om the water offering for washing the feet. O Eternal Padmanābha, O Lord, the water is offered at your feet. O Viṣṇu, with eyes like the petals of a lotus, O Madhusūdana, please accept it. Oṁ namo Nārāyaṇāya (Obeisance to Nārāyaṇa)—thus the Pādya.

28. The holy offering is made as follows :—"O Great Lord, the best among the Puruṣas, the Madhuparka as prepared by Brahmā and other sages is devoutly offered unto you. Please accept it, "Om namo Nārāyaṇāya"—thus the Madhuparka.[1]

---

1. *Madhuparka* : a mixture of honey, curd and butter offered to the guest or the bridegroom on the wedding ceremony.

29. The water for ritualistic rinsing of the mouth is offered to you. The crystaline water of the Gaṅgā is auspicious and it dispels all sins. Accept this water for rinsing your mouth as devotedly offered by me.

30. The ablutionary rite is as under :—

"You are water, earth, fire, wind. O lord of the Universe, I am bathing you with water merely as a routine activity. Om namo Nārāyaṇāya" thus the ablution.

31. The two cloths are offered as follows :—

"O Lord, equipped with the principles, having the lustre and colour of sacrifice, O lord Keśava, two cloths having the lustre and colour of gold are offered to you. Oṁ namo Nārāyaṇāya"—thus the cloths.

32. The unguent is offered as follows :—

"O Keśava, I do not know your body nor your activities. The scent is offered by me. Let it be accepted to smear your body with. Oṁ namo Nārāyaṇāya"—thus the unguent.

33. The sacred thread is offered as follows :—"I dedicate the sacred thread wound into threefolds by the lotus-born deity through the Ṛk, Yajus and Sāman. It has the blessing of Sāvitrī. Oṁ namo Nārāyaṇāya"—thus the sacred thread.

34. Ornaments are offered as follows :—

"O Mādhava, equipped with divine gems, with the lustre like that of fire and the sun, may your body shine splendidly with ornaments. Oṁ namo Nārāyaṇāya"—thus the ornaments.

35-38. When worshipping, the words Oṁ namaḥ shall be used alongwith each of the syllables of the basic Mantra. Or the worship can be performed with the basic mantra alone.

"May this offering of incense be accepted. The divine juice of the plant rendered fragrant by the addition of scents, has been offered by me with great devotion.

Oṁ namo Nārāyaṇāya"—thus the incense is offered.

The light is offered as follows :—

The refulgence "as that of the sun and the moon, the bright-light of the lightning and fire—you alone are that, O Lord of luminaries; may this lamp be accepted. Oṁ namo Nārāyaṇāya"—thus the lamp.

The Naivedya is offered as follows :—

"The four varieties of cooked rice, equipped with six types of tastes O Keśava, this Naivedya (food offering) has been devoutly offered to you. Oṁ namo Nārāyaṇāya"—thus the Naivedya.

39-47. The devotee shall fix Vāsudeva in the petal in the East, Saṁkarṣaṇa in the South, Pradyumna in the West and Aniruddha in the North, Varāha in the South-East, Narasiṁha in the South-West, Madhva in the North-West and Trivikrama in the North-East.

Similarly, he snould fix Garuḍa in front of the Lord of eight syllables; he shall fix the discus at the left side and the couch at the right side. Similarly, he shall fix the great iron club on the right side, the mighty bow on the left. The two divine quivers on the right side and the sword to the left. After establishing Śrī to the right (i.e. the South) he should fix prosperity (puṣṭi) to the North. He should fix the garland of sylvan flowers, the scar Śrīvatsa and the jewel Kaustubha in front. He should fix the weapons of the lord of Devas in the angular points. With the Tāntrika mantras he should fix Indra, Agni, Yama, Nairṛta, Varuṇa, Vāyu, Dhanada and Īśāna in the eight quarters and Ananta and Brahmā beneath and above and worship them.

Worshipping the lord of Devas thus, stationed in the mystic diagram, he shall obtain his cherished desires.

48. He who observes Janārdana who in accordance with this injunction is worshipped in the mystic diagram, shall enter the eternal Viṣṇu.

49. If Keśava is worshipped even for once in accordance with this injunction, the devotee will surmount birth, death and old age. He will attain the region of Viṣṇu.

50. An abode in the white Island (Śvetadvīpa) is allotted to the person who remembers Nārāyaṇa with devout attention.

51. His name with Oṁkāra at the beginning and Namaḥ at the end is called the Mantra of all Principles.

52-53. He should offer scents and fragrant flowers in accordance with this very injunction. For each one of syllables he shall offer flowers in due order. He shall show mystic gestures in the order of their occurrence. Hc should perform the rite of recitation of the bīja Mantra. There are eight mystic gestures viz—lotus, conch, Śrīvatsa, iron club, Garuḍa, discus, sword, and the bow Śārṅga. Repetition of the name may be for eight, twentyeight or hundred and eight times. In accordance with his capacity, or desires entertained or the frequency mentioned, the devotee shall perform the rite of recitation with great concentration and attentively.

The ritualistic dismissal of the deity is as follows :—"O Purāṇa Puruṣottama, go, go to the greatest abode where Devas viz. Brahmā and others live joyfully. Om namo Nārāyaṇāya", thus the dismissal.

Those who do not know this mode of worship of Hari may worship him by reciting the basic Mantra.

CHAPTER FIFTYNINE

The Merit of a holy dip in the Ocean

Brahmā said :

1. After duly and devoutly worshipping the lord thus, the devotee should bend his head thereafter and propitiate the ocean.

2. O Lord of streams you are the vital breath and source of origin of all living beings. O king of sacred waters fond of Lord Viṣṇu, obeisance be to you. Save me.

3-4. O brahmins, by taking the holy dip perfectly in the ocean thus, in that excellent holy centre, by duly worshipping Nārāyaṇa devoid of ailments and by bowing to Rāma, Kṛṣṇa, Subhadra and the ocean the man attains the benefit of performing hundreds of horse-sacrifices.

5-6. He will be rid of all sins. He will be devoid of all miseries. He will be glorious like gods and be justifiably proud of handsome features and blooming youth. He can redeem twentyone generations of his family. He goes to the world of Viṣṇu on an aerial chariot with the lustre and colour of the sun and glorified with the divine sound of music produced by the Gandharvas.

7-9. For the period of a hundred Manvantaras or more he will enjoy excellent pleasures and carry on dalliance with the celestial damsels. He will be devoid of old age and death. When his merit dwindles he returns to the world and is born in a family endowed with noble qualities. He will be handsome, fortunate, glorious truthful and celibate. He conquers his sense-organs. He is born as a brahmin conversant with the meaning of the Vedic and scriptural passages. He will be one who performs sacrifices. He will be a devotee of Viṣṇu. After performing the Yoga pertaining to Viṣṇu he will attain salvation thereby.

10-15. Intelligent devotees give charitable gifts to brahmins at that place on the following occasions. During eclipse of planets, during tropical, equinoctical or other transit of the sun from one zodiac to another, during Yugādi days, (i.e. during the transit of the sun at a particular juncture), during Vyatipāta (ill-owned occasion), when day comes to a close, during the full moon days of Aṣāḍha, Kārttika and Māgha or any other auspicious occasion. For these charitable rites the devotees attain a thousand times more benefit than the very same rites at other holy centres. If the descendants offer balls of rice to the manes in accordance with the injunctions at this place the manes derive everlasting satisfaction. Thus the benefit of holy dip in the ocean has been recounted by me. O brahmins, the benefit of charitable gifts and the benefit offering balls of rice at this centre have also been recounted by me. The holy dip confers the benefit of virtue, wealth and salvation, causes longevity, renown and fame, yields worldly pleasures and bestows salvation upon men. It destroys the evil effects of dreams, despels sins. It is holy and gives all desired benefits.

16-23. O excellent Brahmins, the knowledge of the Purāṇa should not be imparted to an atheist. O Brahmins, so long as the glory of this king of holy centres is not described the other holy centres such as Puṣkara roar with the pride of their manifold glories.

The Puṣkara and other holy centres confer only their respective benefits. But the king of holy centres bestows the benefit of all rivers and holy centres. The rivers, brooks, and other holy spots enter this king of holy centres. Hence, it has acquired excellence. The ocean, the lord of rivers is the king of all holy spots since it bestows all cherished desires and it is more excellent than all other holy centres.

O brahmins, just as darkness perishes when the sun rises, so also the sins perish due to the holy dip in the Tīrtharāja.

There never was nor will ever there be a holy centre on a par with Tīrtharāja where lord Nārāyaṇa is always present. O brahmins, who can recount the excellent qualities of this Tīrtharāja where ninetynine crores of holy centres abide peacefully.

Hence, brahmins, whatever is done there viz., the holy dip, charitable gift, sacrifice, recitation of mantras and the worship of Devas is done with a never-ending benefit.

CHAPTER SIXTY

Glory of five holy spots Pañcatīrthī

Brahmā said :

1. O excellent Brahmins, thence the devotee should go to the holy spot of sacrifices where the splendid and sacred lake Indradyumna is situated.

2. The intelligent devotee should go there with pure mind and body, and meditate mentally on lord Hari, approach the sacred waters, perform the Ācamana rite and repeat this Mantra :—

3. "O holy spot that is sanctified by the performance of horse sacrifice, and which destroys sins, I am taking a holy dip in you. Remove my sin. Obeisance be to you".

4-5. After uttering this, he should duly bathe. With gingelly seeds and water he should perform Tarpaṇa to Devas, Pitṛs and others. He should perform Ācamana rite with restrained speech. He should offer balls of rice to the Pitṛs and worship Puruṣottama. By performing these rites he obtains merits and benefits of ten horse-sacrifices.

6. He redeems seven former generations and seven subsequent generations of his family. Like a God he goes to the world of Viṣṇu on an aerial chariot that can go in all directions.

7. He can enjoy pleasures and happiness there, as long as the moon, sun and stars last. Falling off from that world he returns to the earth and attains salvation thereafter.

8-9. The devotee should conclude his pilgrimage to the five holy spots. He shall observe fast on the eleventh day. He who visits Puruṣottama on the fifteenth day in the bright half of the month of Jyeṣṭha, obtains the benefits and sport in the abode of Lord Viṣṇu. He then goes to that highest region from which he never returns.

The sages said :

10. O lord, great-grandfather, why do you praise the month of Jyeṣṭha in preference to Māgha and other months. Kindly tell us the reason thereof.

Brahmā said :

11. O leading sages, listen, I shall briefly mention why I praise the month of Jyeṣṭha in preference to other months.

12-14. All holy spots, rivers, lakes, lotus, ponds, wells, tanks, eddies, streams and oceans flow into the holy centre of Puruṣottama for seven days beginning with the tenth day in the bright half of the month of Jyeṣṭha. Hence, O branmins whatever rite is performed there at that time such as holy ablution, charitable gifts, visiting the deity etc. should become inexhaustible in merits.

15. O excellent brahmins, the tenth day in the bright half of the month of Jyeṣṭha removes ten sins. Hence it is called 'Daśaharā'.

16. The man who visits Balarāma, Kṛṣṇa, and Subhadrā meditates upon them with concentration and mental purity will get rid of all sins and go to the world of Viṣṇu.

17. O Brahmins, by visiting Puruṣottama, Rāma and Subhadrā during the first day of the northern and southern solar transits the man goes to the world of Viṣṇu.

18. By visiting Govinda, the most excellent of all Gods, seated on the swing, on the full moon day in the month of Phālguna the devotee of great self-restraint shall go to the city of Govinda.

19-20. When the day of Viṣṇu arrives, O brahmins, the devotee will perform the holy pilgrimage to the five holy spots in accordance with the injunctions and visit Saṅkarṣaṇa, Kṛṣṇa and Bhadra. He attains the rare benefit accruing from the performance of various sacrifices. Rid of all sins, he goes to the world of Viṣṇu.

21-22. He who sees Kṛṣṇa smeared with sandal paste on the third day in the bright half of the month of Vaiśākha goes to the palace of Lord Viṣṇu. He who sees Puruṣottama on the full moon day in the month of Jyeṣṭha, when the constellation of Jyeṣṭha occurs will redeem twentyone members of his family and go to the world of Viṣṇu.

CHAPTER SIXTYONE

In praise of Mahājyeṣṭhī Full moon day in the month of Jyeṣṭha

Brahmā said :

1. When the Mahājyeṣṭhī occurs due to the contact of a zodiac and a constellation he should go to the holy place called Puruṣottama.

2. O brahmins, by visiting Kṛṣṇa, Rāma and Subhadrā on the Mahājyeṣṭhī day, the visitor obtains more benefit than that of twelve pilgrimages.

3-16. By visiting Kṛṣṇa on the Mahājyeṣṭhī day he obtains the benefit as is obtained when the rites of ablution and charitable gifts are performed in the following holy places, rivers, etc. during the solar eclipse. They are—Prayāga, Kurukṣetra, Naimiṣa Puṣkara, Gayā, Gaṅgādvāra, Kuśāvarta, the confluence of Gaṅgā and the ocean, Kokāmukha, Śūkara, Mathurā, Marusthala (the holy desert region), Śālagrāma, Vāyutīrtha, Mandara, the confluence of Sindhu and the ocean, Piṇḍāraka, Citrakūṭa,

Prabhāsa, Kanakhala, Śaṅkhoddhāra, Dvārakā, Badarikāśrama, Lohakuṇḍa, Aśvatīrtha that liberates one from all sins, Kāmālaya, Koṭitīrtha, Amarakaṇṭaka, Lohārgala, Jambūmārga, Somatīrtha, Pṛthūdaka, Utpalāvartaka, Pṛthutuṅga, Sukubjaka, Ekāmraka, Kedāra, Kāśī, Viraja, Kālañjara, Gokarṇa, Śrīśaila, Gandhamādana, Mahendra, Malaya, Vindhya, Pāriyātra, Himālaya, Sahya, Śuktimān, Gomanta, Arbuda, Gaṅgā, Tīrthas on the bank of Yamunā, Sarasvatī, Gomatī, seven rivers Brahmaputra, Godāvarī, Bhimarathī, Tuṅgabhadrā, Narmadā, Tāpī, Payoṣṇī, Kāverī, Kṣiprā, Carmaṇvatī, Vitastā, Candra-Bhāgā, Śatadrū, Bāhudā, Ṛṣikulyā, Kumāri, Vipāśā, Dṛṣadvatī, Sarayū, Gaṅgā, Gaṇḍakī Mahānadī, Kauśikī, Karatoyā, Trisrotā, Madhuvāhinī, Mahānadī Vaitaraṇī and other rivers not mentioned there. O excellent brahmins, of what avail is much talk? All holy centres, all holy shrines, oceans, mountains, rivers, lakes, etc. on the earth.

17. Hence, O excellent sages, those who are desirous of attaining their longed-for benefit, will assiduously go to Puruṣottama on the Mahājyeṣṭhī day.

18-20. By visiting Rāma and Kṛṣṇa together with Subhadrā on the Mahājyeṣṭhī day the devotee goes to the world of Viṣṇu after uplifting his family.

After enjoying great and excellent pleasures there, till the dissolution of all living beings he returns to this place when the merit dwindles. He will then be born as a brahmin mastering the four vedas.

He will be devoted to his own duty. He will be peaceful. He will be a devotee of Kṛṣṇa. He will conquer his sense-organs. By adopting the Yoga pertaining to Viṣṇu, he will attain salvation.

CHAPTER SIXTYTWO

Holy Ablution in Propitiation of Kṛṣṇa

The sages said :

1. O lotus-born one, when does the holy dip of Kṛṣṇa take place? By what means and in accordance with what precepts? Mention this, O excellent one among the knowers of precepts.

Brahmā said :

2. O sages, even as I recount, listen to the rules of holy ablution (in propitiation) of Kṛṣṇa, Rāma and Subhadrā. It is meritorious and destroyer of all sins.

3. O brahmins if, in the month of Jyeṣṭha the constella-ation Mārgaśiras coincides with the full moon, that is the auspicious time for the ablution of Hari.

4. There is a pure well devoid of impurities. It is full of sacred water reservoirs. O brahmins, the sacred river Bhogavatī becomes visible there at that time.

5-10. Hence, from that well, the devotee should draw water in golden vessels on the fullmoon day, for the ablution of Kṛṣṇa, Rāma and Subhadrā. O brahmins, the devotee, should make a raised rostrum for the ablution of Rāma and Kṛṣṇa. The rostrum should look splendid and well decorated with flags. It should be firm as well as comfortable to walk upon. It should be beautified with flowers and nice pieces of clothes. It should be spacious and fumigated with incenses. It should be enclosed with white clothes and decorated with pearlnecklaces dangling down. To the accompaniment of musical intruments and auspicious shouts of victory the idols of Kṛṣṇa, Balarāma and Subhadrā should be installed on the platform.

O brahmins, men and women, brahmins, Kṣatriyas, Vaiśyas, Śūdras and people of other castes, householders, religious students newly wed, ascetics and celibate students should pour water over Kṛṣṇa and the ploughshare-armed Balarāma stationed on the platform.

11. O excellent brahmins, all the holy sacred waters mentioned above bathe the deities separately with their waters moved with flowers.

12-14. Loud sounds are then heard from drums of various kinds such as Paṭaha, Bherī, Muraja and Mṛdaṅga, from conches Kāhalas, cymbals, gongs, bells and various musical instruments. Women raise auspicious shouts along with the charming sounds raised by sages in the form of prayers, shouts of victory and sounds of flutes and lutes. The tumult raised there resembles the sound of rumbling sea.

15-16. The sages raise the chanting sound of Vedic Mantras and hymns from holy scriptures accompanied by Sāman songs. At the time of ablution, excellent devas eulogise them with great joy along with ascetics, householders old as well as those newly initiated religious students.

17-18. Rāma and Keśava are fanned with chowries with their handles studded with precious stones by dark-complexioned courtesans bending under the weight of their breasts. They are clad in yellow or red cloths and stoop down by the weight of garlands. They wear jewel-studded divine ear-rings with golden branches.

19-20. Ādityas, Vasus, Rudras, Sādhyas, Viśvedevas, Maruts, guardians of quarters and many others eulogise Puruṣottama. They are surrounded by Yakṣas, Vidyādharas, Siddhas, Kinnaras and Apsaras all occupying the firmament. There are Devas, Gandharvas and Cāraṇas also :—

21. "Obeisance to you, O Lord of the chiefs of Devas, O ancient Puruṣottama, O lord, the cause of creation, sustenance and annihilation, O lord of the world, O lord of the Universe.

22. Devoutly we bow to the lord holding the three worlds, who is favourably disposed to the brahmins, who is the cause of liberation and who bestows all desired benefits.

23. O excellent sages, Devas eulogised Kṛṣṇa, Balarāma of great strength and Subhadrā and remained in the sky itself.

24. Together with Gandharvas they sang auspicious songs while the celestial damsels danced, the divine musical instruments were played and the cool gentle winds blew.

25. The clouds gathered in the sky, showered water and strewed flowers. The sages, Siddhas and Cāraṇas shouted cries of victory.

26. (So also) Lord Indra and other Devas, sages, Pitṛs, Prajāpatis, Nāgas and those others who resided in heaven.

27-45. Thereafter, Deva took the materials of ablution duly inspired by the racitation of Mantra together with other auspicious requisites. Indra, Viṣṇu of great strength, sun, moon, Dhātā, Vidhātā, Anila (Wind God), Anala (fire God), Pūṣan. Bhaga, Aryaman, Tvaṣṭṛ, Aṁśumān and Vivasvat accompanied by his consorts, Mitra, Varuṇa, the lord surrounded by Rudras, Vasus, Ādityas, the two Aśvins, Viśvedevas, Maruts and Sādhyas alongwith the forefathers, were present there. There were Gandharvas, Apsaras, Yakṣas, the Rākṣasas, Nāgas, celestial sages, excellent brahminical sages, Vaikhānasas, Vālakhilyas who subsisted on winds and who drink lunar rays. Bhṛgus, Aṅgiras, the pious ascetics, Vidyādharas, holy persons of Yogic achievement surrounded them. Pitāmaha, Pulastya, Pulaha of great penance, Aṅgiras, Kaśyapa, Atri, Marīci, Bhṛgu, Kratu, Hara, Pracetas, Manu, Dakṣa, seasons, planets, luminaries, rivers in their embodied form, immortal Devas, ocean, eddies, different Tīrthas, Earth, heaven, quarters, trees, Aditi the mother of Devas, the wives of heaven-dwellers such as Hrī, Śrī, Svāhā, Sarasvatī, Umā, Śacī, Sinivāli, Anumati, Kuhu, Rākā, Dhiṣaṇā and others, mountains Himavān, Vindhya and Meru of numerous peaks, Airāvata with his followers. Kāla, Kāṣṭhās, fortnights, month, seasons, day, night, Uccaiśśravas most excellent of horses, Vāmana, Airāvata king of elephants, Aruṇa, Garuḍa, the trees along with the medicinal herbs, lord Dharma assembled together. Kāla, Mṛtyu, Yama and the servants of Yama, groups of Devas who have not been already mentioned because of their numerosity came for bathing the lord, from different quarters. O brahmins, the heaven-dwellers came upon the vessel which contained auspicious articles for ablution. The vessels of gold, O brahmins contained divine articles of requisites as well as holy and divine waters of the river Sarasvatī. Devas stationed in the firmament, bathed Kṛṣṇa and Balarāma with the water vessels mixed alongwith flowers.

46. So also the aerial chariots of Devas moved about in the sky. In these divine chariots they could go wherever they were pleased to go. The cars were of different type high and low. Some of them were stationary.

47. They were of wonderful workmanship with divine jewels studded in them. They were resorted to by Apsaras rendered beautiful by flags. Their charm was enhanced by songs and musical instruments.

48. They, O excellent sages, all these bathed Kṛṣṇa, Balarāma and Subhadrā and eulogised them with great joy.

49. Be victorious,be victorious,protector of the world. O saviour of devotees, be victorious, be victorious, one favourably disposed to one who bows down, be victorious, be victorious. O refuge of living beings, be victorious, be victorious. O primordial lord, O cause of many, be victorious, be victorious O destroyer of Asuras, be victorious, be victorious, be victorious. O most excellent one among the gods, be victorious, be victorious. O deity lying down in the ocean, be victorious, be victorious. O foremost one among the Yogins, be victorious be victorious. O deity with the sun for the eye, be victorious, be victorious. O king of Devas, be victorious, be victorious. O enemy of Kaiṭabha, be victorious, be victorious. O excellent one (eulogized in) the Vedas, be victorious, be victorious. O deity in the form of a tortoise, be victorious, be victorious O excellent deity in the form of sacrifice, be victorious, be victorious. O deity with the umbilical lotus, be victorious. O deity who move about on the mountains, be victorious, be victorious O Yogaśāyin (one who sleep the Yogic slumber), be victorious, be victorious, be victorious. O holder of velocity, be victorious, be victorious, O Viśvamūrti (deity of Universal form), be victorious, be victorious. O holder of discus, be victorious, be victorious. O lord of living beings, be victorious, be victorious. O upholder of the earth, be victorious, be victorious. O Śeṣaśāyin (one lying on the serpent Śeṣa), be victorious, be victorious. O yellow-robed one, be victorious be victorious. O Somakānta (one as lovely as the moon), be victorious, be victorious. O Yogavas (one residing in the Yogic power), be victorious, be victorious, O Dahanavaktra (one whose mouth emits fire), be victorious, be victorious. O abode of piety, be victorious, be victorious. O storehouse of good qualities, be victorious, be victorious. O abode of glory, be victorious, be victorius. O deity going about on the Vehicle Garuḍa, be victorious, be victorious. O abode of

happiness, be victorious, be victorious. O banner of virtue, be victorious, be victorious. O abode of the earth, be victorious, be victorious. O Gahana Caritra (One whose conduct is abstruse); be victorious, be victorious. O Yogigamya (one who can be realised by Yogins), be victorious, be victorious, be victorious. O deity comprehensible through Vedas; be victorious, be victorious. O deity spreading calmness and peace, be victorious, be victorious. O cause of nourishment, be victorious, be victorious, O Jñānamūrti (one whose form is perfect knowledge), be victorious, be victorious. O mine of fortune, be victorious, be victorious. O Bhāvavedya (one who can be understood only through emotional fervour), be victorious, be victorious. O (deity) that causes salvation; be victorious, be victorious. O deity with a physical body devoid of impurities, be victorious, be victorious. O abode of all living beings, be victorious, be victorious. O cause of sacrifices, be victorious, be victorious. O deity devoid of attributes, be victorious, be victorious. O Mokṣakara (Liberator), be victorious, be victorious. Bhūśaraṇya-refuge of the Earth, be victorious, be victorious. O refulgent one, be victorious, be victorious. O refuge of the worlds, be victorious, be victorious. O lotus-eyed one, be victorious, be victorious. O cause of creation, be victorious, be victorious. O deity endowed with Yoga, be victorious, be victorious. O deity whose body is dark-coloured like the Atasī flower, be victorious, be victorious. O Samudrāviṣṭadeva (one whose body has entered the ocean), be victorious, be victorious. O deity acting as the bee in regard to Lakṣmī who is the lotus, be victorious, be victorious. O deity under the control of the devotee, be victorious, be victorious. O lover of the worlds, be victorious, be victorious. O extremely quiescent one, be victorious, be victorious. O greatest deity of essence, be victorious, be victorious, O holder of discus, be victorious, be victorious. O deity accompanied by those who enjoy, be victorious, be victorious. O bluerobed one (i.e. Balarāma), be victorious, be victorious. O bringer of peace, be victorious, be victorious. O liberator, be victorious, be victorious. O dispeller of sins, be victorious, be victorious. O Kṛṣṇa, lord of the universe, be victorious, be victorious. O younger brother of Saṁkarṣaṇa, be victorious, be victorious, O lotus-eyed one, be victorious, be victorious, O bestower of desired benefits, be victorious, be victorious. O deity whose chest is covered with garlands, be victorious, be victorious. O wielder of discus and ironclub, be victorious, be victorious. O lover of Lakṣmī (whose abode is the lotus) be victorious, be victorious, O Viṣṇu, obeisance be to you.

Brahmā said :

50-51. Thus Indra and other Devas were delighted in their minds after eulogising thus. Siddhas, Cāraṇas and others who reside in heaven and the sages Vālakhilyas loved to Kṛṣṇa, Balarāma and Subhadrā. O excellent sages, after bowing to them they stationed themselves in the firmament.

52-53. After visiting, eulogising and bowing to Kṛṣṇa, Rāma and Subhadrā, the heaven-dwellers went to their respective abodes. The aerial chariots of Devas moved about in the sky. Some were lofty. Some were low. Some could go as they pleased. Some were stationary.

54. The aerial chariots were of wonderful workmanship with divine jewels inlaid. They were resorted by the celestial maidens. They were beautified with flags and banners while musical instruments and songs enhanced their charm.

55. The devotees who visit Puruṣottama, Balabhadra and and Subhadrā on that occasion go to the eternal region (whence there is no return to the earth).

56. By seeing Puruṣottama seated on the platform accompanied by Subhadrā and Balarāma the devotees go to the abode of Viṣṇu which is devoid of ailments.

57. O excellent sages, the man who performs auspicious rites and visits the Lord seated on the couch accompanied by Balarāma and Subhadrā obtains the benefit which is equal to the benefit of charitable gift of a hundred tawny cows at the holy centre Puṣkara.

58. By visiting Lord Kṛṣṇa seated on the couch a man obtains the benefit which is equal to the benefit of charitable gift of a hundred virgins.

59. By visiting lord Kṛṣṇa seated on the couch a man obtains the benefit which is equal to the benefit of charitable gift of a hundred pieces of gold coins.

60. By visiting lord Kṛṣṇa seated on the couch a man obtains the benefit which is equal to the charitable gift of a thousand cows.

61. By visiting lord Kṛṣṇa seated on the couch a man obtains the benefit which is equal to the getting of land as prescribed in the Śāstras.

62. By visiting Lord Kṛṣṇa seated on the couch a man obtains the benefit equal to the gifts of cooked rice and due hospitality to guests alongwith Arghya.

63. By visiting Lord Kṛṣṇa seated on the couch a man obtains the benefits which is equal to that of performing Vṛṣotsarga.[1]

64. By visiting lord Kṛṣṇa seated on the couch a man obtains the benefit which is equal to the gift of water in summer or in any other season.

65. By visiting lord Kṛṣṇa seated on the couch a man obtains the benefit which is equal to the gift of Tiladhenu.[2]

66. By visiting Lord Kṛṣṇa seated on the couch a man obtains the benefit which is equal to the gift of elephants, horses and chariots.

67. By visiting lord Kṛṣṇa seated on the couch a man obtains the benefit which is equal to the gift of a cow with its horns plaited with gold.

68. By visiting Lord Kṛṣṇa seated on the couch a man obtains the benefit which is equal to the charitable gift of a water and cow.

69. By visiting lord Kṛṣṇa seated on the couch a man obtains the benefit which is equal to the gift of ghee and a cow.

70. By visiting lord Kṛṣṇa seated on the couch a man obtains the benefit which is equal to that of performing Cāndrāyaṇa[3] according to sacred injunctions.

1. *Vṛṣotsarga* : letting loose a bull or a bull and four heifers as a meritorious deed, especially on the occasion of a Śraddha in honour of deceased ancestors

2. *Tiladhenu*—a cow presented to a Brahmin.

3. *Cāndrāyaṇa* : This is a fast prescribed in the Dharmaśāstra, so called because it is regulated by the moon, the food being diminished everyday by one mouthful for the dark fortnight and increased in like manner during the white fortnight.

71. By visiting lord Kṛṣṇa seated on the couch a man obtains the benefit which is equal to that of monthly observance of facts as laid down in the Śāstras.

72-77. Of what avail is much talk ? O excellent brahmins, the greatness of that lord is as follows. By visiting Kṛṣṇa accompanied by Balarāma and seated on the couch as well as Subhadrā, the man who performs an auspicious rite obtains the benefit which is glorified as the result of holy rites and charitable gifts in all the holy centres. Hence, O excellent sages, the man or woman must see Puruṣottama. Thereby he or she obtains the benefit of holy dip in all the holy centres.

With the water that remains after the ablution rite of Kṛṣṇa the devotee must bathe and sprinkle himself.

A barren lady, a lady whose child is dead, a lady in a wretched state or afflicted by evil planets, those who are seized by Rākṣasas, Bhūtas and Piśācas, those who are afflicted by ailments should be sprinkled with water that remains after the rite of ablution. They then attain their cherished desires.

78. She who seeks sons obtains sons; she who seeks happiness attains happiness. She who is afflicted by ailments is liberated from ailments. She who seeks riches obtains riches.

79. All those sacred waters on the face of the earth do not merit even a sixteenth part of the water that remains after the rite of ablution.

80. Hence, O brahmins, one shall sprinkle one's limbs with the water that remains after the rite of ablution of Kṛṣṇa has been performed. It is the bestower of all desires.

81. Those who visit Kṛṣṇa whose ablution is performed and who proceed ahead facing the south are liberated from the sins of brahmin slaughter and other major or minor sins.

82. By visiting Kṛṣṇa proceeding ahead facing the Ssuth, a man obtains that benefit which is mentioned in scriptures as the result of three circumambulations of the earth.

83. By visiting Kṛṣṇa proceeding ahead facing the South a man obtains the benefit which is derivable from the pilgrimage all over the earth.

84. By visiting Kṛṣṇa facing the South, a man obtains the

benefit which is derivable from visiting Nara and Nārāyaṇa[1] in the penance grove Badarī.

85. By visiting Kṛṣṇa facing the south a man obtains the benefit which results from the holy dip and charitable gift at Gaṅgādvāra[2] and Kurukṣetra.

86. By visiting Kṛṣṇa facing the south a man obtains the benefit which is equal to the benefit of (the holy dip) in Prayāga on the Mahāmāghī day i.e. (full moon day in the month of Māgha).

87. By visiting Kṛṣṇa facing the south a man obtains the benefit which is equal to the ablution and charitable gifts in Śālagrāma on the Mahācaitrī day (i.e. full moon day in the month of Citrā).

88. By visiting Kṛṣṇa facing the south a man obtains that benefit which is equal to the benefit of Mahākārttikī (i.e. full moon day in the month of Kārttika) at Puṣkara.

89. By visiting Kṛṣṇa facing the south a man obtains the benefit which is derivable from the holy dip and charitable gift at the confluence of Gaṅgā and the ocean.

90. By visiting Kṛṣṇa facing the south a man obtains the benefit which is the result of holy bath accompanied by charitable gifts in Kurukṣetra at the time of solar eclipse.

91-92. By visiting Kṛṣṇa facing the south a man obtains the benefit of the holy bath and the charitable gifts at the holy centres on the Gaṅgā, Yamunā, Sarasvatī and also on the banks of holy lakes etc.

93-94. By visiting Kṛṣṇa facing the south a man obtains the benefit that is usually obtained by holy dips and charitable gifts during the eclipse of the sun in the holy centres such as Puṣkara, Gayā, Amarakaṇṭaka, Naimiṣa and other holy shrines.

95-97. Of what avail is much talk ? Of what avail is the repeated talk ? By visiting Kṛsna facing the south along with Subhadra and Balarāma a man or a women obtains the bene-

1. *Nara-Nārāyaṇa* : two hermits who had spent many thousands of years in Badaryāśrama doing penance. Arjuna was the rebirth of Nara and Śrikṛṣṇa was the rebirth cf Nārāyaṇa.

2. *Gangadvāra*—Haridvāra or Haradvāra, identifiable with the place where the river Ganges falls from the Himālayas.

fits mentioned in the Vedas, scriptures, Purāṇas, Bhārata and Dharmaśāstras (Ethical texts) by the learned men as the benefit of meritorious deeds.

CHAPTER SIXTYTHREE

Glory of the Holy Procession : Guṇḍikā Yātrā

Brahmā said :

1. Those who observe Kṛṣṇa, Balarāma and Subhadrā seated in a chariot and going in a procession to the Maṇḍapa called Guṇḍikā go to the abode of lord Viṣṇu.

2. Those who visit Kṛṣṇa, Balarāma and Subhadrā occupying the Maṇḍapa for seven days, go to the world of Viṣṇu.

The sages said :

3. Who initiated the procession to the auspicious Guṇḍikā Maṇḍapa ? What is the benefit of witnessing this procession ?

4-5. Why do Kṛṣṇa, lord of the universe, Saṁkarṣaṇa and Subhadrā leave off their (permanent abode and proceed in a chariot, to the Maṇḍapa in a holy secluded spot on the bank of that lake and stay there for seven nights ?

Brahmā said :

6-7. O brahmins, formerly lord Viṣṇu was requested by Indradyumna :

O lord of Devas, let there be a procession to the bank of my lake. It will yield worldly pleasure and salvation to us.

Puruṣottama the lord of Devas granted him this boon.

The Lord said :

8. O king, there shall be a procession for seven days on the banks of your lake. It will be called Guṇḍikā. It will bestow all desired benefits.

9-12. O king, the devotees, whether Brahmins, Kṣatriyas, Vaiśyas, or Śūdras whether male or female shall worship me,

Saṁkarṣaṇa and Subhadrā occupying the Maṇḍapa. They shall worship with great faith by means of fragrant flowers, scents, incenses, lights, (food offerings), presents, obeisance, circumambulations, shouts of victory, hymns, charming songs, and musical instruments. Nothing is difficult of access to them. O excellent king, whatever benefit is desired by them will certainly befall them due to my favour.

Brahmā said :

13. After saying this to him the lord vanished there itself. That glorious and excellent king was fully satisfied.

14. Hence, O excellent brahmins, one shall by all means visit lord Viṣṇu, the bestower of all desires, at Guṇḍikā.

15. A man if he has no son, obtains sons, if poor, gets riches, if sick, is liberated from ailments. A virgin will get a good husband.

16. The man derives longevity, glory, fame, intelligence, strength, learning, courage and obtains cattle, progeny and the wealth of handsome features and blooming youth.

17. By visiting lord Viṣṇu a man or woman devotee attains whatever pleasure he or she wishes for.

18-19. By witnessing Guṇḍikā-procession with great concentration, O excellent brahmins, and by visiting lord Kṛṣṇa, Rāma and Subhadrā in the bright half of the month of Āṣāḍha, the man or woman derives the benefit of fifteen horse sacrifices or even more.

20-23. He will redeem seven earlier generations and seven subsequent generations of his family—He will be fortunate and handsome as well as heroic. He will be bedecked in all ornaments studded with jewels. He will be served by Gandharvas and Apsaras vying with each other. In an aerial chariot that can go wherever one desires to go the devotee shall go to the city of Lord Viṣṇu. He will freely enjoy the desired pleasures. He will be devoid of old age and death. Till the ultimate dissolution of all living beings he will enjoy excellent pleasures. When the merit decreases he will return to this place and be born as a brahmin who has mastered the four Vedas.

Thereafter, he will adopt Yoga pertaining to Viṣṇu and attain salvation.

CHAPTER SIXTYFOUR

The Twelve Holy Pilgrimages and their Benefits

The sages said :

1. Mention separately the benefit which a man or a woman with perfect self-control acquires by making holy pilgrimage.

Brahmā said :

2. O brahmins, even as I recount, listen to the benefit of holy pilgrimage severally, that a man acquires after undertaking the pilgrimage to that holy centre with great restraint.

3-4. A man who undertakes pilgrimage in accordance with the injunctions, visits and bows to Kṛṣṇa, Saṁkarṣaṇa and Subhadrā at the time of Guṇḍikā, Utthānadvādaśī (twelfth day in the bright half of Kārttika), the full moon day in the month of Phālguna, and during equinoctical transit will acquire the fruit thereof separately. As long as the fourteen Indras reign he will stay in the world of Viṣṇu.

5. A man undoubtedly enjoys pleasures for as many Kalpas as the number of times he undertakes pilgrimages in the month of Jyeṣṭha.

6-8. A devotee should undertake pilgrimage to that sacred excellent and beautiful holy centre of Śrīpuruṣottama, which accords worldly pleasures and salvation to men and which is conducive to the pleasure of every living being. Thereafter, the devotee, whether a man or a woman shall control the sense-organs. He shall continue pilgrimages till twelve such Yātrās are completed with great concentration and mental purity. He who, thereafter, eschews stubbornness and arrogance and instals the idols shall enjoy various pleasures and in the end acquire salvation.

The sages said :

9. O Lord, we wish to hear, even as you recount, the installation and worship of the lord of the universe and the mode of these rites as well as charitable gifts and the fruits thereof.

Brahmā said :

10. O leading sages, listen to the installation of idols urged by Brahmā. By devoutly performing this, the man or the woman acquires the benefit.

11. O excellent brahmins, when the twelve pilgrimages are completed, the devotee should carry out the installation that destroy sin.

12-13. On the eleventh day in the bright half of the month of Jyeṣṭha, the devotee with concentration should go to the holy reservoir. With purity and control he should perform Ācamana and invoke holy centres and sacred waters. Meditating on Nārāyaṇa with full devotion he should perform the rite of holy dip.

14. The rite of holy bath should be performed in accordance with the injunctions prescribed by the sages in regard to him.

15. After taking holy bath perfectly in accordance with the injunction (the devotee) who is conversant with the names, Gotras (spiritual lines) and the procedure, should perform Tarpaṇa rite to Devas, sages and manes as well as others.

16-17. Coming out of water and wearing two newly washed and dried cloths free from impurities, he should ritualistically touch water and stand or sit facing the sun. He should repeat the holy sacred and meritorious Mantra of Gāyatrī, the mother of Vedas, the dispeller of all sins. He should repeat the holy Gāyatrī one hundred and eight time.

18. He should repeat other holy passages and Mantras pertaining to the sun with faith and concentration. After making three circumambulations he should bow down to the Sungod.

19. In regard to the people of the first three castes the rite of holy bath and the repetition of Mantras is in the manner mentioned in the Vedas. The utterance of the Vedic passage is to be avoided by women as well as Śūdras.

20-22. The devotee shall go home silently and worship Puruṣottama after washing his hands and feet and after ritualistically touching and sipping water in accordance with the precepts. He shall bathe the Lord with ghee, milk, honey, scented water and the holy water mixed with sandal paste. Thereafter, the devotee shall dress the lord with an excellent pair of clothes with devotion. He shall smear the lord with sandal paste, Agallochum, camphor and saffron.

23. With great devotion he shall worship Lord Viṣṇu offering lotuses and other flowers pertaining to Viṣṇu (like jasmine etc.).

24. After worshipping the lord the ruler of the universe, the bestower of worldly pleasures and salvation, in this manner, he shall burn incense along with agallochum in front of the lord.

25. O excellent sages, he shall burn aromatic resin too along with scents. He shall light a lamp with devotion using ghee (instead of oil) according to the means.

26. With concentration he shall offer twelve other lamps, O excellent sages, he shall burn it with ghee or gingelly oil.

27. By way of Naivedya (food offering) he shall dedicate milk pudding, sweet Śaṣkulis, Vaṭakas (special kinds of baked or fried cakes) sweets, a little quantity of molasses and fruits too.

28. After worshipping Puruṣottama with five items of service (i.e. bathing, offering cloths, worshipping with flowers, showing lamps and incense and food offerings) the devotee shall repeat "Om obeisance to Puruṣottama" a hundred and eight times.

29-32. Then he shall devoutly propitiate lord Puruṣottama thus :—"Obeisance to you O lord of the worlds, O bestower of freedom from fear on the devotees, save me, O Puruṣottama, I am merged in the ocean of worldly existence. O Govinda, O lord of the Universe, may the twelve pilgrimages undertaken by me to you be perfectly completed owing to your grace".

After propitiating the lord thus and prostrating before him like a log of wood, the devotee shall worship the preceptor by means of flowers, cloths and unguents, since, O excellent sages, there is no difference between the two.

33. With faith and concentration, O excellent sages, the devotee shall make a flowery bowerlike Maṇḍapa over the lord.

34. Thereafter, he shall resolve to keep awake at night. For this purpose he shall arrange for the discourses on the divine story of Vāsudeva or devotional songs.

35-36. The learned devotee shall pass night meditating, reading or eulogising the lord. When the twelfth day dawns he shall invite twelve Brahmins who have mastered the Vedas, who are conversant with Itihāsa and Purāṇas, who have controlled their sense-organs and who have taken holy baths signifying their successful conclusion of holy rites.

37. After taking bath perfectly in accordance with the injunctions, the devotee shall control his sense organs and put on washed (and dried) clothes. Thereafter, he shall bathe lord Viṣṇu with devotion as before.

38-39. He should worship the lord with scents, fragrant flowers, presents, Naivedyas, lights, different items of service, obeisances, circumambulations, repetitions of mantras, eulogies, propitiations, charming songs and instrumental music.

After worshipping the lord of the Universe thus, he should worship the brahmins.

40-41. With faith and devotion he should offer twelve cows, gold umbrellas, and pairs of sandals to them.

O brahmins, he should offer wealth, clothes, etc. to them with great devotion since Govinda is propitiated and honoured with emotional fervour.

42. Thereafter, he should give the preceptor a cow, cloth, gold, umbrella, pair of sandals, foodgrain and bellmetal vessel with devotion.

43. He should feed brahmins. The food served should begin with milk pudding. There should be sweet cooked rice and various kinds of edibles prepared in jaggery and ghee.

44. After the brahmins have been fed to their satisfaction and their minds are at rest, he should give them twelve water pots together with sweets.

45. Devoid of revelry he should give them monetary gifts according to his capacity.

He should hand over the pot and the monetary gifts to the preceptor also.

46. O excellent brahmins, after worshipping those brahmins, he should devotedly worship his preceptor who is the bestower of perfect knowledge and who is on a par with Viṣṇu.

47. The learned devotee should honour him with gold, cloth, cow, foodgrains and other articles. Thereafter, he should repeat this mantra.

48. "May Lord Puruṣottama who has neither beginning nor end, who holds conch, discus and iron club and who is the omnipresent lord of the Universe be pleased with this.

49. After uttering this mantra he should circumambulate brahmins thrice. He should bid farewell to the preceptor by bending his head with devotion.

50. Thereafter, he should follow those brahmins with devotion to the boundary of the village. Thus following them he should pay homage and bid them farewell.

51. Accompanied by kinsmen and relatives he should take meals with proper restriction on his tongue. There may be other devotees, poor people, mendicants and hungry persons in need of food, with whom he should share food.

52. By performing this rite perfectly well, the devotee whether a man or a woman should derive the benefit of thousands of horse-sacrifices and a hundred Rājasūya sacrifices.

53-57. The noble devotee will take a divine form for his departure to heaven and will redeem a hundred generations of his ancestors. He will clear the way for a hundred future generations, O brahmins. He will be richly endowed with all characteristic signs and be bedecked in all ornaments. He will have all his desires realized, he will be devoid of fever like a God. He will be richly endowed with handsome features and blooming youth. He will be embellished with all good qualities. He will be eulogised by the celestial damsels. He will be admired by the Gandharvas who will flock around him. He will go to the world of lord Viṣṇu on the aerial chariot that has a steady speed, that has the lustre and colour of the sun, that can go wherever it is desired to go and that is embellished with all sorts of jewels, flags and banners. He will become a young man of great strength. While traversing the sky he will illuminate the quarters and will not suffer from fatigue. He will grow intelligent.

58-65. In the world of Viṣṇu he will enjoy pleasures in consonance with his desires for the period of a hundred Kalpas. He will stay there devoid of sickness and fever. He will be eulogised by Siddhas, Apsaras, Gandharvas, Devas, Vidyādharas, Nāgas and sages.

O brahmins, he will assume a form with four arms joyfully like Viṣṇu, the lord of the universe, holding conch, discus and iron-club. He will enjoy excellent pleasures there and sport with Devas. Then he will come to the abode of Brahmā that bestows all desires and that is beautified by Siddhas, Vidyādharas, Devas and Kinnaras. He will enjoy there for a period of ninety Kalpas. O leading brahmins, from that he will come to the world of Rudra who bestows the desired benefits to the world which is frequented by Devas, which bestows happiness and salvation, which is adorned with hundreds and thousands of lofty mansions, which is beautified by Siddhas, Vidyādharas Yakṣas, Daityas and Dānavas. The man enjoys happiness there for the period of eighty Kalpas. At its conclusion he goes to the world of rays, Goloka which is equipped with all pleasures and which is charming, being adorned by Devas, Siddhas and Apsaras.

66-71. For a period of seventy Kalpas he enjoys there such excellent pleasures as are difficult of attainment in the three worlds. He is as steady-minded as an immortal being. From these he comes to the excellent world of Prajāpati. He is surrounded by Gandharvas, Apsaras, Siddhas, sages and Vidyādharas.

For a period of sixty Kalpas, he enjoys various pleasures there. At its conclusion he goes to the abode of Indra equipped with different miracles. He is surrounded by Gandharvas, Kinnaras, Siddhas, Devas, Vidyādharas, Nāgas, Guhyakas, Apsaras, Sādhyas and other excellent Devas. After coming there he enjoys happiness for a period of fifty Kalpas. From these he goes to the world of Devas beautified by lofty places. It is sacred, difficult of access and beautified by Devas. The intelligent devotee enjoys for forty Kalpas. Then he comes to the world of Nakṣatras which is also difficult of access.

72. For a period of thirty Kalpas he enjoys excellent pleasures there as he wishes. From there, O excellent brahmins, he comes to the world of the moon.

73-74. He enjoys the rarest of pleasures for a period of twenty Kalpas in that world where the moon shines splendidly in the comapny of all Devas. Then he comes to the world of the sungod which is honoured by Devas, which is divine, which is full of wonderful miracles and which is surrounded by Gandharvas and Apsaras.

75. O excellent brahmins, after enjoying splendid pleasures there for a period of ten Kalpas he comes to the world of Gandharvas which is most difficult of access.

76. After enjoying various pleasures to the fullest satisfaction for the period of a Kalpa, he comes to the earth and becomes a virtuous king.

77-78. He becomes an Emperor of great vigour embellished by noble qualities. After ruling over the kingdom virtuously, and after performing sacrifices where as much monetary gift is distributed he goes to the world of Yogins that is auspicious and bestower of liberation. There he enjoys excellent pleasure till the ultimate dissolution of all living beings. From there he comes to the world of mortals and is born in an excellent family of Yogins. O brahmins he is born in an excellent family of a devotee of Viṣṇu, which is difficult of access and is approved of by good men. He becomes an excellent brahmin mastering four vedas. He performs sacrifices with due monetary gifts. He adopts Yoga pertaining to Viṣṇu and attains liberation.

Thus, O brahmin, the benefit of pilgrimages has been perfectly cited by me. It yields worldly pleasures and liberation to men. What else do you wish to hear ?

CHAPTER SIXTYFIVE

The World of Viṣṇu

The sages said :

1-3. O lord, we wish to hear about the world of Viṣṇu the world which is devoid of sickness, is lovely, delightful to the people and full of mystery.

O lord, mention the magnitude of that world, its pleasure, its splendour and its power. By what holy rites do virtuous men go there ? Is it due to the vision or touch of holiness or due to holy dips in the sacred waters of holy centres ? Mention in detail and factually. We are greatly eager to hear this.

Brahmā said :

4-5. O sages, listen all of you, even as I speak about that highest region which is wished for by the devotees. It is blessed, holy land and destructive of the world. It is most excellent of all the worlds. It is named (Viṣṇu-loka) after the name of Viṣṇu. It is a sacred abode full of all mysteries. It is honoured and worshipped by the three worlds.

6-11. It is filled with many trees such as Aśoka, Pārijāta, Mandara, Campaka, Mālatī, Mallikā, Kunda, Bakula, Nāgakesara, Punnāga, Atimukta, Priyaṅgu, Tagara, Arjuna, Pāṭala, Cūta, Khadira, splendid groves of Karṇikāra, Nāraṅga (Orange citron), Panasa (jack tree), Lodhra, Nimba (Margosa) Dāḍima (Pomegranate), Sarjaka, Drākṣā (Grape, vines), Lakuca, Kharjūra, Madhūka, Indraphala, wood apple, coconut palms, palmyra trees, Śrīphala, innumerable splendid trees of various kinds, Sarala, Candana (Sandal), Nīpa, Devadāru, Śubhañjana, Jāti, Lavaṅga, Kaṅkola, such trees as emitted the odour of camphor, creepers with plenty of betel leaves, Areca palms and various other trees appearing splendid in all seasons with their abundant fruits.

12-17. It is full of various flowers in branches in creepers. It is filled with water-reservoirs of diverse lands and different kinds of beautiful meritorious spots resonant with the chirping sounds of many birds. There are hundreds of tanks and lakes full of water and charming. Lilies, hundred-petalled lotuses, excellent Kokanada (a variety of lotus), Kalhāra flowers and other water flowers, splendid with different colours (are abundant in those ponds). They are full of swans and Kāraṇḍava ducks. They are rendered beautiful by ruddy geese. There are other aquatic birds such as Kāyaṣṭikas, Dātyūhas, Cātakas, Priyaputras and Jivañjīvakas. There are other sweet-voiced divine birds moving about in water or flying in the air. Thus the world is adorned by many divine, miraculous trees and charming and holy water reservoirs.

18-22. In that city of Viṣṇu, worshipped by all, people walk about in divine aerial chariots. They are decorated with various jewels beset with pure gold; they can move about at their will. They are resonant with the divine music of Gandharvas. They are as refulgent as the midday sun. They are adorned by the celestial maidens. The beds and seats therein are made of gold. They are rich in means of pleasures of various kinds. Flags and pearl necklaces are suspended from them. They move about in the sky in groups. They are of diverse colours. The various parts of these aerial chariots are made of gold. They are rendered fragrant by the contact of flowers mixed admirably with sandal and agallochum. The instruments of music fill them with sweet sounds. The passages in these aerial chariots afford comfortable movements. They have the speed of wind and mind. Groups of tinkling bells are attached to them.

23-24. The people sport about with various young women of Gandharvas and the group of celestial clans. The young women look very splendid with their faces as charming as the moon. Their breasts are plump and lifted up. Their waists are beautiful and elegant. Some are dark in complexion and some fair. Their gait is like that of elephants in their rut.

25-28. Those women surround the excellent man and fan him with chowries of golden handles. They are bedecked in variety of jewels. They rejoice singing, dancing and having instrumental music. They are lethargic due to intoxication. This excellent world shines with the Yakṣas, Vidyādharas, Siddhas, Gandharvas, Celestial nymphs, Devas and sages. Those lofty-minded persons by whom the lotus-eyed lord Kṛṣṇa, the lord of the universe, is seen near the royal banyan tree on the shore of the southern sea go to this world of Viṣṇu and enjoy great pleasures.

29. As long as the heaven stands alongwith the moon and stars, they dally with the celestial nymphs. They resemble heated gold. They are devoid of old age and death.

30. They are free from miseries. They are rid of thirst, fatigue and suffering. They assume the form of the lord :—They have four arms. They are adorned by garlands of sylvan flowers. They possess great vigour and power.

31. They have the scar called Śrīvatsa. They hold conch,

discus and ironclub. Some are dark-complexioned like the blue lotus. Some resemble the gold.

32. Some appear worthy of being gazed at like the emerald, some resemble the lapis lazuli; some are dark complexioned with earings. Others are like the diamond.

33. O excellent brahmins, the worlds of other lords, and Devas do not shine in the same manner as does the world of Viṣṇu being full of mysteries and miracles.

34. O brahmins, by the power of that lord, there is no question of return till the ultimate dissolution of all living beings.

35. Those who visit Kṛṣṇa, Rāma and Subhadrā in the holy shrine Puruṣottama move about in the divine city (justifiably) proud of their handsome features and blooming youth.

36. In the middle of the city shines the place of Viṣṇu which resembles molten gold, which has the lustre of the midday sun and which is embellished by jewels.

37. It is beautifully decorated with many hundred and thousands of buntings and banners. It is encircled by a golden rampart extending to ten thousand Yojanas.

38. With the charming well-arranged flags of various colours wonderfully displayed, the city shines like the autumnal moon surrounded by the stars.

39. It has four main gates. It is very extensive and well-guarded by watchmen. It is lofty and charming. It consists of seven city areas.

40-41. The first area is made of gold; the second is fitted with emiralds; the third is full of sapphire and beyond that it consists of dark blue precious stones; the fifth is brightly illuminated by brilliance. O brahmins, the sixth is full of diamonds and the seventh abounds in lapis lazuli.

42. With wonderful, brilliant pillars set with jewels and beautified by gold plates and coral that great mansion shines exquisitely.

43-44. The Siddhas walk about there. They brighten the ten quarters. Just as on the full moon night the moon shines with the stars so also lord Viṣṇu mounting a high seat shines alongwith Lakṣmī. He is dark-coloured, clad in yellow robes. He bears the scar Śrīvatsa.

45. In his right hand lord Viṣṇu holds the terrible and shining discus Sudarśana that destroys all other weapons and that consists of all fiery splendour.

46-47. O excellent sages, in his left hand, lord Viṣṇu holds his conch known as Pāñcajanya.[1] It has the lustre of the Kunda flower, moon and silver. It resembles a white necklace and the cow's milk. By its sound it makes the whole universe agitated. It is adorned by a thousand curls.

48-52. In his right hand he holds Kaumodakī, the iron club which destroys Daityas and Dānavas, which is fiercely terrible and which destroys evil deeds. It has the shape of flame of the blazing fire and is unbearable even to Devas. In his left hand shines the bow Śārṅga that has the lustre of the sun. (It is with this bow and) the excellent arrows that resemble the sun and are agitated by the series of flames that the lord annihilates the three worlds consisting of mobile and immobile beings. He is the cause of each and every bliss. He is glorious. He is expert in all scriptural texts. He is the lord and preceptor of all worlds. He is bowed to by all Devas.

He is the lord of Devas with a thousand heads, a thousand feet and eyes. He has a thousand names, a thousand limbs and a thousand arms.

53-55. The lord with large eyes like the petals of a lotus shines on his throne. The lord of the universe the preceptor of the universe, shines very clearly like the lightning streak. He is surrounded by Devas, Siddhas, Gandharvas, Apsaras, Yakṣas, Vidyādharas, Nāgas, Cāraṇas, glorious sages, Suparṇas, Dānavas, Daityas, Rākṣasas, Guhyakas, Kinnaras and Devas of divine splendour. He shines eulogised by these people.

56-58. The following ladies of immortal beings are stationed there viz—Kīrti (Fame), Prajñā (Wisdom), Medhā (Intellect), Sarasvatī (Speech), Buddhi (Intelligence), Mati (Reasoning power), Kṣānti (Forbearance), Siddhi (Achievement), Mūrti (Form), Dyuti (Refulgence), Gāyatrī, Sāvitrī, Maṅgalā, Sarvamaṅgalā, Prabhā, Matī and Kānti (Lustre) belonging to Nārāyaṇa. Then there is Śraddhā (Faith), goddess Kauśikī, vidyut (Lightning) Saudāmini, Nidrā (Slumber),

1. *Pāñcajanya*—Kṛṣṇa's conch taken from the asura Pañcajana.

Rātri (Night), Māyā and other womenfolk of the immortal beings.

59. All these are established in the abode of Vasudeva. Of what avail is much talk? Everything is established there.

60-67. The following ladies dance every day at the place where Puruṣottama stays :—Ghṛtācī, Menakā, Rambhā, Sahajanyā, Tilottamā, Urvaśī, Nimlocā, Vāmanā, Mandodarī, Subhagā (fortunate one), Viśvācī, Vipulānanā, Bhadrāṅgī, Citrasenā, Pramlocā, Sumanoharā, (very charming), Munisammohinī (one who fascinates sages), Ramā, Candramadhyā, Śubhānanā, Sukeśī (possessed of good tresses), Nīlakeśī (possessed of blue tresses), Manmathadīpanī (one who kindles the fire of love), Alambuṣā, Miśrakeśī, Puñjikasthalā, Kratusthalā, Varāṅgī, (possessed of excellent limbs), Pūrvacitti, Parāvatī, Mahārūpā, Śaśilekhā of auspicious face, Haṁsalīlānugāminī, Mattavāraṇagāminī (one who walks like an intoxicated elephant), Bimboṣṭhī and Navagarbhā—these are the celestial ladies of Devas. These and other celestial ladies are proud of their beauty and youth. Their wrists are fine and their faces are beautiful. They are bedecked in all ornaments. They are endowed with the faculty of singing sweet songs. They are endowed with all noble signs. They are experts in vocal and instrumental music. They perform dance everyday at the place where lord Puruṣottama stays.

68. There is neither sickness nor fatigue. There is neither death nor snow and sunshine. There is no hunger, no thirst, no old age, no deformity, no unhappiness.

69. O brahmins, I do not behold any other world better than the world of Viṣṇu. It is the cause of bliss and it bestows the desired benefits.

70. O brahmins, all those worlds which we hear as the worlds in the heavenly sphere, all those who perform meritorious rites, do not merit even a sixteenth part of the world of lord Viṣṇu.

71. Thus O brahmins is the greatest abode of Viṣṇu endowed with all enjoyable pleasures and attributes. It is conducive to the pleasures of everyone. It is holy and full of mysteries.

72. Atheists and profligates do not go there. Nor do the following go there viz.—the ungrateful and those who are of uncontrollable sense-organs.

73. The devotees of Viṣṇu who worship Vāsudeva the preceptor of the universe with devotion, go to the world of Viṣṇu.

74-77. After visiting Kṛṣṇa, Rāma and Subhadrā in this rarest of holy centres on the shore of the southern ocean, excellent devotees cast off their bodies near the Kalpa tree. Those men who die in the holy centre Puruṣottama go to that world. He who remembers Puruṣottama in between the baniyan tree and the ocean and those who die in Puruṣottama go to that world. They go to that greatest abode.

Thus, O excellent sages, the eternal world of Viṣṇu, the cause of bliss unto all, the bestower of worldly pleasures and liberation, has been mentioned by me.

CHAPTER SIXTYSIX

The Glory of Lord Puruṣottama

The sages said :

1-9. O lord of the universe, the glorious world of lord Viṣṇu has been recounted by you. It has many mysterious features. It yields perpetual bliss, worldly pleasures and liberation. Puruṣottama, the rarest of holy centres in the world has perfectly been glorified by you. By casting off his body there, a man will directly go to the abode of Viṣṇu.

Wonderful, indeed, is this path of liberation that you have mentioned for helping men viz. the abandonment of body in the holy centre named Puruṣottama.

Without any strain, O lord of Devas, excellent men abandon their bodies in that holy centre and go to the region of Viṣṇu devoid of ailment.

O lord of Devas, by bearing the greatness of holy centres

we are extremely amazed. Hairs stand on end and we feel extremely satisfied.

There are other holy centres and shrines viz. Prayāga, Puṣkara etc. There are many holy centres on the earth, rivers and lakes. O excellent Deva, you do not praise them in the same manner as you praise the holy centre Puruṣottama. O grandsire, your intent has been understood by us whereby you praise the holy centres Puruṣottama that bestows liberation.

Certainly, there is no other holy centre on par with Puruṣottama. Hence, O excellent Deva, you praise it over and again.

Brahmā said :

10. O excellent sages, the truth, the very truth has been cited by us on all. There is no other holy centre on Earth that is equal to Puruṣottama.

11. All those holy centres and shrines do not deserve even a sixteenth part of Puruṣottama.

12. Just as Viṣṇu, the lord of all, is the most excellent of all excellent ones so also the holy centre of Puruṣottama is the most excellent of all holy centres.

13. Just as Viṣṇu has been cited as the most excellent one among the sons of Aditi so also Puruṣottama is the most excellent one among the holy centres.

14. Just as the moon among the stars and ocean among lakes so also the holy centre of Puruṣottama is the most excellent among the holy centres.

15. Like (fire) among the Vasus and Śaṅkara among the Rudras, so also Puruṣottama is the most excellent of all holy centres.

16. Like brahmins among the four castes and Garuḍa among the birds, Puruṣottama is the most excellent of all holy centres.

17. Just as the Meru is the most excellent among mountains with lofty peaks, just as the Himālaya is the most excellent among the mountains so also Puruṣottama is the nost excellent holy centre.

18. Like Lakṣmī among young women and Ganga among the rivers Puruṣottama is the most excellent of all holy centres.

19. Like Airāvata among the leading elephants, like Bhṛgu among the great sages, Puruṣottama is the excellent of all holy centres.

20. Like Skanda among the commanders of armies, like Kapila among the saintly men of great achievements Puruṣottama is the most excellent of all holy centres.

21. Like Uccaiśśravas among the horses, like Uśanas among the poets, Puruṣottama is the most excellent of all holy centres.

22. Like Vyāsa among the sages, like Kubera among Yakṣas and (like Vibhīṣaṇa among) Rākṣasas, Puruṣottama is the excellent of all holy centres.

23. Like mind among the organs of sense, like earth among the elements, Puruṣottama is the most excellent of all holy centres.

24. Like the holy big tree among all trees, like wind among those who float and spread, Puruṣottama is the most excellent of all holy centres.

25. O brahmins, just as the crest-jewel is the most excellent of all ornaments, so also Puruṣottama is the most excellent of all holy centres.

26. Like Citraratha among the Gandharvas, like Kuliśa among weapons, Puruṣottama is the most excellent among all holy centres.

27. Like the letter A among all syllables, like Gāyatrī among all vedic mantras, Puruṣottama is the most excellent of all holy centres.

28. O excellent brahmins, just as the head is excellent of all limbs so also Puruṣottama is the most excellent of all holy centres.

29. Just as Arundhatī is excellent among chaste ladies so also Puruṣottama is the most excellent of all holy centres.

30. Just as the doctrine of salvation is the greatest of all doctrines and lores so also Puruṣottama is excellent of all holy centres.

31. Like the king among men, like the Divine cow among cows, Puruṣottama is the most excellent of all holy centres.

32. Like a piece of gold among jewels, like Vāsuki among serpents, Puruṣottama is the most excellent among holy centres.

33. Like Prahlāda among all Daityas, like Rāma among

the wielders of weapons, Puruṣottama is the most excellent of all holy centres.

34. Like the shark among fishes, like lion among violent animals, Puruṣottama is the most excellent among all holy centres.

35. Just as the milky ocean is excellent of all oceans so also puruṣottama is the most excellent of all holy centres.

36. Just as Varuṇa is excellent of all aquatic beings, just as Yama is excellent of all Yogins. so also Puruṣottama is the most excellent of all holy centres.

37. O excellent sages, just as Nārada is excellent of all divine sages so also Puruṣottama is the most excellent of all holy centres.

38. Like gold among metals, like the gift of coins among all sacred gifts, Puruṣottama is the most excellent of all holy centres.

39. Like Dakṣa among Prajāpatis, like Kaśyapa among sages, Puruṣottama is the most excellent of all holy centres.

40. Like the Sun among planets, like Praṇava among Mantras, Puruṣottama is the most excellent of all holy centres.

41. Just as the horse-sacrifice (aśvamedha) is glorified as excellent of all sacrifices, O excellent brahmins, so also that holy centre is the most excellent of all holy centres.

42. Just as the food-grain plant is the most excellent of all plants; like the cocoanut or palmyra among the grassy species, Puruṣottama is the most excellent of all holy centres.

43. Just as the holy rite of all sacred places is the means of redemption from worldly existence so also Puruṣottama is excellent of all holy centres.

CHAPTER SIXTYSEVEN

The Glory of Ananta Vāsudeva

Brahmā said :

1-11. O excellent brahmins, the benefits of Japas, Homas, austerities and charitable gifts in the holy centres and shrines have been mentioned to you.

O brahmins, I do not see a holy centre which is equal to the holy centre Puruṣottama on the earth. Of what avail is much talk and repeated utterance. Truth, it is the truth, really the truth that the holy centre Puruṣottama is extremely great. By visiting the holy centre Puruṣottama but once, by touching the waters of the ocean but once, by knowing the doctrine of Brahman but once, there is no further staying in the womb.

The devotee should stay for a year or at least for a month in the excellent holy centre of Puruṣottama, the place where Lord Viṣṇu is present. In that case the Japa performed or Homa offered by him is great. A great penance has been performed by him.

He goes to the great abode where Viṣṇu the lord of Yogins is ever present. Accompanied by celestial women he enjoys pleasures of various sorts. At the end of Kalpa the excellent man returns to the mortal world. O brahmins, he is born in the house of Yogins. He endeavours to understand what should be understood. After acquiring the Yoga of Viṣṇu, be attains liberation. Know the glory of Kalpa tree, Rāma, Kṛṣṇa, Subhadrā, Mārkaṇḍeya's eddy. Indradyumna's lake is also mentioned. The glory of Śveta Matsya and of the heavenly door and the rules regarding bath in the ocean have been mentioned. The rules regarding ritualistic cleansing mārjana and the proper time of contact with Gaṅgā have also been mentioned by me. What more do you wish to hear ? The glory of Indradyumna has also been recounted. The Purāṇa that enables one to liberate himself, that is full of mysteries and miracles, that is holy and excellent and that is a great secret conducive to richness has also been mentioned fully by me.

The sages said :

12. We are not satiated by listening to the story of the lord. It behoves you to relate once again the great secret doctrine.

13. The details of Vāsudeva the infinite deity have not been explained perfectly by you. O lord, we wish to hear. Kindly mention it in detail.

Brahmā said :

14. O excellent sages, I shall mention the greatest essence, the greatness of the infinite deity Vāsudeva, the rarest in the three worlds.

15. Formerly, in the Ādikalpa (first of the Kalpas), O brahmins, I was born of the unmanifest. Viśvakarman spoke these words.

16-18. I urged Viśvakarmā the leading architect of Devas, whose activities are of the greatest nature—"Make an idol of Vāsudeva, carving it out of a rock. On seeing it, men and women in the South will worship it duly and devotedly. Once, Devas and the lord of Devas Indra sensed danger from Dānavas and Rākṣasas. Being afraid they had come to the peak of Sumeru in heaven. They propitiated Vāsudeva and stayed there without any calamity or agitation.

19-22. After hearing my words, Viśvakarmā made a pure idol holding conch, discus and iron club. It was endowed with all traits. It had eyes as large as the petals of a lotus. It had the scar-Śrīvatsa. The excellent idol was owe-inspiring. The chest was covered with garlands of sylvan flowers. It wore crown and shoulder-lets. It was clad in yellow robes. The shoulders were plump and round. It was bedecked with two ear-rings. Thus the divine idol was got made by me through secret mantras and the time for installation had come.

23-24. At that time, Indra, the king of Devas, came to my abode riding on Airāvata, his excellent elephant. He was surrounded by Devas. By means of ablution, charitable gifts, he propitiated the idol. Taking the idol with him he returned to his capital.

25-28. By propitiating the idol for a long time after restraining his speech, body and mind he gained in strength. He killed Vṛtra and other Asuras as well as the cruel and terrible Dānavas led by Namuci. He then enjoyed the worlds Bhuḥ, Bhuvaḥ, Svar etc.

After the advent of Tretā Yuga, there was a valorous overlord of the Rākṣasas, Daśagrīva (Rāvaṇa). He had great prowess. For ten thousand years he performed holy rites and severe penance, abstaining from food and conquering sense-organs. This penance was very difficult to be performed by ordinary persons. Pleased with that penance I granted him a boon.

29-30. He could not be killed by Devas, Daityas, Nāgas, and Rākṣasas. He could not be killed by the terrible attendants of Yama who had the power to curse beside their infallible weapons. After securing this boon the Rākṣasa defeated Yakṣas and their lord Kubera. He then attempted to conquer Indra.

31-36. He fought a terrible battle with Devas. The Rākṣasa defeated the king of Devas. The son of Rāvaṇa, Meghanāda acquired the title Indrajit by conquering him. Thereafter Rāvaṇa of great strength reached Amarāvatī. In the splendid abode of the king of Devas, Rāvaṇa saw the idol of Vāsudeva as refulgent as collyrium. It was endowed with the characteristic marks of Lord Viṣṇu. It had the scar Śrīvatsa. It had large eyes like the petals of a lotus. The chest was covered by the garlands of sylvan flowers. It was bedecked in crown and shoulderlets. It held conch, discus and iron club in its hands. It was clad in yellow robes. It had four arms. It was bedecked in ornaments. It was the bestower of all benefits. Leaving off the heaps of jewels, (Rāvaṇa) immediately despatched the auspicious idol to Laṅkā by the aerial chariot Puṣpaka.

37. The glorious and righteous Vibhīṣaṇa, the younger brother and minister of Rāvaṇa was a devotee of Nārāyaṇa. He was entrusted with the administration of the capital Laṅkā.

38. On seeing that the divine idol was taken away from the abode of the lord of Devas, he experienced horripilation all over his body. He was struck with surprise.

39-40. With a delighted mind he bowed his head to the lord. After saying—"My birth is fruitful today. My penance is fruitful today", the righteous Vibhīṣaṇa made obeisance again and again. He went to his eldest brother. With his palms joined in reverence he spoke thus :—

41. O king, it behoves you to favour me with this idol. O lord of the worlds, I shall propitiate it and cross the ocean of worldly existence.

42-43. On hearing the words of his brother, Rāvaṇa spoke "O heroic one, take the idol. What shall I do with it? I have propitiated the self-born deity and am conquering the three worlds. I shall also worship Mahādeva who wields various miraculous powers and who is the source of origin of all living beings.

44-45. Then Vibhīṣaṇa of great intellect worshipped the splendid idol for one hundred and eight years and acquired the boon of old age. He attained the attributes of Aṇimā (minuteness) etc. He acquired the realm and overlordship of Laṅkā. Even now, he enjoys all pleasures as he wishes.

The sages said :

46-47. On hearing this extremely immortal narrative the origin of the infinite deity-Vāsudeva, difficult of access on the earth, we are extremely surprised. O lord, we wish to hear the greatness of that lord, precisely and in detail. It behoves you to mention it fully.

Brahmā said :

48-49. That sinful ruthless Rākṣasa (Rāvaṇa) defeated Devas, Gandharvas, Kinnaras, guardians of the quarters, human beings, sages and Siddhas in battle. He kidnapped excellent women and settled them in the city of Laṅkā. Thereafter, he attempted the abduction of Sītā.

50-58. He deceived Rāma through Mārīca in the form of a golden deer.

Rāma and his brother Lakṣmaṇa the son of Sumitrā became infuriated and (resolved to slay Rāvaṇa. After killing Bāli of great prowess, he crowned Sugrīva as the king and Aṅgada as the Heir-apparent. With eyes resembling the petals of a lotus Rāma was surrounded by extremely terrible monkeys of great strength such as—Hanumān, Nala, Nīla, Jāmbavān, Panasa. Gavaya, Gavākṣa and others. They possessed great power and they were pure. With massive boulders of mountains he got the bridge built over the great ocean. With his vast army, Rāma crossed the ocean and fought an unparalleled war against the Rākṣasas. The powerful Rāma slaughtered Yamahasta, Prahasta, Nikumbha, Kumbha, Narāntaka, Yamāntaka, Mālāḍhya, Mālikāḍhya, Indrajit Kumbhakarṇa and Rāvaṇa. He got Sītā the daughter of Janaka, the king of Videha tested by the fire ordeal.[1] He bestowed kingdom on Vibhīṣaṇa and brought the idol of Vāsudeva to Ayodhyā formerly protected (by himself and his ancestors) riding in the aerial chariot Puṣpaka sportingly.

59-61. Out of affection he crowned his younger brother Bharata and Śatrughna as heir-apparents. Rāma who is favourite of his devotee, ruled over the kingdom as an Emperor. Propitiating his own ancient form born of Viṣṇu, Rāma enjoyed the ocean-girt earth for eleven thousand years. Thereafter he attained his own region i.e. the region of Viṣṇu.

62-67. Rāma gave that idol to the lord of oceans (saying) "You are blessed. You will protect this idol in your waters with perfect concentration".

In the Dvāpara Age, the lord the preceptor of the Universe, incarnated in the family of Vasudeva at the request of the earth on account of the emotional instability of the people due to the demons' activities. The lord incarnated for slaying Kaṁsa and was assisted by Balarāma. O brahmins, at that time, with some other purpose in view and for the welfare of worlds, the lord took out that idol, the bestower of all cherished desires and benefits, from the waters of the ocean—the lord of the rivers. He then placed it in that excellent holy centre, Puruṣottama, the rarest of all holy centres. Ever since then, O brahmins, that lord the dispeller of the agony of Devas, the bestower of all desires, stays there itself in that holy centre, the bestower of liberation.

68. Those who devoutly resort to the infinite lord of all, mentally, verbally and physically attain the highest region.

69. By visiting Ananta (infinite) even for once and by devoutly worshipping and bowing to him, the devotee derives ten times more than the benefit of Rājasūya and Aśvamedha sacrifices.

70-71. The man redeems twenty-one generations of his family. He then goes to the city of Viṣṇu seated in a highly

---

1. *Divine Ordeal* (divya-parīkṣā). Yājñavalkya prescribes ten ordeals viz tulā, agni, jala, viṣa, kośa, taṇḍula, tapta-māṣa, phāla, dharma, tulasī.

In the Yuddhakāṇḍa of the Rāmāyaṇa, Vālmiki has described Sītā's entering and standing in fire as a test of her purity.

refulgent aerial chariot that has the lustre and colour of the sun, that is richly furnished with all desirable things, that can go as one desires it to go and that has a row of tinkling bells. He shall be surrounded by the celestial ladies. Gandharvas will be singing in praise of him.

72-74. He will enjoy excellent pleasures there. He will be rid of old age and death. Assuming a divine form the glorious devotee will enjoy pleasures until the dissolution of all living beings.

When his merits dwindle he will return to the earth and be born as a brahmin who has mastered the four Vedas. By adopting Yoga of Viṣṇu he will attain liberation.

Thus, O excellent sages, the infinite deity Ananta has been glorified by me. Who is competent to recount all the merits of visiting the shrine even in hundreds of years ?

CHAPTER SIXTYEIGHT

Glory of the Holy Shrine of Puruṣottama

Brahmā said :

1. Thus, the glory of (Infinite deity) and the holy shrine of Puruṣottama that yields worldly pleasures and liberation unto men has been recounted by me. It is very difficult of access.

2-3. It is the place where the glorious lord stays—the lord whose eyes resemble the lotus, who holds conch, discus and ironclub, who is clad in yellow robes and who has killed Kaṁsa and Keśin.[1]

There is no doubt that those who see there Kṛṣṇa who is bowed to by Devas and Asuras, Saṁkarṣaṇa and Subhadrā are blessed.

1. *Keśin* : a follower of Kaṁsa who at the instruction of Kaṁśa went to Gokula, in the form of a horse, to kill Śrīkṛṣṇa. But Śrīkrsṇa killed him and got the name Keśava.

4. Those who meditate upon Kṛṣṇa the overlord of the three worlds, the bestower of all desired benefits, are liberated souls.

5. Those who are devoted to Kṛṣṇa, those who remember Kṛṣṇa at night (when they go to bed) and again when they get up enter Kṛṣṇa when their bodies are consumed on death like the ghee offering consigned to fire with due repetitions of Mantras.

6. Hence, O excellent sages, the lotus-eyed deity Kṛṣṇa should be assiduously visited in that holy centre by those who seek salvation.

7. The lofty-minded persons who visit Kṛṣṇa, (Balarāma) and Subhadrā at the time when the deities are laid to rest go to the world of Viṣṇu.

8. Those who devoutly visit Puruṣottama, Balarāma and Subhadrā at any time, go to the world of Viṣṇu.

9. He who stays in the holy centres of Puruṣottama for the four months of rainy season derives more benefit than the benefit accruing from the holy pilgrimage to the other centres of the Earth.

10. Those lofty persons who reside there itself during the seasons, after conquering sense-organs and controlling anger, derive the benefit of a penance.

11. Within a month a man obtains at Puruṣottama their benefit which others obtain after performing penance in other holy centres for ten thousand years.

12. Lofty-minded persons always obtain the usual benefit of penance, celibate life eschewed of attachment at the holy centre of Puruṣottama.

13. Lofty-minded persons obtain the benefit which is glorified as the meritorious benefit of ablution and charitable gifts in all other holy centres.

14. Everyday, the pure person derives that benefit which is mentioned as the result of perfectly performed pilgrimage, holy rites and observances.

15. A man of perfectly restrained sense-organs obtains everyday the same benefit as one obtains (on other holy centres) after performing different rites of sacrifice.

16. There is no doubt that the people who resort to the Kalpa tree in the holy centre of Puruṣottama[1] and abandon their bodies become liberated souls.

17. Those who abandon their bodies anywhere between the baniyan tree and the Ocean obtain the greatest liberation which is very difficult to get.

18. Even if the man is forced to give up his life against his wish, he will be liberated from misery. He will attain salvation which is very difficult to get.

19. Even the animals of low strata of species such as germs, worms, moths etc., attain the greatest salvation by abandoning their bodies there.

20. O brahmins, see the illusion of the world in regard to other holy centres. The fruits of all other holy centres are derived from the only holy centre Puruṣottama.

21. The man who faithfully visits Puruṣottama for once will become the most excellent man among thousands of men.

22. The lord is glorified as Puruṣottama in the Vedas, Purāṇas and in the world because he is greater than Prakṛti and more excellent than Puruṣa.

23. He who is cited as Paramātman (the Supreme Being) in the Purāṇas and in Vedānta is present for the uplift of universe. Hence, he is Puruṣottama.

24. Here in this centre whether it is on the road, or in the cemetery or in a house of a pupil or anywhere among different spots in the streets whether willing or otherwise the man who gives up his body derives liberation.

25. Hence, O excellent brahmins, one who gives up his body in this holy centre will achieve liberation.

26. Who can adequately mention the glory of Puruṣottama ? Just by visiting the baniyan tree there a man dispels the sin of brahmin slaughter.

27. Only a part of the good qualities of the holy centres has been related by me. Who can mention the entire merits adequately even in hundreds of years ?

28. O excellent sages, if you seek for perpetual salvation, stay in that holy centre alertfully.

1. *Puruṣottama-kṣetra* : a centre in Orissa, sacred to Viṣṇu.

Vyāsa said :

29. On hearing the words of Brahmā born of the unmanifest one, sages resided there and attained the highest region.

30. Hence, O excellent brahmins, you too stay in this holy centre—Puruṣottama, if you seek for perfect creation hereafter.

CHAPTER SIXTYNINE

Narrative of Sage Kaṇḍu

Vyāsa said:

1-4. O excellent sages, there was a great sage, Kaṇḍū in that holy centre Puruṣottama which is conducive to the happiness of all living beings and which bestows the benefit of virtue, wealth, love and liberation. The sage was extremely virtuous. He had great refulgence. He was truthful in speech, pure and engaged in the welfare of all living beings. He had control over his sense-organs. He had conquered wealth. He was a master of the Vedas and Vedāṅgas. By propitiating Puruṣottama he attained great Siddhi. There were other great sages too who had achieved much. They used to perform great holy rites. They were engaged in the welfare of the people. They had subdued their sense-organs and conquered anger. They were rid of rivalry and malice.

The sages said:

5. Who was this Kaṇḍu? How did he attain the greatest salvation? O excellent one, we wish to hear his story. Please narrate.

Vyāsa said:

6. O leading sages, listen to his interesting story. I shall mention in brief the activities of that sage.

7-9. O excellent sages, the hermitage of Kaṇḍu was on the holy banks of Gomatī[1] river. It was a secluded and charming spot, full of fruits, roots and bulbous roots. It abounded in sacrificial twigs, Kuśa grass and flowers. Many trees and creepers grew there. It was beautified by different kinds of flowers. It was a charming place resonant with the chirping sounds of various birds and those of different kinds of animals. The hermitage was adorned by a grove of plantain trees. It abounded in fruits and flowers in all seasons.

10. The sage performed a great penance. It was extremely wonderful on account of rites, fasts and observances, ablutions, vows of silence and restraint of senses.

11. During the summer he practised fivefold penance with four fires on the four sides and the sun overhead; during the rainy season he slept on the bare ground; during winter he stood in neck-deep water—thus he performed a great penance.

12. On seeing the power of penance of that sage, Devas, Gandharvas, Siddhas and Vidyādharas were struck with wonder.

13. O excellent sages, with the force of his strength Kaṇḍu scorched the three worlds, Earth, firmament and heaven.

14. On seeing him engaged in penance Devas said thus :— "Wonderful is his great courage ! Wonderful is his great penance !"

15. Without excitement they consulted one another. Including Indra they were bewildered and frightened. Hence, they wanted an obstacle to be put in the way of his penance.

16-17. Having come to know their intention, Indra, the destroyer of Bala, the lord of the three worlds, spoke to the beautiful celestial damsel Pramlocā. She was proud of her beauty and youth. She had slender waist and attractive breasts plump and beautiful. She was endowed with all characteristics.

Indra said :

18. O Pramlocā, go quickly to the place where this sage is performing penance. O splendid lady, in order to impede his penance make his mind agitated.

---

1. *Gomatī* : a celebrated river of Purānic fame which flowed through Naimiśa-forest where several sacrifices had been performed by the sages. The word 'Gomati' means 'abounding in water'.

Pramlocā said :

19. O most excellent Deva, O my lord, I always carry out your behests. But in this matter, I have some doubts. My life has to be risked.

20. I am afraid of that excellent sage, who is steadfast in the vow of celibacy. He is very fierce and refulgent as fire and sun. His penance is brilliant.

21. When he comes to know that I have approached him to create impediment in his penance, sage Kaṇḍu of excessive splendour will curse me angrily. It will be unbearable.

22-24. There are many celestial damsels proud of their beauty and blooming youth such as Urvaśī, Menakā, Rambhā, Ghṛtācī, Puñjikā, Sthalā, Viśvācī, Sahajanyā, Pūrvacitti, Tilottamā, Alambuṣā, Miśrakeśī, Śaśilekhā, Vāmanā and others. They are slender-waisted. Their faces are attractive. Their breasts are plump and lifted up. They are experts in the extensive amorous dalliances. Employ them there.

Brahmā said :

25. On hearing her words the consort of Śacī said again;—Let others stay by. O splendid lady, you are very clever in this affair.

26. O lady of fine buttocks, I shall send Kāma, Vasanta (Spring) and the gentle breeze to assist you. Go with them to the place where this great sage lives.

27. On hearing the words of Indra that excellent lady of attractive eyes went with them by the aerial path.

28. After going there she saw the excellent and charming forest. She saw the pious sage, seated in the hermitage performing his brilliant penance.

29. Along with them, she surveyed the beautiful forest comparable to the Nandana forest. It contained excellent flowers of all seasons. It was agitated by groups of monkeys.

30-31. The forest was holy. It was endowed with clusters of lotuses. It was filled with trees with abundant sprouts. She heard sweet songs of birds pleasing to the ears. She saw trees laden with fruits and flowers of all seasons. They were resonant with the songs of birds.

32-37. The lady of wide eyes saw many trees there :—Āmra (Mango), Āmrātaka, coconut, palm, Tinduka, Bilva, Jīva, Dāḍima, Bījapūraka (pomegranate), Panasa (jack tree), Lakuca, Nīpa, beautiful Śirīṣa, Pārāvata, Kola, Arimeda, Amlavetasa, Bhallātaka, Amalaka (Embylic myrobalans), Śataparṇa, Kiṁśuka, Iṅguda, Karavīra, Harītaki, Vibhītaka, Aśoka, Punnāga, Ketaki, Bakula, Pārijāta, Kovidāra, Mandara, Indīvara, Pāṭala in full bloom, Devadāru, Śāla, Tāla, Tamāla, Nicula and Lomaka. These and other trees laden with fruits and flowers she saw there.

38-39. The forest was accompanied by many birds that chirped sweetly such as Cakora, Śatapatra, Bhṛṅgarāja, parrots, cuckoos, sparrows, Hārītas, Jīvajīvakas, Priyaputra, Cātaka and various other birds.

40-42. She saw beautiful lakes with crystal clear waters and full of waterborn flowers such as lilies, lotuses, splendid blue lotuses, Kalhāra etc. The lakes were beautified by these flowers. There were aquatic birds such as Kadambas, Cakravākas (ruddy geese), waterfowls, Kāraṇḍavas cranes, swans, tortoises, porpoises. The lakes were filled with these aquatic beings.

43-45. Alongwith Kāma and others Pramlocā wandered all round the forest. After surveying the beautiful and wonderful forest in their company that excellent lady was extremely wonderstruck. Her eyes beamed with pleasant surprise. O excellent brahmins, she said to Cupid, Spring and the gentle breeze.

Pramlocā said :

Assist me. Ye all severally be prepared.

Brahmā said.

46-49. After saying this, she who was proud of her ability to agitate the passion of everyone said thus:—I shall now go to the place where this sage is present. The sage is like a charioteer with the body as the chariot and the sense-organs as horses. I shall convert him into a bad charioteer with the reins, dropped by the weapons of Kāma. Whether he be a Viṣṇu, a Brahmā or a Śiva, I shall get him split up by the arrows of Kāma".

After saying this she came to the place where the sage was seated. Such was the power of the penance of the sage; the beast of prey in the penance-grove had become quiescent.

50. Standing on the banks of the river, only a very short distance from him, that excellent celestial damsel with the sweetness of the cuckoo in her voice began to sing songs merrily.

51. An untimely but sweet and charming note of the cuckoo was heard and Vasanta exerted his full force.

52. A gentle breeze with his abode in the Malaya mountain blew there making the excellent flowers fall down gently into small or big heaps.

53. Holding the flowery arrows, Kāma went near that sage and made his mind agitated.

54. On hearing the sweet sound of the song the sage was surprised and his mind was afflicted by the arrows of Kāma. He went to the place where the lady of beautiful eyebrows was standing.

55. On seeing her he was delighted with wonder; his eyes beamed. He experienced horripilation all over his body. His upper garment dropped down. He was completely upset.

The sage said :

56. O lady of good buttocks, who are you? Whom do you belong to? O fortunate blessed lady of atrractive smiles, you have captivated my mind. O lady of fine eyebrows and slender waist, tell me the truth.

Pramlocā said :

57. I have come here to collect flowers. I am your servant-maid. Command me quickly? What shall I do at your bidding?

Brahmā said :

58. On hearing her words the sage lost his courage. He was dubed. Taking that damsel by her hand he entered his hermitage.

59. O excellent brahmins, then Cupid, Spring, Breeze became satisfied. They returned to heaven.

60. After going there they spoke to Indra of their activities, on hearing which Indra and Devas became delighted.

61. Immediately after entering the hermitage sage Kaṇḍu assumed a very beautiful form like that of a Cupid.

62. It was richly endowed with handsome features and blooming youth. It was very charming. It was bedecked in divine ornaments. It was the physical form of a blooming youth of sixteen years.

63. Suddenly, due to the power of his penance he assumed a form clad in divine garments, and beautified with divine garlands and unguents. It was lovely and capable of enjoying all pleasures.

64. On seeing his vim and vigour she was excessively surprised saying—"Wonderful, indeed, is the power of penance." She rejoiced much.

65-66. O excellent sages, eschewing his rites of holy bath, prayer during dusk and dawn, repetitione of holy names, sacrifices, study of the Vedas, worship of deities, observances of holy rites, fasts, and meditation he sported with her day and night with great joy. With cupid penetrating into heart he did not know that his penance was getting reduced.

67-68. With his mind drawn to sexual pleasures he was not aware of the passing time. Twilights, nights, days, fortnights, months, seasons and years sped on.

O brahmins, clever in secret amorons dalliance, that lady of fine buttocks, skilled in engaging conversation diverted his mind with various lustful emotions.

69. The sage Kaṇḍu engaged himself in vulgar sexual intercourse with her. Many hundreds of years he stayed with her in the valley of the Mandara mountain.

70. Once she said to that highly blessed sage—"O brahmin, I wish to go to heaven. It behoves you to permit me with a pleasant face."

71. Thus requested by her that sage whose mind was fondly attached to her said—"O gentle lady, please stay for a few days more."

72. Thus requested by him that slender-framed lady enjoyed sexual pleasures in the company of that noble sage for a further period of a hundred and odd years.

73. When requested by her thus—"O holy sir, please

grant me permission. I am going back to heaven," he once again replied—"Stay for some days more."

74. When a further period of more than a hundred years elapsed, that splendid-faced lady said with a lovely smile of great endearment—"O brahmin I am going to heaven".

75. When urged by her thus, the sage said to that lady of large eyes—"O lady of beautiful eyebrows, stay with me for a long time more: you will go later to heaven."

76. Frightened of being cursed by that sage, the lady of fine buttocks stayed with him for a further period of slightly less than two hundred years.

77. Repeatedly requested by that lady for permission to go to heaven that highly blessed sage merely said—"Stay further".

78. The timid lady was afraid of his curse. Amiably submissive she was aware of the agony of frustration in love. So, when requested by him, she did not part from the sage.

79. The great sage sported and diverted himself with her, day and night, with his mind overwhelmed by cupid. The more he indulged himself the fresher became the ways of expressing his affection.

80. Once the sage went out of his hut in a great hurry. As he rushed out the splendid lady said—"Pray, where do you go?"

81. When asked by her thus he said—"O auspicious lady, the day is coming to a close. I shall say my prayers for the dusk. Otherwise, it will be a great omission of my holy rites."

82. The delighted lady then laughed and said to the sage—"is it only now, O sage conversant with all holy rites, that the day is coming to a close? Has it not passed of many times before ?"

The sage said :

83-84. "O gentle lady, you came to this splendid bank of the river this morning. O lady of fine buttocks, you were seen by me and you entered my hermitage, Now it is the dusktime. The day has come to a close. Why do you laugh at me now? Let it be mentioned to me in real feeling of earnestness".

Pramlocā said :

85. "O brahmin, this is true that I came here in a morning. It is not false. But hundreds of years have passed by, since I came to you."

86. Thereupon, the brahmin asked the lady of large eyes in great perturbation—"O timid lady, even as I was engaged in dalliance with you, what period of time did pass by?"

Pramlocā said :

87. "Nine hundred, seven years, six months and three days have passed off till date."

The sage said :

88. "O timid lady, are you telling me the truth or are you jesting with me ? I think I have stayed here with you only for a day."

Pramlocā said :

89. "O brahmin, how will I utter a lie in your presence ? Particularly when asked by you as you proceed ahead along your path ?"

Vyāsa said :

90. O excellent brahmins, on hearing her words that sage censured himself saying—"Fie upon me who have not adhered to disciplined good conduct".

The sage said :

91. My austerities have perished. The spiritual wealth of the knowers of Brahman is doomed. Sense of discrimination has been taken away. A woman has been created by someone only for delusion.

92. The Brahman that is beyond six Ūrmis (billows of worldly entanglement) should have been realized by me by the conquest of self. Fie upon this great evil element of Kāma by whom this adverse goal has been effected.

93. The vedas, and holy rites, all causes of welfare have been damned today by Kāma, the pathway leading to the hell."

94. After censuring himself thus, that sage conversant with piety spoke these words to that celestial damsel who was seated there.

The sage said :

95. O sinful lady, go away as you please. The task of the king of Devas has been duly accomplished by you by causing perturbation in me through your amorous gestures.

96-97. I am not reducing you to ashes by the fire of dreadful anger. Friendship is generated in good people through seven words or seven steps.[1] I have stayed with you for long. Or, what is your fault ? What can I do to you ? This is exclusively my own fault for I could not conquer my sense-organs.

98. Wastage of my austerities has been brought about by you who seek the favour of Indra. Fie upon you the despicable one, the cause of great delusion.

Vyāsa said :

99. When that brahminical sage said this to that lady of fine waist, she trembled excessively and perspired profusely.

100. To that chaste lady who was quaking with fear and whose tender creeperlike body was drenched in sweat, the excellent sage said furiously—"Go. Go away".

101. Rebuked by him she went out of his hermitage and traversing the path of firmament she mopped off her sweat drops by the sprouts of trees.

102. The young damsel moved from tree to tree. She wiped off her body from which perspiration flowed in profuse drops. With the pink sprouts she mopped off the sweat drops.

103. The foetus that had been implanted in her body by sage came out of her limbs in the form of sweat drops and the sense of horripilation.

104. Trees took up that foetus and unified it in a body. Developed through his rays by the moon that child in the womb grew up by and by.

---

1. One can befriend a person by speaking seven words or by footing seven steps together.

105. She became the lovely-eyed daughter of trees, Māriṣā by name. O brahmins, it was she who became the wife of Pracetas and the mother of Dakṣa.

106. When his power of penance was exhausted, the excellent and holy sage Kaṇḍu went to the holy shrine of Viṣṇu named Puruṣottama, O brahmins.

107-111. He saw the rarest of holy centres on Earth that bestows salvation on the shore of the southern sea. It had plenty of flowers in all seasons. It was the bestower of happiness unto all men. It was the receptacle of all good qualities. It was conducive to wealth. Formerly, it had been frequented by Bhṛgu and other great sages and Siddhas. It was the bestower of all cherished desires. It appeared very beautiful with sands scattered all round. Clusters of Ketaki plants enhanced its beauty. Trees and creepers grew there in abundance. The auspicious chirping sound of various birds was heard everywhere. Everywhere the holy spot could be traversed comfortably. (It was always resorted to by Gandharvas, Kinnaras, Yakṣas and other persons seeking salvation. There, he saw Hari adorned by all Devas. He was resorted to by the people of brahmin and other castes in the various stages of their lives.

112. As soon as he saw the holy centre and lord Puruṣottama, the excellent sage considered himself contented as one who had fulfilled his duties.

113. There he sat with fully concentrated mind and propitiated Hari. The excellent sage, a great Yogin stood with his arms lifted up. With a singleminded attention he performed Japa (repetition of holy names) of Brahmapāra (Brahman the great redeemer).

The sages said :

114. O sage, we wish to hear about the excellent and great Brahmapāra whereby lord Keśava was propitiated by Kaṇḍu who performed this Japa.

Vyāsa said :

115. Viṣṇu is the greatest Pāra (the other shore—the destination after crossing the ocean of world by existence). He is Apāra-pāra (It is difficult to cross him—to comprehend him).

He is greater than the greatest Beings. He is of the form of the greatest Ātman. He alone is known as Brahmapāra (Brahman the great redeemer). He is the greatest Pāra (the other shore). He is greater than the greatest. He is Pārapāra (the redeemer of those who redeem).

116. He is the cause and also one who has resorted to the cause, the cause of that too, the greatest cause of cause. Thus, in the effects, it protects all by means of its manifold forms such as Karman (object) and Kartṛ (the Agent).

117. The lord is Brahman, he is identical with every thing; Brahman is the lord of subjects. He is Acyuta (the unswerving). Viṣṇu is the unchanging, unborn, permanent Brahman. He is not contaminated by depreciation and other defects.

118. Just as Puruṣottama is the imperishable, unborn, permanent Brahman so also may the defects of passionate attachment subside.

Vyāsa said :

119-121. O excellent brahmins, on hearing the repetitions of the holy Mantra viz Brahmapāra by the sage and on realizing his great and steadfast devotion, lord Puruṣottama, favourably disposed towards his devotees, approached him with great pleasure riding on his vehicle Garuḍa the son of Vinatā. The slayer of Madhu (=Viṣṇu) spoke to him in a voice as majestic as the rumbling sound of the cloud. He seemed to make the quarters resonant.

The lord said :

122. O sage, mention to me the greatest task that is thought of by you in your mind. I have come to you as the bestower of boons. O sage of good holy rites, choose the boon.

123-125. On hearing these words of the discus-bearing lord of Devas (the sage) opened his eyes and saw Hari in front of him. He resembled the blue Atasi flower in complexion. His eyes were as large as the petals of a lotus. He held conch, discus and iron club in his hands. He wore the crown and shoulderlets. He had four arms and elegant limbs. The lord was clad in yellow robes. He had the Ścar Śrīvatsa. He was bedecked in garlands of sylvan flowers.

(*Extra Verse*) He was endowed with all the characteristic marks. He was bedecked in all jewels. He had smeared his limbs with divine sandal paste. He was embellished with divine garlands.

126. Then the sage was struck with great wonder. His hairs stood on end due to delight. He prostrated himself on Earth like a long staff and made obeisance.

127. After saying—"My birth is fruitful today. My penance is fruitful today," the leading sage began to eulogise the lord.

Kaṇḍu said :

128. O Nārāyaṇa, O Hari O Kṛṣṇa, O lord of the universe with the Śrīvatsa scar, O seed of the universe, O abode of the universe, O witness of the universe, obeisance be to you.

129. O unmanifest one, O victorious one, O source of origin, O chief Puruṣottama, O lotus-eyed one, O Govinda, O lord of the worlds, obeisance be to you.

130. O golden-wombed one, O abode of Śrī, O deity with the umbilical lotus, O eternal one, O deity with the Earth in the womb, O steadfast one, O Īśāna, O Hṛṣīkeśa, obeisance be to you.

131. O deity without beginning and end, O immortal and unconquerable one, be victorious, O most excellent one among those who conquer; O unconquered one, O Indra, O Kṛṣṇa, O resident abode of Śrī, obeisance be to you.

132. O deity with the Yogic Ātman, O incomprehensible Ātman; O soul of the world, you are eternal. O deity difficult to be realised, O deity as immovable and steady as the mountain peak. Obeisance be to you, the lord of Kuśa.

133. O excellent one, O bestower of boons, O infinite one, O source of origin of Brahmā, O mine of good qualities, O lord of dissolution, origin and contact, O Vāsudeva, obeisance be to you.

134. O Parjanya (Lord of Rain), O maker of holy rites, O Duṣpāra (one who cannot be easily comprehended), O Durādhiṣṭhita (one inadequately supported ?); O dispeller of misery and agony, O Hari lying down in the waters, obeisance be to you.

135. O Bhūtapa (lord of Elements), O unmanifest one, O deity not agitated by the elements and principles, O abode of living beings, O soul of living beings. O deity containing living beings in the womb, obeisance be to you.

136. O performer of Yajñas, O upholder of Yajñas, O creator of Yajñas; O bestower of fearlessness; O deity with the Yajña in the womb (?), O golden-limbed one, O deity born of Devakī, obeisance be to you.

137. You are the knower of Kṣetra (Physical form, holy centre) you are the holder Kṣetra; you possess Kṣetra; you are the destroyer of Kṣetra; you are the maker of Kṣetra; you have selfcontrol; O soul of Kṣetra, O deity devoid of Kṣetra, obeisance be to you, the creator of Kṣetra.

138. O abode of good qualities, O receptacle of good qualities, O support of good qualities; O deity who are conducive to good qualities; O enjoyer of good qualities; O garden of good qualities; O deity who abandon good qualities (i.e. attributes), obeisance be to you.

139. You are Viṣṇu; you are Hari; you are the discus-bearing lord; you are Jiṣṇu (victorious); you are Janārdana; you are the Element; and the Vaṣaṭkāra; you are the future one, the lord of the present one.

140. You are the creator of the Bhūtas (living beings); you are the unmanifest one; You are Bhava (source of origin); you are the holder of Bhūtas. You are lord conceiver and creator of Bhūtas. They call you the unborn overlord.

141. You are infinite; you are (deity) conversant with what is done; you are Prakṛti; you are Vṛṣākapi (Viṣṇu). You are Rudra; you are unthwartable; you are never futile; you are the supreme lord.

142. You are identical with Viśvakarman, you are Jiṣṇu. You are Śambhu riding on a bull (?); you are Śaṅkara (benefactor); you are Uśanas, you are the Satya (world); you are the Tapas (world), you are the Jana (world).

143. You are the conqueror of universe, you are welfare; you are one worthy of being sought refuge in. You are the imperishable one; you are the selfborn Śambhu; you are the eldest; you are the greatest resort.

144. You are the sun; you are the Oṁkāra, you are the vital breath; you are the dispeller of darkness; you are Parjanya (god of Rain); you are well reputed; you are Brahmā; you are Indra, lord of Devas.

145. You are Ṛk. Yajus and Sāman; you are Ātman; you are the honoured and approved one, you are fire and wind; you are Kubera; you are Havis (ghee offering).

146. You are the creator; you are the enjoyer; you are the Hotṛ (one who performs Homa offerings), you are Havis (oblation) Kratu (sacrifice); you are the poet, you are Hari; you are the most excellent lord of worlds; you are Acyuta.

147. You are the glorious deity with the vision of everything; you are the destroyer of enemies suppressing everyone; you are the day; similarly, you are the night; learned men call you Vatsara (year).

148. You are the units of time such as Kāla; Kāṣṭhā, Muhūrta, Kṣaṇa and Lava; you are a boy; you are an old man; you are man, woman and eunuch.

149-150. You are the source of origin of the universe, you are the eye, you are Sthāṇu (Śiva, stump); you are the deity of pure ears; you are permanent; you are unconquered; you are Upendra (younger brother of Indra); you are an excellent one.

151. You are Ātman the support of all (?) You are not perceptible to sense-organs.

152. You are Agraṇī (leader); you are Grāmaṇi (leader of groups); you are Suparṇa (Garuḍa); you are one without a beginning, you are the collection; you are very great, you are one who held the Ātman; you are Acyuta (unswerving).

153. You are Yama; (Restraint); you are Niyama (observance of regulations); you are lofty; you are four-armed; you alone are the cooked rice and the immanent soul; you are mentioned as the greatest Ātman.

154. You are the preceptor and the weighty one; you are the weightier being; you are the left one (adverse one); you are the right one (the favourable one, clever one); you are Pippala (a variety of medicinal plant), you are one who do not go, you are the manifest one; you are the Prajāpati (patriarch).

155. You are one with golden umbilicus; you are the lord; you are the moon; you are one whose physical form cannot be specifically pointed out; you are Yama; you are the destroyer of the enemies of Devas.

156. You are lord Saṁkarṣaṇa; you are the eternal maker; you are Vāsudeva of unmeasurable soul; you alone are one devoid of attributes.

157. You are the eldest; you are the most excellent; you are one who endure; you are Mādhava; you are thousand-headed lord; you are unmanifest one with thousand Visions.

158. You are the thousand-footed lord, you are Virāṭ (Immense Being); you are the lord of Devas; O lord of Devas; you alone stand ten Aṅgulas beyond all.

159. You alone are mentioned as that which is past; you are the excellent Puruṣa; Indra; you are Īśāna and that which is going to occur in future; you are the Ṛta Divine law, you are Amṛta (Nectar).

160. It is from you that this world grows up; you art the great being without anyone to excel you; you are the elderly Puruṣa; O lord, you stay in ten forms.

161. A fourth part of yours constitutes the Universe; your nine parts are immortal in heaven; nine parts are stationed in the firmament; this part is the eternal manly being.

162. Two of your parts are stationed on the Earth; four parts were also here. (?) Yajñas originate from you, the cause of rain in the world.

163. The Virāṭ (Immense Being) originated from you; it is the Man who is in the heart of the universe; he excelled the elements by splendour, fam e and glory.

164. It is from you that Pṛṣadājya (ghee mixed with coagulated milk), the diet of Devas originated. The medicinal plants of the village of the forests and the animals etc originated from you.

165. You are devoted to what should be meditated upon and the meditation; you created the medicinal herbs. O lord of Devas, having seven faces you are named Kāla; you have an illuminated physical form.

166. The whole universe mobile and immobile is born of you and established in you.

167. O lord, the most excellent one among Devas, the greatest refuge of the worlds you are Aniruddha, you are Mādhava, you are Pradyumna the destroyer of the enemies of Devas.

168. O lotus-eyed deity, save me O Nārāyaṇa, obeisance to you. O Puruṣottama, obeisance to you.

169. Obeisance to you, O lord of worlds, obeisance to you the abode of Lakṣmī; obeisance to you, O abode of attributes; obeisance be to you; O mine of good qualities.

170. O Vāsudeva, obeisance be to you. O most excellent Deva, obeisance be to you. O Janārdana, obeisance be to you; O eternal one, obeisance be to you.

171. Obeisance to you O deity comprehensible to the Yogins; O abode of Yoga, obeisance be to you. O lord of Lakṣmī; O lord of universe, obeisance be to you.

172. O lord of the universe, O source of origin of the universe, O lord of the men of perfect knowledge, obeisance to you. O lord of heaven, obeisance be to you. O lord of Earth, obeisance be to you.

173. Obeisance to you, to the slayer of Madhu; O lotus-eyed one, obeisance to you; O destroyer of Kaiṭabha, obeisance be to you; O Subrahmaṇya (Excessively favourable to the brahmins). Obeisance be to you.

174. O great Fish, obeisance be to you. O Acyuta, holding up Śrutis on your back. Obeisance to you who agitated the oceanic water and delighted the lotus-born lady.

175. O Horse-headed deity of great snout, O deity, having the great manly frame, O Horse-faced deity, obeisance to you the annihilator of Madhu and Kaiṭabha.

176. Obeisance to you, to the great tortoise, to the deity with the great body of a tortoise, to the deity who lifted up the Earth, to that form that held the mountain aloft.

177. Obeisance to the great Varāha (Boar), to (the deity) who lifted up the Earth. Obeisance to the Primordial Varāha, to the creator of the form of the universe.

178. Obeisance to the infinite one, to the subtle one, to the chief one, to the most excellent one. Obeisance to you of the form of the atom, to one comprehensible to the yogins.

179. Obeisance to the greatest cause of causes; to the abode of the circle of leading Yogins; to the being very difficult to be known. Obeisance to you who lie down on the couch of the great serpent stationed in the milky ocean; obeisance to the deity with fine ear rings made of gold and studded with jewels.

Vyāsa said :

180. Eulogised thus by him Mādhava was delighted and he said—"O excellent sage, tell me quickly what you wish from me.

Kaṇḍu said :

181-185. O lord of the universe, I am deluded by your Māyā. I wander about in the ocean of worldly existence which is very difficult to be crossed, which causes hairs to stand on end, which is impermanent, full of miseries and restless like the plantain leaf. It has no support. It has no base. It is a support. It is as fickle as bubbles in water, it is full of all calamities; it is difficult to be crossed; it is terrible to behold. My mind is drawn to and afflicted by sensual objects. I do not find any end to this worldly Existence, O lord of Devas. I am afflicted by the fear of worldly existence. I seek refuge in you O Kṛṣṇa. Redeem me from the ocean of worldly existence. O lord of Daityas, Dānavas and Devas, I wish to go to that eternal great region of yours from which it is difficult to return.

The lord said :

186. O excellent sage, you are my devotee. Propitiate me continuously. Due to my favour you will certainly attain the desired liberation.

187. Even Kṣatriyas, Vaiśyas, women folk, Śūdras and the lowcaste people attain great Siddhis if they are my devotees. What doubt then about you, O excellent brahmin.

188. Even a caṇḍāla, if he is my devotee and if he is endowed with perfect faith, attains the desired end. What doubt then about others?

Vyāsa said :

189. O brahmins, after saying thus to him, Viṣṇu the lord

favourably disposed to his devotees, the lord whose movement is very difficult to comprehend vanished there itself.

190. After he had gone, O excellent sages, Kaṇḍu eschewed all lustful desires. He became delighted in his mind and he attained a proper mental quietude.

191-92. He restrained all his sense-organs. He was rid of the feelings of "my-ness". He was free from egotism. With single-minded devotion he perfectly meditated on Puruṣottama who is free from smearing attachment, who is devoid of attributes, who is quiescent and who is established in his sole existence. He attained the greatest of liberation that is difficult of access even unto Devas.

193. He who reads or listens to the story of the noble Kaṇḍu shall be liberated from sins. He goes to the heavenly world.

194-195. Thus, O excellent sages, the land of holy rites has been cited by me. So also the greatest holy centre for liberation named Puruṣottama has been recounted. It pertains to Lord Puruṣottama.

Those men devoid of impurities who visit the omnipresent lord, who eulogise the lord who grants boons, and devoutly meditate upon the deity named Śrīpuruṣottama who bestows salvation, who dispels worldly miseries and who is devoid of old age, enjoy the pleasures of a king. Later they enjoy divine pleasures in heaven. Freed of all defects they later go to the unchanging abode of Hari.

CHAPTER SEVENTY

Doubts raised by sages

Lomaharṣaṇa said:

1. On hearing the words of Vyāsa, the sages of restrained sense-organs became satisfied, delighted and struck with wonder again and again.

The sages said:

2. Wonderful indeed are the attributes of the sub continent Bhārata mentioned by you. So also of the shrine named Śrī-puruṣa in the holy centre Puruṣottama.

3. O sage, the most excellent among eloquent ones, who will not be delighted and surprised on hearing about the excellent greatness of the shrine named Puruṣa?

4. We have a doubt in our hearts. It has been there for a long time. Excepting you, there is no one on the Earth to clarify that doubt.

5. O great sage, it is about the origin of Balarāma, Kṛṣṇa and Subhadrā on the Earth that we wish to ask. We would like to understand it thoroughly.

6. Why were the heroic Kṛṣṇa and Saṅkarṣaṇa (Balarāma) born in the house of Vasudeva? Why was she too born in that house there, O sage ?

7-8. How did the terrible ordeal of a stay in the womb appeal to them? The womb that is sling and lubricious due to urine and faeces? It is painful, distressful and miserable. Why were they born in this mortal world that consists mostly of miseries? Though it is devoid of essence and very fickle like a watery bubble, yet it is very terrible and it causes hairs to stand on their ends.

9. O sage, the most excellent among the eloquent ones, recount to us in detail the activities that they pursued on being born on the Earth.

10-12. Mention their wonderful and superhuman story, how did the lord of Devas, the most excellent and intelligent one among Devas attain the state of Vāsudeva in the house of Vasudeva?

He left off the holy world of Devas surrounded by the immortal beings and adorned by meritorious persons and came over to the mortal world here.

Why did that leader of Devas and human beings, the unchanging source of origin of the Earth unite his divine soul with mortal bodies?

13-20. Alone, the lord makes the circle of human beings whirl without ailments. Why did that wielder of discus and ironclub decide to be born among human beings? It is Viṣṇu the lord who protects all living beings in the universe. Why did that lord come over to the Earth and carry on the activity of a cowherd?

He is the soul of Elements. He created and sustained the great elements. He is one whose glory is hidden in the womb. How was it that he was conceived in the womb by an ordinary women who walked about on the Earth? In his incarnation as the Dwarf at the request of Devas he won over three worlds by means of three paces. The excellent threefold path of the three aims of life (virtue, love and wealth) was immediately restored. He is the lord who, at the hour of dissolution, converts the universe into an aquatic body and drinks it up. He makes the world a vast sheet of water and lies therein with his form partly manifest and partly unmanifest.

He is the ancient lord, the soul of ancient beings, the destroyer of enemies. He assumed the form of a Boar. By the tip of his curved fangs, he lifted up the Earth.

He is the most excellent among Devas, who on behalf of Indra conquers the three worlds and gave it over to Devas as their realm.

He assumed the form of a lion and split it further into two (i.e. half man, half lion). The Daitya of great prowess, Hiraṇya-kaśipu was killed by him.

21-26. Formerly, lord Hari became the Aurva and Saṁvartaka fires (submarine fire and fire of dissolution). Stationed in the nether regions he drank the watery essence of the ocean. In every Yuga they call him Brahman with a thousand feet, with a thousand rays. They call him the lord who bestows thousands, the lord with a thousand heads.

In his umbilicus a lotus grew up. It was the abode of Brahmā. It was a lotus of molten gold in the vast sheet of water, in the world of serpents.

In the war called Tārakāmaya,[1] many Daityas were killed by him with the weapons presided over by Devas.

---

1. *Tārakāmaya* : a war which arose in consequence of Soma (Moon) havin carried off Tārā, the wife of Bṛhaspati.

The arrogant demon Kālanemi[1] was struck down by the lord seated on Garuḍa.

He adopts the perpetual Yoga and lies down at the northern end of the milky ocean. He envelops everything in great darkness.

27-28. Aditi conceived the ancient lord in her divine womb. Indra who was challenged by Daityas was held in womb by Aditi and saved.

By his Yogic powers he created regions and made Daityas stay there embedded in waters. After creating Devas and the leaders of Devas he made Indra their lord.

29-30. By Gārhapatya and Anvāhārya rites he created the material essential for Yajñas while his hand was hanging downwards, Āhavanīya fire, Vedas, initiation, sacrificial twig, Prokṣaṇīya vesssel, Sruva ladle, Avabhṛtha, and the persons partaking of their shares in havya.

31-33. He made Devas the partakers of Havya and Pitṛs the partakers of Kavya. He assigned shares to them in the sacrificial rites and laid down rules regarding Yajña. Vessels, monetary gifts, initiation, Caru offerings, Ulūkhalas (Mortars) sacrificial post, Soma juice, Pavitras (ringlike loops made of Kuśa grass), paridhis (sacrificial sticks placed round the fire), articles required for sacrifice such as Camasas, all these the lord created. He classified Sadasyas (audience) and Yajamānas (performers of Sacrifice); He made the various excellent sacrifices such as Medhā etc.

34. He divided sacrifices according to Yugas and the power (of endurance) of the people. The rites of Parameṣṭhin were also classified in accordance with Yugas.

35-38. He created some units of the time such as Kṣaṇas, Nimeṣas, Kāṣṭhās and Kalās. He created three forms of time past, present, future. He created Muhūrtas, Tithis (days of the lunar fortnight), months, days, years and seasons. The various groups of time, units, three types of magnitude (length, breadth, bright), span of life, centres (?) increase, characteristics, beauty of form—all these were created by the lord. Three worlds, three Devas, three lores, three fires, three time factors

1. A great asura, son of Virocana and grandson of Hiraṇyakaśipu.

(past, present, future), three holy rites, three castes and three Guṇas were created by him. Formerly, all the worlds were created by that lord of infinite activities. He is present in all living beings in the form of attributes.

39-40. The lord diverts himself through the contact of sense-organs of men. He is the leader of to-and-fro travel. He is the creator and overlord. He is the goal of those who possess virtue. He is the non-goal of persons of sinful rites. He is the origin of division of four castes. He is the custodian of division of four castes.

41-44. He is one who knows the fourfold division of lores. He is the seat of support for the four divisions of society, four stages of life. He is the intervening space between the quarters, Earth, wind and fire. He is luminary in the forms of sun and moon. He is the lord of Yugas. He walks about at night. He is the greatest luminary; he is (mentioned) as the greatest penance; they call him the greatest without anyone else greater than himself; he is the great Supreme soul. He is the lord of sons of Aditi, the lord is the annihilator of Daityas. He is the destroyer during the concluding days of yugas. He is the smiter of the destroyers of worlds: he is the bridge of bridges of worlds; he is the holiest of all holy rites.

45. He is the deity worthy of being known unto the Vedic scholars; he is the greatest lord among those who are sources of origin; among the gentle he is Soma; among those of fiery refulgence he is fire.

46. He is one who is the overlord of Indra; he is the penance of those who perform penance; he is the humility of those whose behaviour is conditioned by statesmanship, he is the brilliant splendour of those who are refulgent.

47-48. He is the physical form of those who deserve physical forms; he is the goal of those who deserve goal.

The wind originates from Ether, fire originates from wind (that is the vital breath) (?), the vital breath originates from heaven. The lord, (the destroyer of Madhu) is fire and vital breath. From juice originates blood and flesh originates from blood.

49. Fat is produced from flesh; bone is produced from fat;

marrow is generated from bone and semen is produced from marrow.

50-56. Foetus is evolved out of semen, due to that activity at the root of which is Rasa (juice). There the first part is that of waters. It is called heap pertaining to the moon. The second heap should be understood to have been born of the heat of the womb (?) One should know that the semen is of the nature of the moon; and the menstrual blood is of the nature of fire. Emotional fervour follows the Rasa. The moon and fire are present in the seed (?). The semen comes under the category of Kapha (Phlegm) and the menstrual blood in the category of Pitta (bile). The heart is the place of the phlegm and the bile is established in umbilicus. The heat is in the middle of the body and it is remembered as the seat of the mind. The place in between the umbilicus and belly (?) is the place where fire-god is present. The mind is the lord of subject. The phlegm is thought of as the moon. The bile is fire. Thus the universe is of the nature of fire and moon. When the foetus has thus begun to function and when it increases in size like a lump of flesh, the wind enters the body and comes in contact with the greatest Ātman. It becomes split into fire within the body and grows in size.

57-63. The winds are Prāṇa, Apāna, Samāna, Udāna and Vyāna. Prāṇa moves round increasing the great Ātman (?) Apāna increases the hinder body; Udāna (increases) half of the embodied soul (?); Vyāna is so called because it pervades the body. The Samāna makes it return. Then the elements are attained and they become perceptible to the sense-organs. The five elements are Earth, wind, firmament, waters and fire.

The Elements permeating the sense-organs create their respective parts (in the body). They say that the mass body pertains to Earth; Vital breath is the part of air; pores and hollow cavities originate from firmament; exudations function from watery element. Eyes and the warmth of the body is the fiery element. The guide of all these is the mind.

The villages and territories function through the power of the lord. Puruṣa, the lord, creates the eternal worlds.

The sages said :

Why did Viṣṇu attain the form of a man in this mortal world O brahmin, this is our doubt. It gives us a great surprise.

64-65. How did the goal of those who deserve the goal take up the human body? Viṣṇu is mentioned by Devas and Daityas as a great wonder. O great sage, tell us the wonderful story of the origin of Viṣṇu whose splendour is unmeasured and whose strength and prowess are well known.

66-69. May the real principle of Viṣṇu who is a great miracle on account of his activities, be mentioned. How did that lord, the dispeller of the agony of Devas, Puruṣottama (take birth as a human being) ? The lord of the universe is omnipresent; he is the great lord of all the worlds; he is the lord and cause of creation, sustenance and annihilation; he is the cause of happiness of everyone; he is inexhaustible, permanent, infinite. He is devoid of both decline and increase. He is unsmeared, free from attributes, subtle unafflicted and unsullied. He is free from all conditioning factors. He is stabilised in his sole form of Existence. He undergoes no change or transformation; he is the eternal, perpetual great soul. He is unmoving and all-pervading. He is devoid of impurities. He is ever satisfied and he has none to support him.

70-75. In the Kṛta Yuga the state of being Viṣṇu and Hari is heard of; among Devas, he has the state of Vaikuṇṭha and among mortals he has the state of Kṛṣṇa.

We wish to hear about the inscrutable way of activities of this lord for ever, both past and future. The lord is unmanifest but his symbols are clearly manifest. Nārāyaṇa is the infinite Ātman. He is the unchanging source of origin Hari the eternal lord became Nārāyaṇa, Brahmā, Indra, Rudra, Dharma, Śukra and Bṛhaspati. Formerly, this lord in the form of Ātman of Pradhāna created Brahmā. That primordial Puruṣa created Prajāpatis in the previous Kalpa. Thus the lord Viṣṇu is the over-lord of lords of all the worlds. Why, then, did Hari go to the family of Yadus in the mortal world ?

CHAPTER SEVENTYONE

Lord's Incarnation

Vyāsa said :

1-9. Having bowed to Viṣṇu, the lord of Devas, I shall mention the story. Obeisance to the powerful ancient Puruṣa, to the unchanging permanent lord.

Obeisance to the lord in the form of four arrays; to the lord without attributes and to the lord with attributes; to the excellent one, to the weightied one; to the most excellent one, to the unmeasured one; to the deity forming part of the Yajña, to the part of all; to one attainable by Vedas etc; there is nothing minuter than that lord. There is nothing larger than that unborn lord by whom this universe is pervaded—the universe consisting of mobile and immobile beings. The universe is of peculiar nature different from what is manifest and what is unmanifest. It appears and vanishes. They say that such a world is created by the lord and in the same way it is withdrawn by him.

With great concentration I bow down to Brahmā the primordial lord. Obeisance to one without aberration, to the pure one, to permanent and greatest Ātman, to the deity who has the same sole form always; to Viṣṇu the conqueror of every one.

Obeisance to Hiraṇyagarbha (Brahmā), Hari and Śaṅkara to Vāsudeva, the essential one, to the cause of creation, sustenance and dissolution.

Obeisance to the single-formed and multiformed deity; obeisance to the gross-formed and subtle-formed deity; obeisance to the manifest and unmanifest-formed deity; obeisance to Viṣṇu the cause of salvation.

Obeisance to Viṣṇu who is identical with the universe and who is the root cause of creation, sustenance and dissolution of the universe. Obeisance to the greatest Ātman.

10-13. I bow down to Acyuta, Puruṣottama who is the support of the universe; is the minutest of all minute beings; who is stationed in all living beings; whose form is that of knowledge, Who is extremely devoid of impurities in fact but who stands in the form of objects as a result of erroneous perception. I bow down to Viṣṇu who swallows the universe and who is competent to create and sustain the universe; I bow down to the lord of world who has no beginning, who is unborn, who has no decline and who has no change. (After bowing down thus) I shall recount in the same manner as the lotus-born deity Brahmā said when formerly he was asked by Dakṣa and sages.

14-15. After bowing down to the lord Brahmā who sanctifies the three worlds by uttering the Ṛk and Sāman mantras through his mouths who came out of the vast sheet of water and whose behest is certainly carried out by Asuras and human beings, I shall mention fully the opinion of Brahmā born of unmanifest one.

16-20. Holy rites are revealed by him after directing creation The waters are called Nāras by the sages, the seers of the principles since waters constitute his place of resort (Ayana) of lord Viṣṇu as Nārāyaṇa.

Nārāyaṇa, the ommipresent lord, envelops everything. Brahmā who is both Saguṇa (with attributes) and Nirguṇa (attributeless) is stationed in four forms. One form cannot be specifically mentioned. Learned men see it in white form, encircled by clusters of flames. It is the form which Yogins steadfastly adhere to. It should be known as staying nearly as well as far off. It is beyond the Guṇas (attributes). It is called Vāsudeva. It appears free from the felling of myness. Forms, colours and similar things, that are conceivel, but not real are not present in it. It is always pure, single-formed and well-established.

21-25. The second form called Śeṣa upholds the Earth with its head. It stands below in the nether rigions. It is called Tāmasa (having Tamas attribute and hence assumed the status of a lower species of animal.

The third form is interested in protecting the subjects and it performs activities. It should be known as predominatly possessing Sattva attribute. It is the cause of stabilizing Dharma.

The fourth form is stationed in the middle of waters. It lies on the couch of a serpent. Its attribute is Rajas. It always creates.

The third form of Hari is interested in protecting the

subjects invariable. It establishes virtue on the Earth. It destroys the haughty Asuras who break the laws of virtue.

26-28. It protects Devas and Gandharvas and all those who are interested in protecting virtue.

Whenever there is any drawback in virtue and evil gains the upper hand, this form creates itself, that is, it takes up incarnations.

Formerly, it assumed the form of a Boar. With its snout it pierced through the water and lifted up the Earth with single curved fang as though it was a lotus plant. After assuming the form of a man-lion Hiraṇyakaśipu was killed by it.

29-35. Other Dānavas too such as Vipracitti were struck down by it. He assumed the form of a Dwarf; bound Bali by his Māyā. Covered the three worlds with his steps and defeated the sons of Diti.

The valorous son of Jamadagni was born in the family of Bhṛgu. Remembering the murder of his father, Paraśurāma killed Kṣatriyas. Born as Dattātreya, the valorous son of Atri, he related the eightfold Yoga to the noble Alarka. The same lord became Rāma the valorous son of Daśaratha and in a battle killed Rāvaṇa who had terrified the three worlds.

When the lord of Devas, the lord of the universe was lying asleep in the vast sheet of water be adopted the Yogic slumber on the couch of the serpent for the period of a thousand Yugas. He was established in his own greatness.

He had kept the three worlds in his belly, the whole universe consisting of mobile and immobile beings. He was then eulogised by Siddhas and sages who were in the world of Janaloka.

36-42. From his umbilicus there grew up a lotus. The quarters were its petals with which it was adorned. It had the refulgence of fire and the sun. It was embellished by the mountains that acted as the filaments. The winds were its blossoms. It was the excellent abode of Brahmā. It was there that four-faced lord of Devas, Brahmā was born.

At that time, two Dānavas, Madhu and Kaiṭabha were born of the impurities from his ears. Those two Dānavas of great strength and prowess attempted to kill Brahmā. The lord got up from his bed in the ocean and killed them. I do not attempt to enumerate these and other activities fully. But the incarnation of the unborn lord at Mathurā is relevant to the context now.

Thus the form of Sattvaguṇa undertakes incarnations. It is called Pradyumna and is engaged in the activity of protection. It can assume the forms of Devas, human beings and lower animals. It will have the respective nature (of the species where incarnation is taken). It is due to the will of Vāsudeva.

O excellent brahmins, if it is worshipped it bestows desired benefits. Though the lord is contented he undertakes the form as human beings. Listen to the sequal now.

CHAPTER SEVENTYTWO

Incarnations of Hari

Vyāsa said :

1. Listen, O leading sages, I shall recount to you briefly the incarnations which Hari took up in order to remove the burden of the Earth.

2-4. O brahmins, whenever there is increase in evil and virtue dwindles down, lord Viṣṇu takes incarnation by dividing his body into two in order to protect the good, establish virtue and chastise the wicked and other enemies of Devas. He is born in every Yuga for protecting the subjects.

5-6. O brahmins, formerly, the Earth was afflicted by excessive burden. The Earth went to the assembly of heaven-dwellers. After bowing down to Devas including Brahmā, the Earth narrated every thing speaking piteously in her grief.

The Earth said :

7. Fire is the preceptor of gods; sun is the preceptor of cows, Nārāyaṇa is the preceptor of those worthy of being saluted by me as well as other people.

8. Now, Daityas, the followers of Kālanemi have come to the mortal world. Day and night they harass the subjects.

9. That Asura Kālanemi who was slain by all powerful Viṣṇu is now born as Kaṁsa the great Asura and a son of Ugrasena.

10-11. There are many other very powerful asuras such as Ariṣṭa, Dhenuka, Keśin, Pralamba, Naraka, Sunda, Bāṇa, the fierce son of Bali and many others. They are wicked souls born in the abodes of kings. I do not attempt to enumerate them all.

12. O Devas holding divine forms, there are many Akṣauhiṇīs (huge armies, of haughty leading Daityas of great strength), on me.

13-14. O lords of immortal beings, afflicted and distressed by their excessive burden I am unable to steady myself. I hereby submit to you, O highly blessed ones, may the extra burden be removed from me lest I should sink into the nether worlds in my bewilderment.

Vyāsa said :

15. On hearing these words of the Earth Brahmā was requested by Devas to remove the burden of the Earth.

Brahmā said :

16-18. O heaven-dwellers whatever the Earth says is true. You all, I and Hara—all of us are the excellent and elegant powers of Nārāyaṇa. Among these powers there is superiority and inferiority complex by way of hindering others and being hindered by them. Hence come ye. We shall go to the excellent shore of the milk ocean. There we shall propitiate Hari and intimate everything to him.

19. That lord is the Ātman of all. He is identical with the universe. He will always work for your benefit. With a small part of himself he will be born over the Earth and he will establish virtue.

Vyāsa said :

20. After saying thus Brahmā went along with Devas. With full concentration, he eulogised the Garuḍa-emblemed deity.

Brahmā said :

21. O lord with thousand forms, obeisance, obeisance be to you; O thousand-armed one, O many-armed and many-footed one, obeisance, obeisance to you, O lord engaged in creation, maintenance and destruction of the universe, O incomprehensible one.

22. You are the subtlest of all subtle beings; you have a great magnitude, O lord, you are weightier than the weightiest. O lord, possessed of Pradhāna, cosmic intellect and sense-organs, O lord identical with the chief worlds, be pleased.

23. On account of the mighty Asuras born on the Earth, O lord, this Earth is extremely afflicted. She is pained under the heavy weight of suffering. In order to get the burden removed she has approached you the ultimate resort of worlds, the redeemer without any other greater being.

24-25. O lord of Devas, all of us are ready to carry out your orders viz—Indra, the slayer of Vṛtra, Nāsatya and Dasra (Aśvins), Varuṇa, Rudras, Vasus, Sun, wind, fire and Devas. What should be done by these and by me, O lord, command us. We shall await your behest for even eschewing defects.

Vyāsa said :

26-27. O excellent brahmins on being eulogised thus, the great lord, plucked out two hairs from his head, one white and the other black. He then spoke thus to the Devas. "These two hairs of mine will incarnate on the Earth distressed due to excessive burden.

28. May all Devas incarnate on the Earth. Let them fight with the mighty proud Asuras who are already born before.

29. Then, there is no doubt about it, all those Asuras on the Earth will be exterminated after being reduced to powder by means of different weapons.

30. O immortal ones, this hair of mine will be born as the eighth child in the womb of Devakī, the wife of Vasudeva who is comparable to a goddess.

31. After birth on the Earth it will kill Kaṁsa born of Kālanemi. After saying this, Hari vanished there itself.

32. Those Devas then bowed down to the noble lord who became invisible, went to the top of Meru and then descended on the Earth.

33. The holy sage Nārada said thus to Kaṁsa—"The eighth child in the womb of Devakī born in the Earth will kill you".

34. On hearing it from Nārada, Kaṁsa became infuriated. He kept Devakī and Vasudeva as prisoners in their own house and guarded them well.

35. O brahmins, whenever a son was born Vasudeva immediately handed over that son to Kaṁsa as he himself had told him before.

36. The sons of Hiraṇyakaśipu became well known as these six children in the womb. Urged by Viṣṇu, his (Yogic) slumber joined them gradually to the womb of Devakī.

37. This Yogic slumber pertaining to Viṣṇu is also called Mahāmāyā and Avidyā. The entire universe is deluded by her.

Lord Hari said to her :

38. O slumber, go hence. One by one take these children (of Hiraṇyakaśipu) who are in the nether worlds now to the belly of Devakī at my behest.

39. When they have been killed by Kaṁsa, my sinless part named Śeṣa will become the seventh child in the womb of Devakī by means of a small part.

40-41. In the cowherds' colony, there is another wife of Vasudeva named Rohiṇī. At the birth of Devakī's child, it should be taken to the belly of Rohiṇī. People will then say that there was an abortion of the seventh child in the womb of Devakī due to her fear from Kaṁsa and also due to the rigours of imprisonment.

42. Since the child in the womb has been dragged away, the heroic boy comparable to the peak of Meru, Saṅkarṣaṇa will be born in the world.

43. Then, I shall be born in the auspicious womb of Devakī. You should also go to the womb of Yaśodā without delay.

44. I shall be born at night on the eighth day in the dark half of the mouth of Śrāvaṇa during the rainy season. You will be born on the ninth day.

45. O uncensured lady, urged by my Śakti, Vasudeva will take me to the bed of Yaśodā and you to that of Devakī.

46. O gentle lady, Kaṁsa will seize you and hurl you against a rocky slab. Thereafter, you will attain an abode in the firmament.

47. With due deference to me, Indra will bow down to you a hundred times; with his head bent down in obeisance he will accept you as his sister.

48. Thereafter, you will kill thousands of Daityas. With various abodes (i.e. shrines) you will adorn the entire Earth.

49. You are identical with the following deities :—Bhūti (Existence), Sannati (Obeisance), Kīrti (Renown), Kānti (Splendour), Pṛthivī (Earth), Dhṛti (Courage), Lajjā (Bashfulness), Puṣṭi (Nourishment), Umā and other goddesses whoever they may be.

50-51. If the devotees eulogise you in the morning and in the afternoon with their forms bent down in humility, and address you as Āryā, Durgā, Vedagarbhā, Ambikā, Bhadrā, Bhadrakālī, Kṣemyā and Kṣemakarī, they will have whatever they desire, due to my favour.

52. Worshipped by means of wine, meat and other presents and various items of foodstuffs you will become delighted and fulfil all desires of men.

53. Undoubtedly, all of them will have welfare always due to my favour. It need not be suspected at all. O gentle lady, go, in the manner mentioned before.

CHAPTER SEVENTYTHREE

The nativity of Śrīkṛṣṇa

Vyāsa said :

1. In accordance with what was mentioned by the lord of Devas formerly, the mother of the universe i.e. the Yogic slumber Māyā took the six children to the womb of Devakī one by one and removed the seventh forcibly.

2. When the seventh child in the womb was transferred to the womb of Rohiṇī, Hari entered the womb of Devakī for helping the three worlds.

3. On the same day the Yogic slumber took birth in the belly of Yaśodā in accordance with what was mentioned by Brahmā.

4. O brahmins, when the part of Viṣṇu entered the Earth the seasons became auspicious. The planets in the sky moved perfectly (and favourably).

5. No one dared to look at Devakī due to her excessive refulgence. On seeing her blazing splendidly, the minds of onlookers became excited.

6. Day and night the deities eulogised Devakī who held Viṣṇu in her womb.

Devas said :

7. You are Svāhā, you are Svadhā, you are Vidyā, you are Sudhā (Nectar), you are splendour. For the protection of worlds, you have incarnated on the Earth.

8. Be pleased, O gentle lady, do what is auspicious to the universe. For the delight of all, bear Īśāna in your womb. It is by him that the entire universe has been sustained.

Vyāsa said :

9. Thus eulogised by Devas, she conceived the lord in her womb, the lotus-eyed lord, the cause of safety and security of the world.

10. The entire universe is like the lotus. In order to make it bloom the noble deity Acyuta manifested himself like the sun. It was Devakī's womb that bore him even as the sky at dawn bears the sun.

11. When at midnight, Janārdana the support of all, was born, the clouds produced gentle sounds and Devas showered flowers.

12-13. On seeing the lord born, the lord whose lustre was like that of the petals of a full-blown blue lotus, who had four arms and whose chest was marked by the Śrīvatsa scar, Vasudeva eulogised him.

O excellent brahmins, after eulogising him with pleasing

words, the highly intelligent Vasudeva who was afraid of Kaṁsa intimated to him thus :

Vasudeva said :

14-15. O lord of the chiefs of Devas, bearing conch, discus and iron-club, you have been realised by us as the lord. O lord, be pleased to withdraw this divine form. O lord, today itself Kaṁsa will begin to torture me on coming to know that you have incarnated in my abode.

Devakī said :

16. May that lord of Devas be pleased, the lord of Devas who has now revealed an infant's form by means of his own Māyā, whose form is endless, whose form is this entire universe and who bears the world in his womb.

17. O lord, the Ātman of all, withdraw this four-armed form. O destroyer of Asuras, sons of Diti, let not Kaṁsa know about your incarnation.

The lord said :

18. Formerly, O gentle lady, I had been eulogised by you, desirous of a son. Since I am now born of your womb, your prayer has become fruitful.

Vyāsa said :

19. O excellent sages, after saying thus, the lord became silent. During the night itself Vasudeva took him and went out.

20. When Vasudeva set out, the watchmen became deluded. The porters and watchmen of the city of Mathurā were enchanted and deluded by the Yogic slumber.

21. When the clouds discharged a heavy and fierce downpour during that night, Śeṣa shielded Vasudeva by means of his hoods.

22. Bearing Viṣṇu, Vasudeva waded through Yamunā with the waters reaching only upto his knees though the river was majestic and agitated due to whirlpools.

23. On the bank of Yamunā he saw Nanda and other elderly cowherds who carried revenue to be paid to Kaṁsa.

24-25. At that time, O sages, Yaśodā too was deluded by Yogic slumber. She gave birth to a girl who was Māyā herself. When the people were enchanted, Vasudeva of unmeasured lustre, placed the boy on the bed of Yaśodā, took the baby girl and came away quickly.

26. On waking up, Yaśodā saw her new-born son, dark in complexion like the petals of a blue lotus. Thereat she rejoiced very much.

27. Taking the baby girl back to his abode, Vasudeva placed her on the bed of Devakī.

28. O brahmins, thereafter the watchmen heard the crying sound of the infant and got up suddenly. They intimated to Kaṁsa about the birth of a child to Devakī.

29. Kaṁsa rushed to Devakī and seized the baby girl from her even as Devakī tried to prevent him crying aloud "Leave off, leave off" till her throat ached.

30. He hurled her on the top of a rocky slab. On being hurled thus she flew up and took up a position in the sky. She assumed a formidable form with eight large hands armed with weapons. She laughed aloud (in derision) and furiously spoke to Kaṁsa thus :

Yogamāyā said :

31-32. O Kaṁsa, what do you gain by seizing me ? He who will kill you is born. He is the entire possession of Devas. Formerly, he had been Death unto you. After considering this, you may do something quickly that may be conducive to your own welfare.

Vyāsa said :

After saying this, the goddess with divine garlands, scents and ornaments went away through the sky even as Kaṁsa stood watching. She was eulogised by Siddhas.

CHAPTER SEVENTYFOUR

Kaṁsa takes steps to ward off his danger

Vyāsa said :

1. Distressed in mind (due to this) Kaṁsa called all Asuras, Pralamba, Keśin and others and spoke to them thus :

Kaṁsa said :

2. O Pralamba of great arms, O Keśin, O Dhenuka, O Pūtanā, may my words be heard by Ariṣṭa and others.

3. It seems attempt is made by the wicked immortal beings, to kill me. Of course they are scorched by my prowess. I do not consider them heroic.

Indra's younger brother (i.e. Viṣṇu) has been sent by Devas due to the words of the Earth. O my heroic friends, he is already scorched by my valour. I do not mind him at all.

4. O leading Daityas, I am surprised at what is mentioned by that girl. O my heroic friends, the fact that they are straining themselves provokes only my laughter.

5. Still O leading Asuras I have to exert myself to harm those wicked ones, more than what those evil ones may do.

6. "The lord of the past, present and future is born to bring about my death", So says the girl born of the womb of Devakī.

7. Hence, we have to endeavour very much in regard to boys on the Earth. If any extraordinary strength is visible in any boy he should be killed assiduously.

Vyāsa said :

8. After commanding the Asuras thus Kaṁsa came back to his abode. Without any ill will unto them he spoke to Vasudeva and Devakī.

Kaṁsa said :

9. It was in vain that all your children were killed by me. An entirely different boy has been born to bring about my death.

10. Hence grieve not for what has happened. Who is not

killed when his span of life comes to a close? Moreover, it is certain that more sons will be born to you two.

Vyāsa said :

11. O excellent brahmins, after consoling them thus, Kaṁsa delighted them by releasing them. Thereupon, he entered his inner apartment.

CHAPTER SEVENTYFIVE

Pūtanā slain and Cart smashed

1. Vasudeva who was released went to Nanda's cart. He saw Nanda who was delighted because a son was born to him.

2. Vasudeva then said to him with great respect :—Good luck, good luck, even in your old age a son is now born to you.

3. The yearly revenue to the king has been paid: The purpose for which you all came here has been served. Hence, my noble friends should not stay here.

4. O Nanda, the task for which you came here has been accomplished; why do you tarry then? You must all go back to the cowherds' colony quickly.

5. That son of mine born of Rohiṇī should be looked after by you in the same manner as your own son.

Vyāsa said :

6. Thus urged, the powerful cowherds led by Nanda paid the revenue and went back after loading their carts with vessels and articles of trade.

7. While they were staying in the cowherds' colony a certain (ogress) named Pūtanā who had been going about killing children took up Kṛṣṇa who was asleep at night and fed at her breasts.

8. All the childern whom Pūtanā fed at her breasts during the night used to die instantaneously.

9. Kṛṣṇa seized her breasts and pressed them forcibly with both of his hands. He sucked the breast furiously and drank up even her vital breath.

10. The terrible Pūtanā groaned loudly as she died with the nervous cards snapping one by one. She fell on the ground.

11. Frightened on hearing her loud cry the residents of the cowherds' colony woke up and saw Pūtanā lying dead and Kṛṣṇa was in her lap.

12. O brahmins, then the extremely frightened Yaśodā took up Kṛṣṇa from her (dead body). She warded off the evil effects on the boy by whirling the cow's tail over him and by similar rituals.

13. Nanda the cowherd took some cow-dung and smeared Kṛṣṇa's forehead with it, according him protection thereby. Even as he did so he uttered these Mantras :—

Nanda said :

14-20. May Hari the source of origin of all living beings save you; the universe originated from the lotus that grew up from his umbilicus. May lord Keśava who assumed the form of a boar and by whom the Earth was held at the tip of his curved fang, protect you. The whole universe was thus supported by the Earth. May the lord Keśava in the form of Man-lion protect you everywhere; the lord who split open the chest of his enemy with his claws. May Viṣṇu protect your private parts along with the belly; may Janārdana protect your calves and feet. May Vāmana protect you always, Vāmana who instantaneously became very huge, covering up the three worlds in as many steps and whose weapons shone (in all the three worlds). May Govinda protect your head. May Keśava protect your neck. May the unchanging Nārāyaṇa whose prowess is unimpeded, protect your face, arms, forearms, mind and the sense-organs. May Govinda protect you in all the quarters. May Madhusūdana protect you in the intermediary quarters. May Hṛṣīkeśa protect you in the sky and may Mahīdhara protect you on the Earth.

Vyāsa said :

21. The boy for whom the benedictory rites were performed

by Nanda the cowherd, was laid in the child's cradle beneath a cart.

22. On seeing the huge body of the dead ogress Pūtanā, the cowherds were frightened and surprised.

23. Once (the infant) Śrīkṛṣṇa who was lying beneath the cart cried out for breast milk and kicked up his legs.

24. Hit by his legs the cart was upset. With all the vessels and utensils broken the cart lay there topsy turvy.

25-29. O brahmins, all the cowherds and the cowherdesses came there crying, "Alas, Alas." Knowing that the child was safely lying supine, the cowherds asked—"By whom was the cart upset?" The boys there said—"It was kicked down by this infant boy who was crying. We saw the cart being overturned when struck by the legs of the boy. No one else has done this."

Thereat the cowherds became still more surprised. Nanda who was extremely surprised caught hold of the boy and held him close to himself.

Yaśodā who too was bewildered worshipped the broken cart with curds, flowers, fruits and raw rice grains.

CHAPTER SEVENTYSIX

Cowherds' colony shifted to Vṛndāvana

Vyāsa said :

1. Thus urged by Vasudeva, Garga went to the Cowherds' colony disguised and unknown to the cowherds. He performed the postnatal ceremonies and rites for the two boys.

2. The highly intelligent Garga, the most excellent among the wise ones, gave the name Rāma to the elder boy and Kṛṣṇa to the younger one.

3. O brahmins, in a short while the two boys became well known as very powerful. They began to crawl on their knees.

4. With their bodies smeared with the ashes of cowdung cakes they roamed about here and there. Neither Yaśodā nor Rohiṇī was inclined to stop them.

5. They played about in the middle of the kine-enclosure. Then they stepped into the folds of calves. They were eager to pull the tail of the new-born calf.

6-7. When Yaśodā could not prevent those restless boys from playing about and walking about as they pleased, she bound Kṛṣṇa of unimpaired activities to the middle of a mortar by means of a rope and then spoke in anger.

Yaśodā said :

8-15. Now, O restive one, go about if you are strong enough.

Vyāsa said :

After saying thus that housewife became busy with her household activities. As she was engaged thus the lotus-eyed lord dragged his mortar through a pair of Arjuna trees. As he drew the mortar sideways between the two trees two Arjuna trees with lofty branches broke down. On hearing the 'Kaṭa-kaṭa' sound of the snapping trees the frightened people of the Cowherds' colony came there and saw the trees lying down on the Earth with broken branches. They saw the smiling infant boy with a tooth or two in his mouth, lying in between the trees with a rope tied firmly round his belly. Since he was tied with a rope round his belly he became to be called Dāmodara.

The elderly cowherds, Nanda and others took counsel together in their great dejection. They were excessively frightened due to the great calamities.

"We have nothing to do with this spot. We shall go to some other place."

16-19. "Many evil portents are seen here indicating destruction, such as the death of Pūtanā and the upsetting of the cart. Without any such cause as gust of wind the two trees have fallen down. Hence, we shall go away from this place. We shall go to Vṛndāvana. Do not delay. Better to get away before these portentous great calamities overwhelm the Cowherds' colony completely."

After deciding to go thus, the residents of Vraja spoke to their family members. "Hurry up. Do not tarry."

Thus in a trice, they set off with their cattle wealth and carts.

20-24. Thus the residents of Vraja went along with their herds of cattle and calves in groups.

O brahmins, within moments, that place of cowherds' colony became scattered with multitudes of male and female crows as broken bits and remnants of various articles lay strewn about.

Kṛṣṇa of unimpaired activities desired the prosperity of the cows. In his auspicious mind the lord meditated upon Vṛndāvana. Thereat, O excellent brahmins, fresh shoots of grass grew all round as if in the rainy season although it was the middle of summer when everything remained parched up.

The cowherds now colonized Vṛndāvana with their carts, cattle enclosures and camping sites arranged in the form of a big crescent. Rāma and Kṛṣṇa then began to tend the calves.

25-28. Continuing their childish sports they stood or moved about (as they pleased) among the cattle. Peacocks' tail embellished their crests. They adorned themselves with the flowers of the forest. They made noise among the cowherds with their flutes and various musical instruments evolved out of leaves and twigs of trees. With hanging forelocks, the boys shone like fire. They roamed about in that great forest laughing and playing (as they pleased). They played together as well as with other children. Along with them they tended the calves and moved about here and there. As time passed they reached the age of seven.

29-32. The protectors of the universe tended the calves in that great colony of cowherds.

Then the rainy season arrived with patches of clouds covering up the sky. It seemed to bind the quarters by the currents of downpours of rain. Fresh blown flowers and glowworms covered the Earth. So it appeared as though set with emerald and adorned with rubies. Everywhere the river waters flowed down and astray like the minds of indisciplined persons immediately after inheriting a large fortune. The powerful boys reached the colony at the proper time and played in the company of cowherd boys equal to them in age. They played like the immortal beings.

CHAPTER SEVENTYSEVEN

Suppression of Kāliya

Vyāsa said :

1. Once, Kṛṣṇa went to Vṛndāvana forest without Rāma. Surrounded by cowherd lads he moved about. He shone splendidly in garlands of forest flowers.

2. He went to the river Kālindī that had gently moving ripples and waves and that appeared to be smiling all round by the clusters of foams sticking to the banks.

3. There he saw a hideous and extremely terrible whirlpool of serpent Kāliya, which had been defiled by sparks of poisonous fire.

4. As the fire of poison spread, the great trees that grew on its banks were burnt. Even the birds (that flew over it) had been burnt when they came into contact with its watery spray as the wind wafted it up.

5. On seeing that highly terrible serpent which was like another jaw of Death lord Kṛṣṇa thought thus :

6-7. In this whirlpool lives that wicked Kāliya with poison for his weapon. Formerly, he had been left in the ocean by me. The evil fellow had not been conquered then as he disappeared in the ocean. The whole of the ocean-going river Yamunā has now been defiled by him. Hence, the water of Yamunā is not being used by the thirsty travellers or cows that constitute our wealth.

8. This king of serpents should be curbed and restrained by me whereby the residents of the cowherds' colony who are continuously frightened now should move about with comfort.

9. It is for this purpose that I have incarnated in the world of human beings. So I should chastise these wicked souls who have gone astray.

10. Therefore, I shall climb this great tree of Kadamba which is not very far off from it, I shall jump into the eddy of the serpent that causes destruction.

Vyāsa said :

11. After thinking thus and girding up his loins, he quickly fell into that whirlpool of the king of serpents.

12. As he jumped into it, the great eddy was stirred up by him. He sprinkled even the trees growing far away.

13. Those trees that were sprinkled with the hot water heated by the flames of the defiled person of the serpent blazed suddenly. The flames then spread over all the quarters.

14. Lord Kṛṣṇa clapped and dashed against the whirlpool with his arms. On hearing that sound the king of serpents approached him.

15. His eyes turned red due to wrath; his hoods became agitated through poisonous flames. He was surrounded by pink-coloured serpents of great poison.

16. There were hundreds of wives of the serpent. They appeared splendid by their attractive necklaces. Their earrings sparkled as they moved along with their jerking trembling bodies.

17. Kṛṣṇa was then encircled by those serpents which bound him with their bodies. With their fangs rendered nasty by poisonous flames, they bit Kṛṣṇa.

18. On seeing him fallen there afflicted by the bodies of serpents, the cowherd lads went back to Vraja (the colony of cowherds) and lamented in their excessive grief.

The Cowherds said :

19. In his delusion Kṛṣṇa went into the eddy of Kāliya. He has sunk into it. He is being bitten by the king of serpents. Hence, all of you come. Do not delay.

Vyāsa said :

20. On hearing these words comparable to the stunning blow of the thunderbolt, the cowherds and the cowherdesses, Yośodā and others, hastened to the eddy.

21. "Alas, Alas where is this (beloved) person of cowherdesses (lying) extremely perturbed ?" Saying thus, the people accompanied Yaśodā. They were confused. They were faltering in their steps.

22. Rāma of wonderful exploits, Nandagopa and other cowherds hastened to Yamunā, desirous of seeing Kṛṣṇa.

23. And surely did they see Kṛṣṇa, but he was encircled

by the serpent. He was completely under his control. His eflort to release himself had been made ineffective.

24. O excellent sages, staring anxiously at the face of his son, Nandagopa stood motionless. The highly blessed Yośodā was also like that.

25. The cowherdesses and others looked on helplessly. In their extreme distress and grief they wept continuously owing to their love for Keśava. Those ladies said in the frightened timidity of their minds:

26. All of us shall now enter this great eddy of the king of serpents alongwith Yaśodā. It is not proper on our part to go back to our colony.

27. What is that day without the sun? What is that night without the moon? What are those cows without milk? What is that cowherds' colony without Kṛṣṇa? We will never go back to the cowherds' colony without Kṛṣṇa.

28. *Vyāsa said* :

On hearing these words of cowherdesses, the son of Rohiṇī of great strength steadily looked at those distressed cowherds and said.

29. He saw Nanda extremely distressed with his eyes fixed to his face. He saw Yaśodā perturbed and fainting without being fully aware of his greatness.

Balarāma said :

30-33. O lord of the chiefs of Devas, why is this human feeling revealed too much? Don't you know own Ātman? You are the pivot of this universe: you are the support of Devas. You are the maker, protector and distroyer of the three worlds. You are identical with the three Vedas. To both of us, O Kṛṣṇa, who have taken incarnations here the cowherds are the real kinsmen. So also the cowherdesses. Why then do you neglect them, your kinsmen who are distressed? You have exhibited the human traits. You have demonstrated puerile fickleness. So, O Kṛṣṇa, may this wicked fang-weaponed serpent be suppressed.

Vyāsa said :

34. Kṛṣṇa who was thus reminded kept his legs slightly

parted in a gentle smile with a sudden dash and blow. He released his body from the bondage of the serpent's coil.

35. With both of his hands he made the middle hood bend down. As the head of the serpent king became bent he rode and danced on it.

36. The hood of the serpent became wounded due to the kicks from the feet of Kṛṣṇa whenever the hood was raised. After the kick his head bent low.

37. By frequent hits and blows from Kṛṣṇa the serpent became unconscious and deluded. Due to the fierce kickings he vomited blood.

38. On seeing that serpent had been compelled to bend his head and neck to shed blood from his mouth the wives of the serpent lord sought shelter in Kṛṣṇa.

The wives of the Serpent lord said :

39-42. O lord of the chiefs of Devas, you have been understood. You are the excellent lord of all. You are the greatest and inconceivable splendour, a portion of which is Parameśvara. You are that lord not born of anyone else. Even Devas are not competent to eulogise you (adequately). How can women describe his form? The whole cosmic Egg consisting of the entire Earth, sky, water, fire and wind is only a bit of a part of that lord. How can we describe him and eulogise him adequately. Hence, O lord of the universe, be pleased with one who is distressed and fatigued. This serpent is about to die. May our husband be given to us even as alms are given to the beggars.

Vyāsa said :

43-49. After this had been mentioned by them, the serpent with the timid eyes and exhausted body spoke slowly.

"Be pleased, O lord of Devas, your eight-fold lordship is very natural. It has nothing else that surpasses it.

How can I eulogise it ? You are the greatest being, the first among the great. You are of the nature of great being. You are the greatest, greater than the greatest. How can I eulogise you? O lord, I am created by you with certain form in a certain species with certain traits in the characters and my activities have conformed to them. If I had acted contrary to that, O lord of Devas, the punishment that had been meted out to me has been endured by me. It is not punishment but only a boon. Let there not be any other boon for me. O Acyuta, my vigour has been destroyed; my person has been dispelled, I have been suppressed. May life be spared unto me. Commend me, what shall I do?

The lord said :

50. O serpent, you must not stay any longer in the waters of Yamunā, go to the waters of the ocean along with your sons and attendants.

51. O serpent, when he sees the imprints of my feet on your head during your stay in the ocean, Garuḍa the enemy of serpents will not strike you.

52. After saying this lord Hari released the king of serpents. The serpent lord bowed down to Kṛṣṇa and went to the ocean.

53. Even as all the living beings stood watching, the serpent king abandoned his white eddy and went away along with servants, children and kinsmen accompanied by all his wives.

54-57. When the serpent had gone, the cowherds embraced Kṛṣṇa with a joy as though the dead man had come to life. They sprinkled Govinda on his head with tears of joy. The joyous cowherds and others eulogised Kṛṣṇa of unimpaired activities with surprised minds. On seeing the river flowing with auspicious water once again they were glad. Kṛṣṇa returned to the colony of cowherds with the cowherdesses singing songs about his charming activities and the cowherds eulogising him.

CHAPTER SEVENTYEIGHT

Dhenuka and Pralamba are slain

Vyāsa said :

1. Once again, Bala and Keśava started tending the cows together. Wandering along the forest they came to the beautiful grove of palmyre trees.

2. The Asura Dhenuka occupied that palmyra grove after assuming the form of a donkey. Human flesh and beef constituted his diet.

3. On seeing the beautiful palm grove richly endowed with plenty of fruits, the cowherds became desirous of plucking those fruits. They said thus:

The cowherds said :

4-5. "O Rāma, O Kṛṣṇa, this spot of land is always guarded by Dhenuka. Hence, these fruits of palm trees had been avoided by us. These fruits have a joyous fragrance. We wish to let them be struck down if it pleases you.

6. On hearing these words of the cowherd lads, Saṁkarṣaṇa and Kṛṣṇa knocked down the palm fruits to the ground.

7. On hearing the sound of the falling palmyra fruits the evil-minded king of Asuras, a son of Diti who had assumed the form of a donkey came there in great fury.

8-9. With the pair of his hind legs the powerful asura kicked him in the chest. He was immediately seized by means of those two legs. After catching hold of him thus Kṛṣṇa whirled him in the sky. When he lost his life thus, he hurled him on a big palm tree.

10. As he fell down from the top of the palm tree the dead donkey brought with him many fruits on the Earth like a gust of wind bringing down clouds.

11. Kṛṣṇa and Balabhadra playfully seized other asuras too in the form of donkeys—this asura's kinsmen came there (to attack them) and hurled them on to the top of the palm trees.

12. Within a short while, O sages, the Earth was adorned by the ripe palm fruits and the dead bodies of the asura donkeys. The whole area shone well.

13. O brahmins, thereafter without any obstruction the cows comfortably grazed fresh shoots of grass in that palmgrove where they had not been grazing before.

14. When that asura donkey had been struck down along with his younger brothers, the palmgrove appeared splendid and fearless to the cowherds and cowherdesses.

15. Then those two sons of Vasudeva much delighted after killing asura Dhenuka, went to the Bhāṇḍīra forest.

16. Jesting and shouting, singing and collecting the fruits of the trees those two noble boys shone splendidly like two bulls with tiny horns.

17-21. They grazed the cows in the forest. When they strayed far off (into the forests) they used to call them by their names. They kept a noose ready on their shoulders in order to bind the straying cows. They were adorned by garlands of sylvan flowers. They were clad in robes of golden colour or of the colour of collyrium. (i.e, yellow and blue). They resembled the weapon of lord Indra (i.e. the thunderbolt). They were like the black and white clouds. They moved about delighting each other by means of sports usually indulged in by the people. They were the lords of worlds. They were engrossed in human activities and they honoured human qualities. They roamed about in the forest with sports having human traits and attributes. They engaged themselves in various exercises through swings or through wrestling bouts or through hurling huge stones. Thus the powerful lords performed exercises.

22. An Asura named Pralamba, desirous of catching them, came there, even as both of them were sporting about thus. He was disguised as an ordinary cowherd.

23. That inhuman being, the excellent Dānava Pralamba, unhesitatingly entered the midst of those cowherds assuming a human form.

24. He considered ways and means to find about a vulnerable point in them very quickly. He desired to kill Kṛṣṇa and Balarāma.

25-26. The boys were playing a children's game called Hariṇa Krīḍana (Deer play). In this game the boys jumped in pairs, Govinda with Śrīdāman, Bala with Pralamba (the asura in disguise) and the other cowherds with similar other cowherds. Thus they jumped together.

27-28. Kṛṣṇa defeated Śrīdāman; the son of Rohiṇī defeated Pralamba. Other cowherds were defeated by those belonging to Kṛṣṇa's side. (According to the rules) those who were defeated carried victors upto the stem of Bhāṇḍīra tree and returned to the starting place).

29. The Dānava carried Saṁkarṣaṇa on his shoulders and walked quickly. He did not stop (at the stipulated plaee). He appeared like the cloud carrying the moon.

30. Unable to bear the weight of Rauhṇeya the excellent asura increased in size with his body like a cloud in the rainy season.

31-32. On seeing him with a huge body comparable to a burnt mountain, with garlands suspended round the neck as his ornament, with a crown over his head Balarāma was dismayed. The asura was terrible. His eyes were like the wheels of a cart. When he walked, the Earth appeared to shake. As he was thus carried off Balarāma said to Kṛṣṇa:

Balarāma said:

33-34. O Kṛṣṇa, O Kṛṣṇa, I am being carried off by a certain Asura with a terrible form like that of a mountain. See, he is disguised like a cowherd. O slayer of Madhu, what should be done now—please tell me. This wicked one is going at a rapid pace.

Vyāsa said:

35. The noble Kṛṣṇa who was aware of the magnitude of strength and prowess of Balarāma said to Rāma with a gentle smile splitting his lips apart:

Kṛṣṇa said:

36-39. Why is this human feeling resorted to so very specifically? O soul of all, you are the most worthy of being concealed among all concealable persons. O lord of the entire universe, O elder brother, remember the cause, the one Ātman and similarly that person who is in the universe turned into a vast sheet of water (i.e. supreme Being). You and I, O soul of the universe, are the only cause. For the sake of the universe, for the sake of Earth, we are stationed as separate ones. Let the Ātman be remembered O unmeasurable Ātman and kill the Asura. Resorting to human trait alone let what is conducive to the welfare of the kinsmen be carried out.

Vyāsa said:

40-42. O brahmins, reminded thus by Kṛṣṇa the great Ātman, the powerful Balarāma laughed and then began to injure pralamba; with his eyes turned red due to anger he bit him on his head with his fist. Due to this blow his eyes came out. The brain was expelled. Vomitting blood the excellent Asura fell down on the ground dead.

43-44. On seeing Pralamba killed by Balarāma of wonderful deeds the cowherds were delighted. They eulogised him saying "well done, well done. Pralamba.".

When Pralamba the daitya was killed Rāma was eulogised by the cowherds and Kṛṣṇa. They then came back to the cowherds' colony.

CHAPTER SEVENTYNINE

Worship of Govardhana Mountain

Vyāsa said :

1. Even as Rāma and Keśava sported about thus, the rainy season passed off and the season of Autumn set in when lotuses blossomed forth.

2. The season in which the sky was devoid of impurities and the stars sparkled arrived at the cowherds' colony. Kṛṣṇa then saw the residents of Vraja engaged in preparations for Indra's festival.

3. On seeing the cowherds enthusiastic and desirous of celebrating the festival the highly intelligent Kṛṣṇa spoke to the elders out of curiosity.

Kṛṣṇa said :

4. "What is this festival of Indra wherein you are so very delighted?"

As he asked thus with great eagerness, Nandagopa said to him :

Nanda said:

5. Śatakratu, king of Devas, is the lord of clouds and waters. It is on being urged by him that the clouds shower juice in the form of rain.

6. Plants and foodgrains are produced by that rain. We and other embodied beings sustain ourselves by eating them. So we propitiate the Deities.

7. It is through the plants and foodgrains grown by him that these cows become nourished and delighted. They yield calves and produce milk in plenty.

8. The land without plants and grass and people afflicted by hunger are not seen in the places where rain-bearing clouds are seen.

9. The cloud squeezes the terrestrial water through the rays of the sun. Parjanya, lord of the cloud, showers it on the Earth for Existence and growth of the world.

10. Hence, during the rainy season, the joyous kings, we and other embodied beings, worship Indra the lord of Devas in the festival.

Vyāsa said :

11. On hearing the words of Nandagopa in regard to the worship of Indra, Kṛṣṇa spoke thus, in order to rouse the anger of the lord of Devas.

Kṛṣṇa said :

12. O dear father, we are not agriculturists. Nor do we sustain ourselves by trading activities. The cows are our deities since we are persons roaming about in the forests.

13. The four lores are Ānvīkṣikī (Metaphysics), Trayī (The three Vedas), Vārtā (Profession for livelihood) and Daṇḍa Nīti (Civil and Military administration). Of these listen to (the divisions of) Vārtā from me.

14. O highly blessed one, the lore Vārtā consists of three main professions viz. Agriculture, trading activity and cattle breeding.

15. Cultivation is the occupation of agriculturists, trade that of businessmen. To us, cows provide the greatest of occupa-

tion. With these three different activities, the lore of Vārtā is practised by people.

16. Whatever be the calling one has adopted, it should be considered as his great deity. It should be honoured and worshipped. Only that calling renders him true help.

17. If after reaping the fruits of one profession a man honours another, O dear father, he does not derive any thing splendid both here and hereafter.

18. Let our borderlands and outskirts be worshipped ; our forest extends to them, the mountains mark the boundary of the forests ; and the mountain is our ultimate goal.

19. Let a sacrifice unto the mountain or a sacrifice unto the cows be performed. What have we to do with Mahendra? The cows and the mountains are our deities.

20. The brahmins are devoted to Yajñas with the chanting of Mantras; the farmers are devoted to Yajñas with their ploughshares. We who depend upon the mountains and forests shall practise Yajñas of the mountains and cows.

21. Hence, let the mountain Govardhana be honoured and worshipped with all due offerings after killing the sacrificial animal in accordance with injunctions.

22. Let the whole quantity (of milk and milk products) of the entire colony of the cowherds be taken. Do not be anxious and worried over anything. Let the brahmins and other persons who desire be fed thereby.

23. When it is worshipped, the homas are performed, the brahmins are fed. Let herds of cows, with the autumnal flowers adorning their crests go round the mountain that has been worshipped.

24. O cowherds, this is my proposal. If this is carried out with pleasure, the cows, mountain and I myself would have been propitiated.

Vyāsa said:

25. O brahmins, on hearing these words of his, Nanda and other residents of the colony became delighted with their faces beaming with pleasure. They said "Well said, well said, my boy."

26. "O dear one, your suggestion is very splendid. All of us

shall carry out what has been proposed by you. Let the sacrifice unto the mountain be performed.

27. Accordingly the residents of colony performed Yajña unto the mountain. They offered oblations unto the mountain by curds, milk puddings, meat etc.

28-32. They fed hundreds and thousands of brahmins. The cows that were duly decorated and worshipped circumambulated the mountain. So also the bulls that bellowed like the rainbearing rumbling clouds.

O brahmins, saying "I am Indra" Balarāma stood on the top of the mountain and ate many kinds of food-stuffs brought by the leading cowherds. Then Kṛṣṇa climbed up to the top of the mountain and worshipped the mountain. The cowherds had secured boons after performing the festival of the mountain. Once again, they returned to their colony.

CHAPTER EIGHTY

Caronation of Lord Kṛṣṇa

Vyāsa said :

1. When his festival was thus hindered, Indra became extremely infuriated. He spoke thus to the clouds named Saṁvartaka.

Indra said :

2-5. O clouds, even as I speak, listen to my words and immediately thereafter carry out my behest without any lingering thought or hesitation.

The wicked Nandagopa, puffed up with the pride of the strength he derives from the support of Kṛṣṇa, and assisted by other cowherds has now broken (the line of) my festivals.

Hence, at my instance, let their cows be harassed due to a heavy downpour. It is the cow that supports them to a large extent and contributes to their successful cattle breeding.

I too shall assist you, riding on my lofty elephant that resembles the peak of a great mountain. You will have the collaboration of winds as well.

Vyāsa said :

6. O brahmins, on being commended thus by the lord of Devas, those clouds let down a terrible gust of wind and downpour for the annihilation of cows.

7. Then, O brahmins, Ear h, sky and quarters became one as it were, due to the great showers that filled them all.

8. The cows began to tremble as the winds blew and the showers fell. They gave up their lives and fell down with their heads and faces directed sideways.

9. O excellent brahmins, other cows stood over their calves covering them with their laps. Still other cows were deprived of their calves by the heavy downpour of water.

10. The distressed calves exhibited their wretched faces. The chill wind made their necks shiver. They seemed to tell Kṛṣṇa "O save us, O save us" by uttering few feeble words.

11. On seeing the entire cowherds' colony bewildered with the cows, cowherds and cowherdesses in utter confusion, Hari thought of the means of saving them. Hc said.

12-13. "This is wrought by lord Indra who is opposed to us due to the break in the sense of festivals in his honour. Hence this entire cowherds' colony should be protected by me now. I shall uproot this mountain with my prowess. I shall hold up its big rocky ridge over the cowherds' colony like a big umbrella."

Vyāsa said :

14. After thinking thus, Kṛṣṇa uprooted the Govardhana mountain and playfully held it aloft with a single hand.

15-16. The lord of the universe said to the cowherds after uprooting the mountain: "Enter ye all together. The shower has been prevented (here). Be seated in befitting places where there is no terrible gust of wind. Be fearless. After entering this place you should not be afraid of this that the mountain may fall.

17. On being advised thus by him the cowherds and the cowherdesses who had been afflicted by the heavy downpour, entered the sheltered spot along with their cattle wealth. They kept their utensils and belongings loaded in carts.

18-19. Kṛṣṇa held the mountain, aloft very steedily. He was then watched by the residents of the cowherds' colony with delight and wonder manifest in their eyes. He was observed by cowherds and cowherdesses with their eyes widely dilated due to joy. His conduct and exploit was eulogised by them. Thus Kṛṣṇa held the mountain aloft.

20. The great clouds prompted by Indra who was desirous of destroying the cowherds showered for seven nights in the cowherds' colony.

21. As the great mountain was thus held aloft and the herds of cows were saved, Indra's vow became falsified. So he withdrew the clouds.

22. When the sky was cleared of clouds, when Indra's advice became futile and the lord of Devas became disappointed the delighted colony of cowherds was re-established in its own place.

23. Kṛṣṇa then released the great mountain Govardhana and replaced it in its spot, closely watched by the residents of Vraja with wonderment evident in their faces.

Vyāsa said :

24. When the mountain Govardhana was held up and the herds of cows were saved by Kṛṣṇa, the chastiser of Pāka (i.e. Indra) desired to visit Kṛṣṇa.

25. The lord of Devas, the conqueror of enemies rode on Airāvata his great elephant and paid a visit to Kṛṣṇa on the mountain Govardhana.

26. The lord of great prowess, the protector of the universe had assumed the form of a cowherd. Surrounded by cowherd lads he was grazing the cows there.

27. O brahmins, he saw Garuḍa the leading bird, who had created a shadow over the head of Hari from above by means of his wing and who remained invisible for others.

28. Dismounted from his elephant Airāvata, with his eyes enlarged due to pleasure Indra smilingly spoke to Viṣṇu.

Indra said :

29. O Kṛṣṇa, O Kṛṣṇa of mighty great arms, listen, why I have come near you. This should not be misunderstood (and thought otherwise) by you.

30. You are indeed the great lord, the support of everything. You have incarnated on the surface of the Earth in order to remove the burden of the Earth.

31. Becoming inimical to you because of the break in the series of my festivals great clouds had been directed by me to destroy herds of cows. This great havoc was perpetrated by them.

32. The cows were saved by you by uprooting the great mountain. O heroic one, I am delighted by this extremely wonderful feat of yours.

33. O Kṛṣṇa, I think, the purpose of Devas has been served today. This excellent mountain has been held aloft with a single hand by you.

34. Moreover, O Kṛṣṇa, I have come near you, after being prompted by the cows saved by you. It is very much for your sake also, you are the cause of causes.

35. Urged by the words of cows, I shall crown you as Upendra (younger brother of Indra). You shall become Govinda, the lord of cows.

36. Then he brought the bell from his vehicle, Airāvata. Filling it with sacred waters he performed the rite of coronation.

37. When Kṛṣṇa's coronation was performed, the cows made the Earth wet with the milk flowing from their udders.

38. After crowning Śrī Kṛṣṇa at the instance of cows, the husband of Śacī, Devendra spoke to Kṛṣṇa again humbly and lovingly.

Indra said :

39-41. This has been done due to the utterance of cows. Similarly, listen to another matter also which I am going to say, O Highly blessed one, due to my desire to remove the burden of the Earth.

O sustainer of the Earth, my own part, a tiger among men

named Arjuna has incarnated on the Earth. He should always be protected by you.

He will be your associate and friend in the act of removing the burden of the Earth. O slayer of Madhu, he should be protected by you in the same manner as your soul.

The lord said :

42. I know Pārtha born into the Bharata family from a part of yours. As long as I continue to live on the surface of the Earth, I shall protect him.

43. O Indra, lord of Devas, O suppressor of foes, as long as I stay on the Earth, no one will conquer Arjuna, in battle.

44-45. O lord of Devas, when the asura of mighty prowess named Kaṁsa, other ones (named) Ariṣṭa, Keśin, Kuvalayāpīḍa and Naraka have been killed there shall be a great battle. O thousand-eyed one, know that in the course of that battle the burden of the Earth shall be removed.

46. Go, it does not behove you to be sad and anxious for the sake of your son. No enemy of Arjuna, howsoever great, will be too powerful in my presence.

47. For the sake of Arjuna I shall protect Yudhiṣṭhira and others also. When the Bhārata battle is concluded I shall hand over to Kunti all these persons led by Yudhiṣṭhira, (safe and) unwounded.

Vyāsa said :

48. On being assured thus the king of Devas embraced Kṛṣṇa and mounted on his elephant Airāvata went back to heaven once again.

49. Accompanied by cowherds and cows Kṛṣṇa returned to the Vraja along the path sanctified by the loving glances of cowherd lasses.

CHAPTER EIGHTYONE

Ariṣṭa is slain

Vyāsa said :

1. When Indra went away, the cowherds who had witnessed Kṛṣṇa of unimpaired activities holding aloft the mountain Govardhana said to him lovingly.

The Cowherds said :

2. O highly blessed one, from this great danger all of us and the cows have been protected by you through this activity of holding up the mountain.

3. (If this is only) a childish play, it is (really) unrivalled. O dear one, tending of the cows is a profession viewed at with abhorrence. But your activities are divine. How is this ? May it be explained to us.

4. Kāliya was suppressed in the water. Pralamba was struck down. (Now) this Govardhana has been lifted up. (Really) our minds are full of doubts.

5. Truth. It is the truth : O excessively valorous one, we swear by the feet of Hari, on observing your prowess we do not think that you are an ordinary person.

6. Whether you are a Deva or a Dānava, whether you are a Yakṣa or a Gandharva—You are our kinsman in our consideration. Obeisance be to you.

7. O Keśava, the love of the entire cowherds' colony including women and children is heaped on you. This feat is impossible to Devas too.

8. Your boyhood and this excessive valour, your birth amidst us, not very splendid in itself—all this, on being considered, O Kṛṣṇa of immeasurable Soul, produces suspicion in us.

Vyāsa said :

9. On being addressed thus by the cowherds, O excellent brahmins, Kṛṣṇa remained silent for a while with feigned anger (in spite of his) love and said.

Śrikṛṣṇa said :

10. O cowherds, if due to your relationship with me you are not ashamed and if I am worthy of being praised, of what avail is your pondering over other matters ?

11. If you have any love for me, if I am worthy of being praised by you, O my kinsmen, let that venerable offering befitting a kinsman be made unto me.

12. I am neither a Deva nor a Gandharva, neither a Yakṣa nor a Dānava. I have become your kinsman. Hence, nothing other than this should be thought of me.

Vyāsa said :

13. On hearing these words of Hari and realizing that he had feigned anger due to love, the highly blessed cowherds kept quiet. They gained in strength thereby.

14-15. Kṛṣṇa observed that the sky was clear and devoid of impurities; that the bright light of the autumnal moon spread everywhere; that the cluster of lilies was full-blown rendering the quarters fragrant and that the forest region was charming due to the humming swarms of bees. He was therefore inclined to indulge in amorous sports with the cowherd lasses.

16. The lotus-footed lord sang sweet songs in the company of Rāma, pleasing to the womenfolk. He feigned that he was observing holy rites there.

17. On hearing the sweet and charming sound of the songs, the cowherd lasses left off their abodes and hurriedly came to the place where Kṛṣṇa stood.

18. A certain cowherd lass followed his footsteps and sang slowly. Another one listened to it attentively and mentally remembered him.

19. A certain lass uttered "O Kṛṣṇa O Kṛṣṇa" and became bashful. A certain lass who was blindly in love with him went near him without shame.

20. A certain lass who was standing within her abode saw her father (father-in-law) standing outside. She closed her eyes and meditated on Govinda completely identifying herself with him.

21. Surrounded by the cowherd lasses and eager to begin the charming dance of Rāsa, Govinda approved of the night, charming with the autumnal moon.

22. The cowherdesses were fully engrossed in the activities of Kṛṣṇa. When Kṛṣṇa went to a different spot those lasses walked about in the forests of Vṛndāvana in groups.

23. Eager to see Kṛṣṇa, the cowherdesses wandered here and there, O brahmins, on seeing the footprint of Kṛṣṇa during that night.

24. Thus in the course of different types of activities and sports of Kṛṣṇa, the cowherd lasses became agitated simultaneously and roamed about in the beautiful forest of Vṛndāvana.

25. From there the cowherd lasses losing their hopes of seeing Kṛṣṇa, came back to the banks of Yamunā and sang about his conduct.

26. Thereupon, the cowherdesses saw Kṛṣṇa of unimpaired activities, the saviour of the three worlds coming to them with his face beaming like a full-blown lotus.

27. A certain lass became extremely delighted on seeing Kṛṣṇa coming. With wide open eyes she shouted "Kṛṣṇa, Kṛṣṇa, Kṛṣṇa".

28. A certain lass looked at Hari with knit eyebrows over her broad forehead. She seemed to squeeze honey from his lotus face through her bee-like eyes.

29. A certain lass closed her eyes after seeing Govinda. Meditating on his own form she appeared to be in Yogic slumber.

30. Then Kṛṣṇa humoured, delighted and consoled some ladies with pleasing conversations, some by glances with knit eyebrows and some by gently touching them with hands.

31. Hari of elegant conduct sported about and diverted himself with those cowherd lasses who were delighted in their minds by means of Rāsa dances enthusiastically pursued.

Extra Verses : (*According to another reading*)

[Women of the cowherds' colony assembled together for the group dance of Rāsa. They tried to be by his side. They never stayed steadily in any single spot. Hari caught each of the cowherd lasses by her hand from the midst of group assembled for the Rāsa and made each close her eyes by gently stroking her with his hand.]

32. Then began to function a series of music with songs of autumn along with the sounds of the moving bangles.

33. Kṛṣṇa sang about the autumnal moon, the moonlight and the lily pond, but the womenfolk of the cowherds uttered the name of Kṛṣṇa alone again and again.

34. One (of those ladies) after dancing round and round became fatigued. The heat warmed up her moving bangles. That cowherd lass put her creeper-like arms on his shoulders.

35. A certain cowherd lass whose arms moved about gracefully and who was an expert in singing, eulogising found pretexts, embraced and kissed him emotionally.

36. Hari's arms came into contact with the cheeks of cowherd lasses and acted like the clouds. The downpour from these clouds was the series of sweat drops and the plants issuing therefrom were the hairs standing on end.

37. When Kṛṣṇa sang the usual songs of Rāsa in highly shrill notes, the ladies shouted "Well done, Kṛṣṇa, O Kṛṣṇa" with notes twice as shrill.

38. When he went anywhere they followed him; when he moved in a circle they stood in front of him. The womenfolk of the cowherds' colony resorted to Hari both directly and inversely.

39. At that time Kṛṣṇa sported himself together with the cowherd lasses. Even when he was away from them for a moment they felt that period of time equal to a crore of years.

40. Though prevented by their fathers, husbands and brothers the cowherdesses who were fond of sexual intercourse delighted Kṛṣṇa during the nights.

41. The slayer of Madhu, whose soul is immeasurable who had destroyed his enemies and who was in the prime of youth honoured them and sported together with them.

42. He was the lord in the form of Ātman. He permeated all living beings including them and their husbands. He stood pervading everything.

43. Just as Ether, Earth, fire, water, wind and Ātman are present in all living beings so also he stood pervading everything.

Vyāsa said :

44. Once in the evening when Kṛṣṇa was engrossed in Rāsa the asura Ariṣṭa came there, arrogantly terrifying the people of the cowherd colony.

45-50. The asura had assumed the form of a bull, with sharp horns. His eyes sparkled like the sun. His form was like that of a rain-bearing cloud. He was kicking and tearing up the surface of the Earth with his hoofs. With lips, often rubbing and striking them, in his fury he raised his tail. The muscles of his shoulders were hard and tough. The hump on his back was large and raised up. He could never be surpassed in majestic magnitude. Dung and urine stuck to his hind quarters. He was repulsive to the cows of that colony. The loose dewlap hang down from his neck. There were markings of his butting against trees in front of him. He appeared as though he would cause abortion among the cows. He hit and killed everything on his way with great force. He always roamed through the forest (?). His eyes were terrifying. On seeing him the cowherds and the cowherdesses were excessively frightened. They shouted "Kṛṣṇa, O Kṛṣṇa." Thereupon Kṛṣṇa roared like a lion and clapped hands to make a loud report.

51-56. On hearing that sound the bull ran towards Kṛṣṇa. With the tips of his horns pointed ahead and his eyes fixed to the belly of Kṛṣṇa, the evil-minded Daitya in the form of a bull rushed along. On seeing the demonaic bull of great strength rushing towards him Kṛṣṇa did not move from his seat. Smilingly and playfully he stood there with contempt towards the asura. But when he approached him, Kṛṣṇa seized him like a crocodile seizing his prey. Catching hold of his horns he made him incapable of moving. Then he hit his belly with his knee. After catching hold of him by his horns he dispelled his arrogance and strength. He seized and twisted the neck of Ariṣṭa in the manner as one does with a wet cloth (in order to squeeze out water). Thereafter Kṛṣṇa uprooted one of his horns and struck him with the same.

Thereat, the great asura vomited blood through his mouth and died. When the asura was killed the cowherds eulogised

Kṛṣṇa like Devas who praised the thousand-eyed Indra formerly when Vṛtra was killed.[1]

CHAPTER EIGHTYTWO

Keśin is slain

Vyāsa said :

1-4. When Ariṣṭa was killed thus, when Dhenuka had been struck down, when Pralamba had been slain, when the mountain Govardhana was held up, when the serpent Kāliya had been suppressed, when the two lofty trees had been broken, when Pūtanā was killed and when the cart had been overturned, Nārada narrated everything to Kaṁsa in the manner it had happened. He narrated the exchange of children between Yaśodā and Devakī and all other details in full. On hearing these details from Nārada of divine vision, the wicked Kaṁsa became furious with Vasudeva.

5. Due to his excessive wrath he taunted everyone in the assembly of Yādavas. He rebuked Yādavas and thought of what should be done next.

6. "Bala and Kṛṣṇa are small boys (now). Before they grow stronger they should be killed by me. Once they attain youth they cannot be checked from their evil activities.

7. Here I have Cāṇūra of great prowess and Muṣṭika of great strength. I shall get those two haughty boys killed through these two in a wrestling bout.

8. Under the pretext of a great sacrifice in the name of Dhanurmaha (festival of bows) I shall fetch them here from the cowherds' colony. I shall do those things strenuously that will reduce their power and destroy them.

Vyāsa said :

9. After thinking like this, the wicked Kaṁsa decided to

---

1. Refers to the Ṛgvedic legend (Ṛv 1.80) of Vṛtra and Indra. Vṛtra was more powerful than Indra but the latter killed him deceitfully.

kill Balarāma and Kṛṣṇa. Accordingly he said to the Valorous Akrūra.

Kaṁsa said :

10. O lord of charitable gifts, may the following task be carried out at my instance for my pleasure. Drive in a chariot from here and go to the cowherds' colony of Nanda.

11. There, two sons of Vasudeva are born from the parts of Viṣṇu. They are born for my destruction. The wicked ones are flourishing day by day.

12. The great sacrifice the festival of bows will take place on the fourteenth day of the lunar fortnight. They should be brought by you there for taking part in the wrestling bout.

13. My wrestlers Cāṇūra and Muṣṭika are experts in duels. Let the people see duel between the two combatants.

14. Then there is the elephant Kuvalayāpīḍa. Prompted by its mahout the elephant will kill the wicked boys the sons of Vasudeva.

15. After killing them I shall kill the wicked Vasudeva and Nanda too. I shall kill my father Ugrasena as well.

16. Thereafter, I shall seize the cattle-wealth of the cowherds. I shall confiscate the wealth of all those wicked ones who are desirous of killing me.

17. O lord of charitable gifts, excepting you all these Yādavas are wicked in my opinion. I shall endeavour to kill them also one by one.

18. Thereafter, I shall make this kingdom devoid of Yādavas. As it is rid of all thorns I shall rule it through you. Hence, O heroic one, go for my love.

19. You should speak to them in such a manner as to make the cowherds bring as present unto me ghee and curds the products of buffalo's milk.

Vyāsa said :

20-21. O brahmins, thus commanded, Akrūra the great devotee of the lord became delighted because he could see Kṛṣṇa the next day. Saying 'So be it' he (Akrūra) who was fond of seeing Kṛṣṇa got into a chariot and hurried out of the city of Mathurā.

Vyāsa said :

22. Keśin who too was urged by Kaṁsa as his powerful messenger came to Vṛndāvana desirous of killing Kṛṣṇa.

23. He came to the colony of cowherds. With his hoofs he dug up pits on the ground. When he waved his manes he shook and scattered the clouds. He traversed through the aerial path of the moon and the sun.

24. Frightened by the neighing sound of the asura in the form of a horse the cowherds and cowherdesses sought refuge in Kṛṣṇa.

25. On hearing their words—"Save us, O save us", Kṛṣṇa spoke in a loud tone like the rumbling sound of the rain-bearing cloud.

Kṛṣṇa said :

26. O cowherds, do not be afraid. You belong to the clan of cowherds, why are you so afraid of Keśin ? Why are you losing courage and prowess befitting the heroes ?

27. This wicked horse has only very little strength. He is making a proud display of the loud neighing sound. He is only an ordinary messenger in the army of asuras. He is vaunting and galloping—Of what avail is this ?

28. O wicked one, come. come. I am Kṛṣṇa. Just as the Pināka-bearing lord knocked off the teeth of Pūṣan, so also I shall knock off the teeth from your mouth.

Vyāṣa said :

29. After saying thus, Kṛṣṇa stood face to face with Keśin. The asura too rushed at him with a wide open mouth.

30. Then Kṛṣṇa enlarged his arm and thrust it into the mouth of the wicked horse, Keśin.

31. His teeth were knocked off by the arm of Kṛṣṇa that was thrust into the mouth of Keśin. They looked like the bits of white clouds.

32. O brahmins, Kṛṣṇa's arm that went into the body of Keśin became the cause of his destruction like the ailment that is neglected in the early stages by trustworthy persons (attendants, relatives or oneself).

33. His lips were torn off. The corners of the mouth were made gapingly wide. He vomited frothful blood. The tendons were loosened and untied.

34. Stretching his legs he fell on the ground and discharged dung and urine in plenty. His body was drenched in sweat. He became exhausted and ultimately ceased to struggle for life.

35. With his mouth torn apart by the arm of Kṛṣṇa, that extremely terrible Asura fell down like a tree that is severed into two by the lightning stroke.

36. The two halves of the dead horse Keśin, each having two legs, one ear, one eye, one nostril and a moiety of the back and the tail shone remarkably.

37. After killing Keśin, Kṛṣṇa was surrounded by the joyous cowherds. His body had no sign of strain. Hale and hearty he stood there laughing.

38. When Keśin was killed, the cowherds and the cowherdesses were surprised. They eulogised the lotus-eyed lord in charming words indicative of their love.

39. The sage Nārada hurriedly came there seated on a cloud. On seeing Keśin killed his mind was extremely delighted.

Nārada said :

40. Well done. Well done, O lord of the universe, O Acyuta ! Keśin, the tormentor of heaven-dwellers, has been killed by you playfully.

41. (?) You were eager to bring about his death in this battle between a man and a horse. Killed by you here that wicked asura has gone to heaven.

42. O slayer of Madhu, good rites have been performed by you in this incarnation that caused surprise in me (?) But by virtue of this action, my mind is delighted and satisfied.

43. O Kṛṣṇa, Devas and Indra had been afraid of this horse that used to shake off his manes, neigh (loudly) and see the clouds high up in the sky.

44. O Kṛṣṇa, since this wicked Keśin was killed by you, you will become worthy of being sung about in the world by the name of Keśava.

45. Hail to you. I shall go now. O slayer of Keśin, day

after tomorrow I shall meet you once again in the course of battle with Kaṁsa.

46. When Kaṁsa, the son of Ugrasena, is struck down along with his followers, O supporter of the Earth, you will remove the burden of the Earth.

47. O Kṛṣṇa, I shall be there witnessing matches, old duels as told by you.

48. I shall now go, O Kṛṣṇa, great task of Devas has been accomplished by you. I have been honoured by you. Hail to you. I shall go now.

Vyāsa said :

49. When Nārada had gone, Kṛṣṇa who was not dismayed entered the cowherd's colony as the sole receptacle of beverage to be drunk by the eyes of the cowherd lasses.

CHAPTER EIGHTYTHREE

Akrūra comes to the Cowherds' colony

Vyāsa said :

1. Akrūra who was eager to see Kṛṣṇa set off in a chariot that went very fast to the cowherds' colony of Nanda.

2. Akrūra thought thus :—There is no one more blessed than I am because I shall be seeing the face of the discus-bearing lord who has incarnated with a part of his.

3. Today my birth is fruitful. My night has turned into a bright morning, since I shall be seeing the face of Viṣṇu which has the eyes resembling the petals of a full blown lotus.

4. I shall be seeing that face of Viṣṇu which has lotus-like eyes and which dispels the sin of men even if it is fancied.

5. I shall be seeing the face of the lord from which the Vedas and Vedāṅgas have come up and which is the greatest abode of Devas.

6. I shall be seeing that lord of the universe who is worshipped as the best of Puruṣas to whom the offering is made in the sacrifice and who is the support of every one.

7. I shall be seeing that Keśava who has neither a beginning nor an end and by worshipping whom with a hundred sacrifices, Indra attained the overlordship of immortal beings.

8. I shall see that lord of the universe whose form neither Brahmā nor Indra nor Rudra nor Aśvins nor Vasus nor Ādityas nor Maruts know.

9-10. He will speak to me, he who is the soul of all, who is omnipresent, who is all, who is stationed in all living beings, who is unchanging, who is all-pervading, who is Existence, alone, who is himself the lord, who performed Yogic feat and who stationed himself in the forms of Fish, Tortoise, Boar, Man-lion, etc.

11. The lord of the Universe has attained a human form and is stationed in the cowherds' colony for certain (specific) tasks. He is the unchanging lord who can take up any form as he wishes.

12. That infinite lord who holds the Earth stationed on the top of the peak and who has incarnated himself for removing the burden of the Earth will call me—'O Akrūra'.

13. Obeisance, obeisance to the lord whose Māyā the universe is incompetent to dispel, the Māyā that consists of kinship with father, kinsman, friend, brother, mother and other kindred relations.

14. Obeisance to that soul of learning by keeping whom in the heart, the mortal beings surmount ignorance, the Yogic illusion.

15. I bow unto him who is called Yajñapuruṣa by the sacrificial priests, who is called Vāsudeva by devotees and who is called Viṣṇu by those who are experts in Śāstras.

16. He is the receptacle of universe in whom Existent-non-existent is retained. May he of the Sattva Guṇa be gentle to me?

17. Continuously do I seek refuge in Hari the most excellent of Puruṣas; On remembering him one becomes the recipient of all auspicious things.

Vyāsa said :

18. Thinking about Viṣṇu thus, humbly and devoutly in his mind, Akrūra reached the cowherds' colony when there was still some sunlight (a little before sunset).

19-22. There he saw Kṛṣṇa engaged in milking the cows. He was in the midst of calves. His lustre was like the lustre of petals of the blue lotus. His eyes resembled the petals of a full blown lotus. His chest was marked with the scar Śrīvatsa. His arms were long hanging down (on either side). His chest was broad and raised up. The nose protruded (prominently). He possessed a lotus-like face that supported a graceful smile. His nails were red and raised. He had fixed his legs steadily on the ground. He wore a pair of yellow garments. He was bedecked in sylvan (flowers) and peacock feathers. His hands resembled creepers and were of dark blue colour. He embellished himself with white lotuses.

23. O brahmins, near him he saw Balabhadra, a scion of the family of Yadus. He was white in complexion like the swan, moon and Kunda flower. He was clad in blue robes.

24. He was tall with prominent arms; his face was like a full-blown lotus. He appeared like another Kailāsa mountain surrounded by layers of clouds.

25. On seeing them, O brahmins, that highly intelligent Akrūra experienced horripilation all over the body. His face beamed like a blowing lotus flower.

26. Akrūra then thought within himself thus :—Here is the greatest of splendours. Here is the greatest of regions. Vasudeva is stationed here in two forms.

27. May both of my eyes simultaneously attain fruitfulness when the creator of the universe in the form of Kṛṣṇa is seen. Will this limb (of mine) on coming into contact with his body due to the grace of the lord be on the path of fruition ?

28. Touching my lotus-like hand today itself the lord of infinite form will make it glorious. Excellent achievement is attained by men whose sins are entirely dispelled by a touch of his fingers.

29. With his large hands be will embrace me, the greatest friend, the kinsman who has no other deity. Then itself my soul will be sanctified. The bondage of the nature of Karman breathes thereby (?)

30. After getting into contact with his limbs when I bow down with palms joined in reverence, he of big ears (of great

renown) will say to me 'Akrūra'. At that time alone do we feel that we are alive. Fie upon the birth of that person who is not at all respected by the great one.

31. To him there is no one who is the most beloved, the greatest of friends. He has no one who cannot be a friend or who has to be hated or who has to be neglected. Still the lord resorts to his devotees in the same manner as the divine trees which when sought after bestow riches.

32-33. (Defective) Devas led by Aśvins, Rudras, Indras and Vasus grant boon when they are delighted. The spaces between the eyes (?) of the womenfolk of asuras were removed by him as he struck the army of the lord of asuras. By pouring water therein (i.e. into the hands of the lord) Bali attained charming pleasures even when staying on the Earth. Similarly, Indra, the lord of immortal beings, attained the lordship of Devas for the duration of a Manvantara.

34. Still it is possible he may not honour me because although I have no defects, I am considered blameworthy for I have been taken over by Kaṁsa. Fie upon that person who is excluded by good men.

35-36. Is there anything which is not known to this lord who is of the nature of perfect knowledge, who is a mass of Sattva elements, who has no defects, who is always unmanifest and who is stationed in the heart of all persons in this world. Hence, I shall go unto the lord of the Universe with a devoutly humble body. He is the lord of lords. He is the partial[1] incarnation (*aṁśāvatāra*) without beginning, middle or end, of Puruṣottama the unborn lord Viṣṇu.

---

1. But the devotees consider Kṛṣṇa Pūrṇa avatāra (complete incarnation) and not the partial incarnation (aṁśāvatāra).

CHAPTER EIGHTYFOUR

Return of Akrūra

Vyāsa said :

1. Thinking thus on his way and approaching Kṛṣṇa, that scion of the family of Yādavas bowed his head to the feet of Hari saying - 'I am Akrūra'.

2. The lord too stroked him with his hand marked by the lines of flag, thunderbolt and lotus. He dragged him with love towards himself and closely embraced him.

3. Balarāma and Kṛṣṇa were duly greeted and honoured by him. The two who were delighted took him with them and entered their chamber.

4-6. After being greeted by them and having taken his meals Akrūra precisely mentioned everything to them; how Vasudeva was rebuked by Kaṁsa; how Devakī was insulted by that wicked Kaṁsa, how that wicked Kaṁsa behaved towards Ugrasena and why he had been sent by Kaṁsa.

7. On hearing everything in detail the lord, the slayer of Keśin said—"O lord of charitable gifts, all this has been understood by me.

8. O highly blessed one, I shall undertake what is the most proper expedient in this matter. It should not be considered otherwise. Know that Kaṁsa is already killed by me.

9. Rāma and I shall go to Mathurā along with you, tomorrow. The elderly cowherds will accompany us taking many presents with them.

10. O heroic one, let this night be passed off. It does not behove you to worry over anything. Within three nights I shall kill Kaṁsa alongwith his followers."

Vyāsa said :

11. After directing cowherds in regard to Akrūra, Keśava and Balabhadra went to the abode of Nandagopa and slept there.

12. When the day dawned with pure atmosphere, the extremely powerful Balarāma and Kṛṣṇa began their preparations to go to Mathurā in the company of Akrūra.

13. On seeing this, the cowherd folk were full of tears. The bangles in their hands got loose. They heaved sighs in their misery and spoke to one another thus:

14. "After reaching Mathurā how will Kṛṣṇa return to the cowherds' colony? He will imbibe honey of the sweet tale of the city-lasses by his ears.

15. After getting involved in the net of elegant speech of the city lasses how will his mind revert to the cowherd boys and cowherd lasses of vulgar nature?

16. The ruthless wicked Fate has struck at the cowherd damsels since it removes Kṛṣṇa who is the essence of our colony.

17. The following attributes of the city lasses are extraordinary—their words are uttered with smiles couched in emotional fervour; their movement is graceful and elegant; their side-glances are very attractive.

18. If our rural and vulgar lord is held up by the fetters of their seductive charms, by what expedient will he return to us.

19. This Keśava goes to Mathurā driving in a chariot. He has been duped by Akrūra who is really Krūra (cruel) and who is one who has dashed our hopes.

20. Does not this wicked Akrūra know us earnestly in love with him? Wherefore does he take our lord elsewhere, lord who provides us with imperishable delight?

21. This excessively merciless Kṛṣṇa is going away accompanied by Rāma and seated in a chariot. May steps be taken hurriedly to prevent him.

22. What do you say? Is it this—"It is not proper on our part to say anything in front of our elders"? But what will the elders do to us who already are burnt by the fire of separation?

23. All these cowherds, led by Nandagopa, are ready to accompany him. No one attempts to make Govinda return.

24. In regard to the womenfolk residing in Mathurā the night has turned into a bright morning. The lotus like face of Acyuta can now be enjoyed by their eyes which resemble the bees.

25. All those persons are blessed who will unobstructedly view Kṛṣṇa on the way, as he starts from here and will experience the sense of horripilation.

26. It will be a festive occasion to the eyes of the residents of Mathurā, after seeing the face of Kṛṣṇa.

27. What auspicious dream was seen by those fortunate ladies? Without any impediment they will see the lord with their wide attractive eyes.

28-30. Alas, after showing them a great treasure the eyes of the cowherd lasses have been plucked by the merciless Fate. Love for us (in the heart) of Kṛṣṇa who is going to Mathurā has become feeble. Even the bracelets in our hands have become loose suddenly. Akrūra with a cruel heart is hurriedly driving the horses. Is there a man who will not have any sympathy for the women who are distressed thus?

31. May this column of dust raised up by the wheels of Kṛṣṇa's chariot be seen. Now even that dust is not seen—the dust by which Kṛṣṇa has been taken away from us."

32. So lamented the cowherd lasses. Even as they were watching him with great sincerity and affection, Keśava left that land of cowherds' colony (far behind) in the company of Rāma.

33. Travelling thus in a chariot fitted with quick horses, Rāma, Akrūra, and Śrīkṛṣṇa reached the banks of Yamunā at midday.

34. Then Akrūra said to Kṛṣṇa:—"Both of you be waiting here, until I complete rites in the waters of Yamunā."

35. O brahmins, after they had consented saying "So be it", Akrūra of great lustre entered the waters of Yamunā, had his bath and then performed Ācamana.

35-45. There in the waters of Yamunā he saw Balarāma with a thousand hoods. His physical form was as pure and white as the Kunda flower. His eyes were large resembling the petals of a full blown lotus. He was surrounded by a large number of serpents, sons of Vāsuki.[1] He was being eulogised by them. He was bedecked in garlands of fragrant sylvan flowers. He was clad in blue garments. He had handsome features and

1. King of Nāgas with a thousand heads; according to Puranic legend he was incarnate in Balarāma.

beautiful ornaments. His ear-rings were fine. He was inebriate and was stationed on the bottom bed of the river water. In his lap he saw Kṛṣṇa. He was dark in complexion like the cloud. His large eyes were copper-coloured. He had graceful limbs and four arms. The discus and other weapons were like ornaments unto him. He wore two yellow clothes. He was bedecked in garlands with flowers of onion colour. He was like a cloud rendered wonderful by Indra's bow (i.e. rain-bow) and many streaks of lightning. The Śrīvatsa scar marked his chest. He shone with beautiful armlets and coronet. He was unafflicted and bedecked in lotus. He was being meditated upon by Sanandana[1] and other sages who had achieved yogic power, who were devoid of sins and who were seated there with their eyes fixed to the tips of their noses on recognizing Balarāma and Kṛṣṇa. Akrūra was struck with wonder. He thought within himself—"How did they come here so quickly?" As he was about to say something, Kṛṣṇa stunned his faculty of speech. Thereafter, he came out of the water and went near the chariot. There too he saw both of them seated in the chariot. Balarāma and Kṛṣṇa were there as before, in human form. Coming back and diving under the water once again he saw them in the same manner as before. They were being eulogised by Gandharvas, sages, Siddhas and Nāgas.

47. Thereupon, he understood the real nature of the lord as existence. The lord of charitable gifts then eulogised lord Acyuta full of all perfect knowledge.

Akrūra said

48. Obeisance, obeisance to the great Ātman of the form of Cit (Consciousness) alone; to the all-pervading lord of unimaginable greatness, to one of single form, to one of many forms.

49. O unimaginable one, obeisance to you, of the form of sound; obeisance to you who have become identical with the sacrificial offering of ghee, obeisance to the lord of the form of perfect knowledge, O lord, greater than Prakṛti.

1. *Sanandana* : belonged to the Sanakādi group and was the mental son of Brahmā, having taken incarnation long before Brahmā started his work of creation.

50. Though one, you are stationed in five different forms viz—the Ātman of Elements, the Ātman of sense-organs, the Ātman of Pradhāna; the Ātman (i.e. individual soul) and the supreme soul.

51. Be pleased, O lord identical with all virtuous rites, O Maheśvara, O imperishable being amongst the perishable ones. You are praised with the conception of Brahmā, Viṣṇu and Śiva.

52. O deity whose form, nature, purpose and aim cannot be adequately expressed; O deity whose name cannot be specifically mentioned, I bow to you, the greatest lord.

53. O lord, you are the unborn one. You are the greatest eternal Brahman without aberrations wherein there are no imposed ideas of name, caste and the like.

54. Since, without some sort of conception, no matter can be comprehended, you are being worshipped under the names: Kṛṣṇa, Acyuta, Ananta and Viṣṇu.

55. O unborn lord, O soul of all, by means of these different conceptions, you are identical with Devas and the Universe. O soul of the universe, you are devoid of differences and aberrations. In every object of the world there is nothing which is different from you.

56-58. You are Brahmā, Paśupati, Aryamā, Vidhātā, Dhātā, lord of Devas, wind-god, fire-god, lord of waters, lord of wealth and annihilator. Although you are the one and only Being, you are differentiated through different Śaktis and rule over the whole universe. In the form of a ray (?) you create and destroy the universe. O unborn lord, this universe is full of your attributes. Your greatest form is imperishable; it is expressed by the word 'sat'. I bow into that deity of perfect knowledge, the existent and the non-existent. Om obeisance to Vāsudeva; obeisance to Saṁkarṣaṇa; obeisance to Pradyumna; obeisance to Anuruddha".

Vyāsa said :

59. After eulogising Kṛṣṇa thus under the water that scion of the family of Yādavas worshipped the lord of all by means of incense and flowers mentally conceived.

60. After eschewing other objects, fixing the mind therein

in the deity who had become identical with the Brahman and staying there for a long time he returned from Samādhi.

61. Considering himself contented and blessed, O excellent brahmins, he came out of the waters of Yumunā and approached the chariot once again.

62. There he saw Rāma and Kṛṣṇa seated as before. Kṛṣṇa spoke thus to Akrūra who was evidently surprised as was indicated by his eyes.

Śrīkṛṣṇa said :

63. O Akrūra, what wonderful thing was seen by you within the waters of Yamunā ? Since your eyes are wide open due to surprise (I ask you thus).

Akrūra said :

64. O Acyuta, here itself standing in front of me in its embodied form I see the same miracle as was seen by me inside the water.

65. This universe itself is a great wonderful form of yours, O noble Kṛṣṇa. I had come into contact with you who are interested in miracles.

66. But, of what use is this ? O slayer of Madhu, we shall go to Mathurā. I am afraid of Kaṁsa. Fie upon one's life if one has to sustain oneself by the doles offered by others.

Vyāsa said :

67. After saying this, the scion of the family of Yadu drove those horses as swift as the wind. In the evening Akrūra reached the city of Mathurā. Observing the city of Mathurā and looking at Kṛṣṇa and Balarāma he spoke this.

Akrūra said :

68. You two of great vigour and prowess will go on foot. I shall alone go in with my chariot. You two should not go to the house of Vasudeva. It is for your sake that the old man is expelled by Kaṁsa.

Vyāsa said :

69. After saying this Akrūra entered Mathurā. Balarāma

and Kṛṣṇa too entered the city and reached the Royal Highway.

70. They were glanced at with delighted eyes by the citizens men and women. The two heroic boys went ahead sportingly like two elephant cubs.

71. As they wandered here and there they saw a washerman and dyer. They requested him for beautiful clothes of good colour.

72. He was the special washerman of Kaṁsa. He was very arrogant because he had the special favour of Kaṁsa. He hurled many abuses against Balarāma and Keśava.

73. With a blow of his palm in anger, Kṛṣṇa struck down the head of that wicked washerman and let it fall on the ground.

74. After killing him and taking clothes from his house Kṛṣṇa and Balarāma, clad themselves in yellow and blue robes, joyously and went to the gardener's abode.

75. Seeing them with a wide gaping eyes, the gardener was struck with wonder and he thought mentally—"In which family are these two born ?"

76. On seeing those two charming boys clad in yellow and blue robes he resolved that they were two Devas who had come to the Earth.

77. He was requested for flowers by those two boys whose faces beamed like full-blown lotuses. Thereupon, he supported himself on his hands and touched the ground with his head.

78. That gardener who maintained himself by selling garlands spoke to them—"O my lords, you two have come to my house with delighted gentle faces. I am blessed. I shall worship you."

79. Then with his face beaming with delight he gave them whatever flowers they desired. He tempted them by offering them more.

80. The excellent gardener bowed to them again and again and gave them beautiful fragrant and pure flowers.

81-85. Kṛṣṇa was delighted and granted a boon to the gardener—"O gentle one, Śrī (Goddess of glory) who is supported by me will never forsake you. O gentle one, you will never have loss of strength or of wealth. Your progeny, sons and grandsons, will continue (to be born as long as the earth and sun last. After enjoying extensive pleasures, you will in the end attain my bliss due to my grace. You will then attain divine world. O gentle one, at all times your mind will dwell in virtue. The children born as your progeny will have longevity. Among your progeny there will never be calamities and faults. O highly blessed one, your family will last as long as the sun and moon last.

86. After saying this, O excellent sages, Kṛṣṇa came out of that house in the company of Balarāma. He was duly worshipped by the gardener.

CHAPTER EIGHTYFIVE

Kaṁsa is slain

Vyāsa said :

1. Thereafter, Kṛṣṇa saw a hump-backed lady in the prime of her youth, coming along the royal high-way with the vessel of unguent in her hand.

2. Kṛṣṇa gracefully said to her :—"O lady with the eyes like the blue lotus, to whom is this unguent being taken by you ? Speak the truth.

3. She was addressed by him with love. She too had the feelings of love towards Kṛṣṇa. That hump-backed lady looked at him attentively and said gracefully.

The hump-backed lady said :

4. O loving one, why don't you know me ? I have been employed by Kaṁsa in the task of preparing unguents. I am well known as Naikavakrā.

5. The unguent ground and pasted by anyone else is not conducive to the delight of Kaṁsa. I am highly favoured by him and I am given much wealth too.

Śrīkṛṣṇa said :

6. May this fragrant unguent beautiful and befitting kings, be given to us at least as much as will suffice our bodies.

Vyāsa said :

7. On hearing that, she spoke to Kṛṣṇa with respect and eagerness "May it be taken." She gave them unguent enough for their bodies.

8. Embellished and smeared with the unguents, the two leading mainly ones shone like a white and a black cloud adorned with the rain-bow.

9. Thereafter, Kṛṣṇa who was well conversant with the mode of suggestive talks and hints, talked to her lovingly, caught hold of her chin with two of his fingers and raised it up.

10. Kṛṣṇa then pulled both of her legs and made her straight. With the body straightened she became the most excellent one among women.

11. In a charming and graceful manner she caught hold of Kṛṣṇa by his robes and said in lingering words couched in love

—'Come to my house'.

12. "I will come to your house", said Kṛṣṇa to her and bade her farewell. Looking at Rāma's face he laughed aloud.

13. With their bodies embellished and smeared with unguents, clad in blue and yellow garments and with their handsome features enhanced by garlands of flowers of various colours—the two went towards the chamber of bows.

14-15. After occupying (the chamber) they asked the guards there, about the most excellent bow. When that was mentioned by the guards Kṛṣṇa immediately took up that bow and bent it. As he was stringing it, the bow broke and made a loud report. The whole of Mathurā was filled with that sound.

16. When the bow was broken they were asked by the guards to explain. They hit the army of the guards and came out of the chamber.

17. After getting information of the return of Akrūra, and after hearing that a bow was broken, Kaṁsa said to Cāṇūra and Muṣṭika.

Kaṁsa said :

18. "The two cowherd boys have come. They are the destroyers of my life. Just in my presence they should be killed by you in a wrestling bout.

19. If they are destroyed in a mutual combat by you, I will be satisfied and will give you all desired benefits. This cannot be otherwise, O strong ones.

20. Whether by just or unjust means, these enemies of mine should be killed by you. By their death the kingdom will be common to you both."

Vyāsa said :

21-23. After commanding the wrestlers thus, he called the mahout and told him loudly—"The intoxicated elephant Kuvalayāpīḍa should be placed by you at the entrance to the assembly. With that those two cowherd lads who will be coming to the stage door for the purpose of wrestling, should be killed." After commanding him also thus and seeing that all the couches and cushioned seats had been brought, Kaṁsa whose death was imminent awaited sunrise.

24. Then all the citizens occupied the common couches and seats and the kings occupied the royal couches and sofas along with their attendants.

25. The wrestlers, umpires and judges were kept in the middle of the stage by Kaṁsa, very near him. Kaṁsa himself occupied a raised sofa.

26. Separate couches, seats and platforms were assigned to the residents of the royal harem, the chief courtesans and the ordinary ladies of the city.

27. Nandagopa and other cowherds were seated in their (specially reserved) couches. Akrūra and Vasudeva occupied extremities of the platform.

28. In the middle of the common ladies of the city was seated Devakī who was very fond of her son. Though it be the time of death, I shall see the face of my son.

29-31. The instruments of music were played; Cāṇūra jumped and bounced frantically, the common people shouted "Ha Ha", Muṣṭika slapped and clapped his arms. After killing Kuvalayāpīḍa who was driven against them by the Elephant driver, Balarāma and Kṛṣṇa entered the stage. Proudly and playfully they looked on, like two lions in the midst of deer. Their limbs had been smeared with the ichor and the blood of elephant. The elephant's tusks now became their excellent weapons.

32. Afterwards there was a tumultuous loud sound all over the stage, along with the wonder of the people—"O this is Kṛṣṇa. O this is Balarāma."

33. "This is the boy by whom the terrible ogress Pūtanā had been killed; he by whom the cart had been upset and the pair of Arjuna trees were broken."

34. "This is the boy who mounted the serpent Kāliya and danced; this is he by whom the great mountain Govardhana was lifted up and held for seven nights."

35. "Here is seen that Kṛṣṇa the noble lord, by whom the wicked asuras Ariṣṭa, Dhenuka and Keśin were playfully slain."

36. "This lad of great arms is Balarāma, his elder brother. He sportingly goes ahead delighting the minds and eyes of the womenfolk."

37. "It is he who is mentioned by wisemen who survey the topics in the Purāṇas as follows "Gopāla will redeem the entire Yādava family".

38. "He is that part of Viṣṇu which has incarnated on the Earth; of Viṣṇu who is identical with everyone; of Viṣṇu who is the source of origin of everything. Indeed he is the dispeller of burden of the Earth".

39. When Rāma and Kṛṣṇa were described thus, the breasts of Devakī instantaneously exuded milk due to affection.

40. On seeing his sons, Vasudeva felt as if he was witnessing a great festival. Due to delight he dispelled the old age that had descended on him.

41. The ladies of the royal harem and the ordinary ladies of the city made their eyes wider. They never ceased from looking at him.

The woman said :

42-50. O friends, see the face of Kṛṣṇa with the eyes resembling the lotus. It is embellished by drops of sweat due to his exertion in his battle with the elephant. It is like the full blown autummal lotus with the snow drops clinging to it.

O eyes, may your birth be made fruitful (by looking at him).

O beautiful lady, may the chest of this boy he looked at. It has attacked even imperishable beings. (?); it is marked by Śrīvatsa scar; it is the abode of universe and it is competent to destroy enemies. May his pair of arms too be seen. O immature lady, don't you see this Balarāma whose face is white as the lotus stalk ? He has come here with a blue garment. Balarāma is put on an equal footing with Muṣṭika who swaggers as well as with Cāṇūra, O friend; Just, see this, please. O friends see Kṛṣṇa approaches Cāṇūra for a mutual combat. Are there no elderly persons here who will do what is proper ? Where is Kṛṣṇa of a very tender body who is just approaching his youth ? Where is that great Asura whose body is as hard and tough as an adamant ? The two fresh youths stay on the stage with their graceful charms. But the asura-like wrestlers, Cāṇūra and Muṣṭika are excessively terrible. It is highly improper on the part of judges and umpires to function at this wrestling bout because an unequal fight between a boy and a strong person has been arranged for (?) by these umpires.

Vyāsa said :

51-52. Even as the womenfolk of the city were talking like this, lord Kṛṣṇa generated much delight in them. He entered the stage making the ground quake. Balarāma clapped his arms and bounced gracefully. The fact that the ground did not crumble down at every step was a great wonder.

53. Kṛṣṇa of unmeasured valour fought with Cāṇūra. Muṣṭika the asura who was an expert in wrestling, fought with Balarāma.

54-55. Kṛṣṇa fought with Cāṇūra. The duel was very terrible and awful without any weapon being used. Other recourses were Sannipātas (causing the opponent to fall down), Avadhūtas (Shaking up), Kṣepaṇas (Hurlings), Muṣṭis (Fisting) Kīlavajranipātana (hitting with the elbows and knees as though with a thunderbolt ?) and neat thrusts with the feet).

56-57. (Defective) In the course of that festival of assemblies they had to show their strength. The more Cāṇūra fought with Kṛṣṇa, the loss of vital breath he sustained was the more. He did not get any kinsman to encourage him. Kṛṣṇa, identical with the universe fought with him playfully.

58-63. On seeing the decreasing power of Cāṇūra and the increasing power of Kṛṣṇa, Kaṁsa was dejected and angry. To get some respite the infuriated Kaṁsa waved his hand and stopped instrumental music. When thus Mṛdaṅgas (drums) and other instruments were suspended, the instruments of Devas in the sky, were played instantaneously. "Be victorious, O Kṛṣṇa kill Cāṇūra, O Keśava. Devas who remained hidden to the view eulogised thus in their delight. After playing with Cāṇūra for some time, Kṛṣṇa lifted him up and whirled him in his attempt to kill him. After whirling the asura wrestler in the sky for a hundred times, the conqueror of foes dashed him on the ground (though he had died even in the atmosphere itself. When he was hit on the ground Cāṇūra's body broke into a hundred pieces.

64-68. He made the Earth marshy and slushy with the flow of blood.

At that time Balarāma of great strength fought with Muṣṭika in the same manner as Kṛṣṇa fought with the asura Cāṇūra. He too hit his head and chest with his fist and knee. He threw him on the ground, and killed him. Thereafter, with a flow of his left fist Kṛṣṇa made Tośalaka of great strength, the king of wrestlers, fall on the ground. When the wrestler Cāṇūra was killed, when Muṣṭika had been struck down and when Tośalaka was slain the other wrestlers ran away. Then Kṛṣṇa and Saṁkarṣaṇa jumped and bounced on the stage.

69. They dragged other cowherds of the same age to themselves in their delight. With his eyes turned red Kaṁsa spoke to his men who had gathered in large.

70. Let these two cowherds be forcibly removed from the the assembled group. Let the sinful Nanda be seized and bound with fetters.

71. Let Vasudeva also be punished in the same manner as one not old. Let all these cowherds too who vaunt and swagger along with Kṛṣṇa, be punished suitably.

72-77. Let their cows and wealth be taken away ?

When Kaṁsa was commanding thus Kṛṣṇa laughed. With great speed he jumped on to the couch and seized Kaṁsa. When he caught hold of his hair his crown dropped down. Kṛṣṇa felled Kaṁsa on the ground and himself fell over him. Kaṁsa, son of Ugrasena, was deprived of his vital breath as Kṛṣṇa with his enormous weight fell on him. Being the support of entire universe Kṛṣṇa had that enormous weight. Catching hold of the hair of the dead Kaṁsa, Kṛṣṇa of great strength dragged the body of Kaṁsa to the middle of the stage. It was itself very great and weighty. A weighty thing fell over it. Further it was dragged. Thus Kaṁsas's body was disfigured due to the speed activity of noble Kṛṣṇa. When Kaṁsa was thus killed, his brother came there furiously.

78-80. Sunāmā (i.e. the brother of Kaṁsa) was playfully thrown on the ground by Balarāma. On seeing the king of Mathurā contemptuously killed by Kṛṣṇa, there was a great hue and cry everywhere around the stage.

Immediately Kṛṣṇa of great arms accompanied by Balarāma touched the feet of Vasudeva and Devakī. Vasudeva and Devakī lifted him up and they themselves bowed to him and stood steady as they remembered his words at the time of his nativity.

Vasudeva said :

81. Be pleased, O lord of Devas, O most excellent one, O lord, O Keśava, favouring us you have lifted us up.

82. Since after being propitiated by me the lord has incarnated in my house for destroying the wicked ones, thereby our race is sanctified.

83. You remain within living beings. You are stationed within living beings, O soul of everyone, it is from you that the past and future function, invariably.

84. O Acyuta, identical with Devas, O incomprehensible and unimaginable one, you are worshipped in the course of a Yajña. O lord of Yajñas, you are the Yajña and the performer of Yajña.

85. O son of Devakī, the fact that out of affection, my mind is full of vague notions in respect of you is great deception.

86. You are the maker of all living beings. You have neither beginning nor end. Where is the tongue pertaining to me, a mere human being, which says—'O son'.

87. By what expedient, excepting Māyā, will that person be born of us, O lord of the Universe, that person from whom all this universe has evolved?

88. How can that lord be borne by a female human being, that lord in whom the entire universe consisting of mobile and immobile beings has been established ?. How can he be made to lie down in the womb or in the lap ?

89. O great lord, be pleased. Protect the universe. Since you are having the partial incarnation you are not my son, O soul of the great lord, O lord of the universe, why do you delude the mind of every one from Brahman to an ordinary tree.

90. My eyes had been deluded by Māyā. I had the feeling "Here is my son." Much afraid of Kaṁsa at that time, you were taken to the cowherds' colony. O lord of cows, you entered then my intellect, even as I was afraid and agitated due to the enemies.

91. You are Viṣṇu, O lord, you have attained what cannot be attained by Rudras, Maruts, Aśvins and Indra for rendering help to the worlds. Our great delusion had surrounded us hitherto.

CHAPTER EIGHTYSIX

The Son of Sandīpani restored

1-5. On seeing Devakī and Vasudeva as persons who had attained perfect knowledge by annihilating Karmans, Kṛṣṇa sretched his Vaiṣṇavī Māyā once again in order to fascinate the multitude of Yadus. He said "O mother, O father, for a long time Saṁkarṣaṇa and I were eager to see you but we could not because we were afraid of Kaṁsa. Now after a long time you are seen by us.

That portion of one's life which is spent without worshipping one's parents is indeed futile in the case of good sons ?

O father, if an embodied being performs the worship of preceptors, Devas, brahmins and parents, his life becomes fruitful. Hence, O father, all our defaults and transgressions should be excused. We had been overwhelmed by Kaṁsa's prowess and exploits. Hence, we were helpless and at the mercy of others.

Vyāsa said :

6. After saying this, both of them bowed down to the elderly persons of Yadus. After worshipping them duly they made them contented.

7. Then Kaṁsa's wives surrounded the dead body of Kaṁsa and lamented. His mothers too were fully overwhelmed by sorrow and misery.

8. They were upset in various ways. They were agitated due to repentance. Kṛṣṇa consoled them. His own eyes became turbid due to tears.

9. He then released Ugrasena from prison. He crowned Ugrasena whose son had been killed. He crowned him in his own kingdom.

10. After being crowned in the kingdom he, the lion among the descendants of Yadu clan, performed the obsequies of his son as well as of others who were killed there.

11-13. As he concluded the post funeral rites and re-occupied the throne, Kṛṣṇa said—"O lord, unhesitatingly command us in regard to any task. As a result of the curse of Yayāti this family does not deserve a kingdom. Still now, when I am ready as your servant, you can command even Devas, why not kings ?" After saying this to Ugrasena, lord Kṛṣṇa who had assumed human form for a specific task said to Vāyu in the human speech.

Śrīkṛṣṇa said :

14-15. O Vāyu, go to Indra and tell him thus—"O Indra, enough of your pride and arrogance. Let your Assembly hall named Sudharmā be given to Ugrasena by you. It is Kṛṣṇa who says—This excellent jewel as befitting a king, this Assembly hall is named Sudharmā. It is proper for Yadus to sit in it".

Vyāsa said :

16. Thus urged, the wind god went to Indra and spoke everything to him. Indra gave the assembly hall Sudharmā to Vāyu.

17. All those leading Yadus, having Kṛṣṇa's arms for support enjoyed that divine assembly hall decorated with jewels and brought over there by Vāyu.

18-19. The two heroic lads, Balarāma and Kṛṣṇa had already acquired perfect knowledge. They were perfectly wise. But these excellent scions of the family of Yadu were desirous of maintaining the utility of the contact of disciples and preceptors. Accordingly they went to Sandīpani of the spiritual lineage of Kāśya and resident of the city of Avanti for learning the use of weapons.

20. They accepted his discipleship. They were duly engaged in serving the preceptor. To all the people they thus practically demonstrated their proper conduct.

21. Within sixtyfour days and nights they learned the science of Archery alongwith its secrets and digests. O brahmins, it was miraculous indeed.

22. Considering their super-human activity that could not at all have been imagined (in persons of their age) Sandīpani thought that the moon and the sun had come to him.

23. The moment they were uttered, (the two brothers) learned the Mantras of all miraculous missiles. They said—"What monetary gift should be paid as the preceptor's fees ? That may be mentioned."

24. Observing their ability to act beyond the pale of sense-organs the highly intelligent preceptor requested (the resuscitation) of his son who was dead in the holy centre of Prabhāsa on the shore of the briny sea.

25. Equipped with their arms they went to the briny ocean. They said to the sea—"May the son of our preceptor be restored".

26-27. With palms joined in reverence and having the vessel of Arghya with him, the great ocean said—"The son of Sandīpani has n t been abducted by me. An asura named Pañcajana, assumed the form of a conch and abducted the child. O slayer of Asuras, he is staying in my waters."

28. On being told thus, Kṛṣṇa went inside the water, killed Pañcajana and took the excellent conch originating from his bones.

29-32. The conch Pāñcajanya's sound reduced the strength of asuras, increased the refulgence of Devas and destroyed evil. Kṛṣṇa and the powerful Balarāma blew the conch Pāñcajanya and went to the city of Yama. There they conquered Yama, son of Vivasvat and regained the boy who was in the tortures of hell, who now got back a body as before. Kṛṣṇa and Balarāma, the most excellent among the strong ones, gave the boy to his father. Balarāma and Kṛṣṇa returned to Mathurā protected by Ugrasena. They delighted men and women there.

CHAPTER EIGHTYSEVEN

The Onslaught of Jarāsandha

Vyāsa said :

1-2. Kaṁsa of great strength had married the two daughters of Jarāsandha named Asti and Prāpti. O brahmins, Jarāsandha the powerful king of Magadha came there in great fury surrounded by a great army. It was to kill Kṛṣṇa together with the Yādavas that he came there, for Kṛṣṇa had killed the husband of his two daughters.

3. The lord of Magadha attacked the vicinity of Mathurā. He was accompanied by twentythree Akṣauhiṇīs[1] of the army.

4. Surrounded by only a limited number of soldiers, the powerful Balarāma and Kṛṣṇa came out of their city and fought with the strong soldiers.

5. Thereafter, O excellent sages, Balarāma and Kṛṣṇa of great strength thought of taking up their ancient weapons.

6-8. The discus, the śārṅga bow, two quivers with inexhaustible supply of arrows and the iron club named Kaumodaki—all these came from the firmament to those heroes.

The ploughshare came into the hand of Balarāma from the sky. O brahmins, it resembled the Saṁvarta fire. So also the Musala (iron-club) called Sunanda came over to them.

In the battle, the heroic lads Balarāma and Kṛṣṇa defeated the king of Magadha together with his army.

1. An army consisting of 21,870 elephants, 21,870 chariots, 65,610 horses, 109,350 feet is called Akṣauhiṇī.

9. O excellent brahmins, although Jarāsandha of evil design was conquered, Kṛṣṇa did not consider him defeated because he returned alive.

10. O excellent brahmins, Jarāsandha came again accompanied by his huge army. He was conquered by Balarāma and Kṛṣṇa. He fled from the battlefield.

11. Thus, the arrogant king of Magadha fought eighteen battles with the descendants of Yadu led by Kṛṣṇa.

12. Although Jarāsandha had more armies he was defeated by the heroes of Yadu clan who had only a small army. He was defeated in all battles and he fled on all occasions.

13. The fact that the army of Yādavas won all times indicates the greatness of discus-bearing Viṣṇu (i.e. Kṛṣṇa)

14. It is a mere sport on the part of the lord of universe to discharge many forms of weapons on the enemies because the lord had human attributes and activities.

15. In fact with his mere mental thought he can create and annihilate the universe. What detailed attempt need he make in destroying the enemy's sides ?

16. Still the lord follows the activities of human beings. Allying himself with the strong persons he fights with the weaker ones.

17-18. He uses the four strategic expedients such as peaceful overtures, gifts, threats or creating dissention in enemies ranks and the actual striking. In some places he resorts to fleeing. The sport of the lord of universe functions according to his will. He imitates the activities of embodied human beings.

CHAPTER EIGHTYEIGHT

Mucukunda's Prayer

Vyāsa said :

1. O brahmins, Śyāla called a brahmin of the cowherds colony (named) Gārgya by the (ignoble remark) Śaṇḍha

(impotent) in the presence of Yādavas and all the Yādavas laughed at it.

2. Thereupon, the infuriated brahmin went to Southern territory and performed a penance. He was desirous of a son who would be a terror to the Yādavas.

3. Propitiating lord Śiva he ate powdered iron. The lord was pleased with him in the twelfth year and he granted him a boon.

4. The Yavaneśa (a Greek King) who had no son honoured him. As a result of sexual intercourse with his wife a son of fiery splendour was born to him.

5. He was named Kālayavana. The Greek king crowned the boy who had a chest as hard as the adamantine tip and went to the forest.

6. Proud and arrogant by virtue of his prowess, he asked about the powerful kings on the Earth. Nārada told him about the Yādavas.

7. He was surrounded by crores and thousands of crores of Mlecchas (alien tribes) who were richly equipped with elephants, horses and chariots. He made an elaborate attempt thus.

8. O sages, he was ceaselessly thinking of the Yādavas everyday. He became very furious with them. He marched against the city of Mathurā.

9-12. Kṛṣṇa thought thus :—"On observing the Yādava army destroyed by Kālayavana, the king of Magadha will strike at us. The powerful Kālayavana will destroy the exhausted army of the king of Magadha. Thus two types of calamity are likely to befall us. Hence I shall make a very invincible fort for my clan. Even ladies can fight from within it. What then about the leading Vṛṣṇis ? May not the wicked enemies harm the Yādavas much when I am inebriate, erring, sleeping or out of the territory."

13. After thinking thus Kṛṣṇa begged of the great ocean a piece twelve Yojana. He created the city of Dvārakā there.

14. It had great parks and outer walls. It was beautified by hundreds of lakes. It had hundreds of thick ramparts. It resembled Indra's city Amarāvatī.

15. Lord Kṛṣṇa brought the people of Mathurā there. When Kālayavana was expected he alone went to Mathurā.

16. When the army (of Kālayavana) encamped outside Mathurā, he came out without any weapon and the Yavana saw him.

17-18. Knowing that he was Vāsudeva, the king too with his arms alone for weapons, followed the lord who is not attained even by the minds of great Yogins. Followed by him Kṛṣṇa entered a cave where king Mucukunda was lying asleep.

19. The Yavana also entered the cave. He saw a man lying on a bed. Thinking him to be Kṛṣṇa, the wicked Yavana kicked him with his foot.

20. The moment the Yavana was seen by him he was consumed by the fire of anger. O sages, he was instantaneously reduced to ashes.

21. That king had taken part in the battle between Devas and Asuras and defeated Asuras. He had to remain for many nights without sleep and so was distressed. He requested Suras for the boon of slumber.

22. He was also informed by Devas thus—"He who wakes you up when you are asleep will soon be reduced to ashes by the fire issuing from your body.

23. After reducing that sinner he looked at Kṛṣṇa and said—"Who are you ?" Kṛṣṇa said : "I am born of the lunar race.

24-25. I am the son of Vasudeva, the scion of the family of Yadu".

On hearing it Mucukunda remembered the words of the elderly Gārgya. After recollecting everything he bowed down to Kṛṣṇa, the lord of all identical with everyone. He said—"You are the greatest Īśvara. You are born of Viṣṇu's part.

26. Formerly, this was mentioned by Gārgya—Hari will take birth in the line of Yadu towards the end of Dvāpara Yuga in the twentyeighth cycle of four Yugas.

27-30. Therefore, there is no doubt at all. You are the one come to me. You are the one that render help to all men. I am unable to endure your great splendour. He uttered words unto him so bold and resonant as the rumbling sound of the rain-bearing cloud, to him who was petted and fondled by you.

However, in the great battle between Devas and Asuras the heroic Devas and Asuras were incompetent to endure your great refulgence. I too am unable to bear that refulgence. You are the greatest refuge to the creature that has fallen in the ocean of worldly existence. You are the sole dispeller of agony of those who resort to you. Be pleased. Remove my inauspiciousness.

31. You are everything viz—oceans, mountains, rivers, forests, Earth, sky, wind, water, fire, you are the highest being.

32-35. You are the one devoid of sound etc., the unageing one devoid of birth and destruction. All beings attain their series of births from you who pervade everything. The immortal beings, Pitṛs (Manes) Yakṣas, Gandharvas, Rākṣasas, Siddhas, Apsarās—attain their births from you—men, animals, birds, reptiles, deer, trees, and the time-scale divided into past, present and future—everything mobile and immobile, all those things with or without forms, those which are gross and subtle—O creator of the universe, you alone are all those things; there is nothing without you.

36. O lord, no peace or happiness was attained by me anywhere; by me who wandered amidst the cycles of worldly existence and who had been attacked by the three forms of scorching agonies.

37. O lord, miseries alone were taken up by me as pleasures, like the mirages that are understood as water-reservoirs. They were conducive to my agony alone.

38-39. Kingdom, Earth, army, treasury, allies, sons, wives, attendants, and the objects of senses beginning with sound—all these, O unchanging one, were taken by me to be the cause of happiness. O lord of Devas, in effect they were sources of distress, of a scorching nature.

40. O lord, even Devas attaining the goal of the common world became desirous of help from me. Where is permanent happiness (available)?

41. Without propitiating you, the basis and source of origin of all the worlds, by whom is permanent happiness attained?

42. People whose minds are deluded by your Māyā attain

birth, death, old age etc. of a sinful nature. They see the King of the dead in the middle.

43-45. Then those men are bound by means of hundreds of nooses in hells. They attain very terrible misery. This is your cosmic form. I am very much sensuous. I am deluded by your Māyā, O great lord, I wander amidst deep pits of 'my-ness'.

I have sought refuge in you. You who have no other side (? a vast one), the primordial Īśa, than whom there is no other greater region. My mind is distressed due to exhaustion and agony of worldly existence. I am desirous of attaining the transformed (?) shelter, being disgusted with worldly affairs."

CHAPTER EIGHTYNINE

Balarāma returns to the cowherds' colony

Vyāsa said :

1. Eulogised thus by that intelligent Mucukunda, the lord of all living beings, the lord who has no beginning or death spoke thus.

Śrikṛṣṇa said :

2. O lord of men, go to divine worlds as desired by you. You will be strengthened by my grace and your prosperity and prowess will be unimpeded.

3. After enjoying the great divine pleasures, you will be born in a great family. By my favour you will be able to remember your previous births. Thereafter, you will attain salvation.

Vyāsa said :

4. Thus blessed by the lord the king bowed to Acyuta; the lord of the worlds came out of the cave. Then he saw short-statured men.

5. The king understood that the Kaliyuga had arrived. He went to the abode of Nara and Nārāyaṇa in order to perform penance (on the mountain) Gandhamādana.

6. Slaying the enemy by means of a stratagem, Kṛṣṇa captured his army shining with horses, elephants and chariots after arriving at Mathurā.

7. After bringing it to Dvāravatī he offered it to Ugrasena. (Thereby) the army of the Yadus had no fear of the onslaught of enemies.

8. O leading brahmins, having subdued all quarrels Baladeva became eager to see his kinsmen and so went to the cowherds' colony of Nanda.

9. As before, the conqueror of enemies spoke to the cowherds and cowherdlasses with affection and respect.

10. He was embraced by them. He embraced some of them. With some cowherds and cowherdesses he cracked jokes.

11. The cowherds spoke many pleasing words to Balarāma. Some cowherdesses spoke joyously in their love and others spoke with malice.

12. Other cowherdesses asked thus :- "Is Kṛṣṇa the lover of womenfolk of the city happy ? Is he agitated by stirring emotions of love.

13. Does not Kṛṣṇa whose affection is momentary, deride our activities and increase the good fortune and pride of the ladies of Mathurā.

14. Does Kṛṣṇa ever remember our following him and singing alongwith him ? Will he come here at least once to see his mother ?

15. Or, of what avail is this talk regarding him ? May other stories be mentioned, for without us his (life) is possible and without (him) our (life) is possible.

16. Father, mother, brother, husband and kinsmen—who is not abandoned by us for his sake. (But) he had been ungrateful.

17. Still, does Kṛṣṇa ever (mention) anything about his coming here ? Nectar-like words must be uttered by you.

18. He appears to be devoid of love towards us because his mind is attached to the ladies of the city. It seems it will be difficult to see him."

Vyāsa said :

19. He (Balarāma) was called (by the cowherdlasses) by the words Kṛṣṇa, Dāmodara etc. The cowherdlasses whose minds were attracted by Kṛṣṇa laughed in good tune.

20. The cowherdlasses were consoled by Rāma through gentle and sweet messages of Kṛṣṇa couched in loving emotions and devoid of arrogance. The notes were as sweet as honey.

21. As before Balarāma continued funny stories and jokes with the cowherds whose minds were attracted by Kṛṣṇa, the cowherds who were the residents of Vraja.

CHAPTER NINETY

Balarāma's sport with Ploughshare

Vyāsa said :

1-2. The noble lord Balarāma was thus roaming about in the forest alongwith the cowherds. He was Śeṣa the supporter of the Earth, who had assumed the false guise of a human being. He had accomplished great tasks. It was for fulfilling a great task that he had taken up this incarnation. Hence, for the purpose of his enjoyment Varuṇa spoke to Vāruṇī (wine).

Varuṇa said :

3. O wine, you have always been liked by (Balarāma) of great prowess, O auspicious one, go now for his joy and enjoyment of pleasures.

Vyāsa said :

4. Thus advised by him Vāruṇī (wine) stationed herself in the hollow of a Kadamba tree growing on the banks of Yamunā in Vṛndāvana.

5. Roaming about that spot Balarāma inhaled the intensive odour of wine. After smelling it he experienced the delight that he previously used to have in wine.

6. O sages, thereafter, Balarāma saw a current of liquor suddenly falling from Kadamba. He derived great joy therefrom.

7. He drank it joyously in the company of cowherds and cowherdesses while experts in songs and instrumental music sang elegantly.

8. Shining with the pearl-like drops of sweat due to excessive heat and fatigue he became agitated and said - "O Yamunā, come hither. I wish to take my bath".

9. The river disregarded those words of inebriated person. She did not approach him. The infuriated Balarāma (thereupon) seized his ploughshare.

10. Agitated due to inebriation he caught hold of her by the tip of his ploughshare - "O evil-minded one, won't you come, won't you come ? Then go elsewhere as you please".

11. Dragged by him suddenly the river left her usual path and flooded the forest where Balarāma was present.

12. She approached him in an embodied form. Due to fear her eyes were agitated. She said to him "O you having lionclub as your weapon, be pleased, leave me off".

13. He said :- "If you disregard me in spite of my heroism and strength I shall split you into a thousand bits with the blows of my ploughshare".

Vyāsa said :

14. When he said thus, he was propitated by the river. When the ground there was flooded, Balarāma released Yamunā.

15-16. Splendour came to him in the forest when he had his bath. Lakṣmī took with her a blue lotus as his ornament, an ear-ring, a garland of never-fading lotus flowers sent by Varuṇa and two blue cloths having the lustre of the sea and gave these presents to him.

17. Having aborned himself with the blue lotus, embellishing himself with the beautiful ear-ring and clad in blue garments, the glorious one shone with splendour.

18. Thus embellished, Rāma sported there in the cowherds' colony. After two months he went to Dvārakā.

19. Balarāma married Revatī the daughter of king Raivata. Two sons, Niśaṭha and Ulumuka were born of her.

CHAPTER NINETYONE

Return of Pradyumna

Vyāsa said :

1. Bhīṣmaka was the king of Kuṇḍina in the realm of Vidarbha. His son was Rukmin and his daughter was Rukmiṇī.

2. Kṛṣṇa loved Rukmiṇī and the lady of beautiful smiles loved him in return. Due to hatred, Rukmin did not give her to the discus-bearing lord.

3. Urged by Jarāsandha and Rukmin together, Bhīṣmaka of great exploit gave Rukmiṇī to Śiśupāla.

4. Then for the purpose of marriage the kings led by Jarāsandha, and Śiśupāla went to Kuṇḍina the city of Bhīṣmaka.

5. Surrounded by Balarāma and other scions of the Yadu, Kṛṣṇa went to Kuṇḍina to witness the marriage of Śiśupāla, the king of Cedī.

6-12. On the eve of marriage day Kṛṣṇa abducted that virgin even as Rāma and other kinsmen were opposed to it. Then the glorious Pauṇḍraka, Dantavaktra, Vidūratha, Śiśupāla, Jarāsandha, Śalva and other kings became infuriated. Allying themselves with Balarāma and other leading scions of the family of Yadu they made earnest attempts to kill Kṛṣṇa but they were defeated. Taking the vow - "Without killing Kṛṣṇa in the battle I shall not re-enter Kuṇḍina", Rukmin rushed at Kṛṣṇa to kill him. After killing his army fully equipped with elephants, horses, foot-soldiers and chariots the discus-bearing lord playfully hurled him on to the ground.

After defeating Rukmin Kṛṣṇa married Rukmiṇī duly in accordance with the injunctions regarding Rākṣasa type of marriage. The valorous Pradyumna, a part incarnation of cupid, was born of her. Śambara kidnapped him but he killed Śambara.

The sages said :

13. How was that heroic one kidnapped by Śambara and how was Śambara killed by him ? O highly intelligent one, narrate this divine anecdote to me.

Vyāsa said :

14. On the sixth day after his birth, O brahmins, Kālaśambara kidnapped Pradyumna from the lying-in-chamber thinking—"O this one will be my killer".

15. Taking the boy with him he hurled him into the briny sea, infested with crocodiles, the awful abode of sparks that abounded in eddies and whirlpools generated by billows.

16. As the boy fell down there a fish caught hold of him. Though burned by its gastric fire the boy did not die.

17. O brahmins, this fish alongwith other fishes was caught by fishermen and offered to Śambara the most excellent one among the Asuras.

18. His wife named Māyāvatī, the uncensured queen of his household, supervised over the work of cooks.

19. When the belly of the fish was ripped open she saw an excessively splendid boy who was the first shooting sprout of the tree of cupid that had been burned.

20. "Who is this ? How did he happen to come into the belly of the fish ?"

Nārada spoke to her :-

Nārada said :

21-22. This is the son of Kṛṣṇa abducted from the lying in-chamber by Śambara who is capable of creating and annihilating the worlds. He was cast off into the ocean, was swallowed by a fish and now he has come under your control. O lady of good eyebrows, look after this jewel of a man confidently.

Vyāsa said :

23-24. Informed thus by Nārada she looked after the boy.

Ever since the boyhood of the child she was fascinated by his excelling handsome features and overwhelmed by excess of love. O excellent brahmins, when he was embellished by extensive youthful features, that lady of graceful elephantine gait, became very much attached to him.

25. Māyāvati taught all the Māyās (illusory tricks) to the noble Pradyumna who was befitting her and in whom she had fixed her heart and the eyes. The lotus-eyed son of Kṛṣṇa told her who was attached to him.

Pradyumna said :

26-31. Setting aside the emotions of a mother why do you behave like this in an entirely different manner ?

Vyāsa said :

She told him - "You are not my son. Kālaśambara kidnapped you, the son of Kṛṣṇa. You were cast off into the ocean. You were obtained by me from the belly of a fish. Your mother is crying now but your beloved is extremely fond of you".

Vyāsa said :

Thus informed Pradyumna challenged Śambara for a fight. With his mind turned turbulent due to fury the powerful one fought. After killing the entire army of that asura, Pradyumna, son of Kṛṣṇa passed over seven Māyās and employed the eighth one too. With that Māyā he killed Śambara.

Then he returned to the city of his father accompanied by her.

32. On seeing him present in the harem accompanied by Māyāvatī, Kṛṣṇa's wives had delightful ideas. The uncensured lady Rukmiṇī said with her eyes fixed on him with affection.

Rukmiṇī said :

33. This is the son of a fortunate lady. He is in the freshness of his youth. If my son Pradyumna were alive he would be of this age.

34. O my beloved child, your mother is fortunate whoever she be, she is embellished by you. Or, (considering

from the way) my affection turns and from your physical features, it it clear that you are Kṛṣṇa's son.

Vyāsa said :

35. In the meantime, Nārada came there along with Kṛṣṇa. Delighted he said to the gentle lady Rukmiṇī who was moving about in the harem :

Śrīkṛṣṇa said :

36. O lady of fine eyebrows, this is your son who has come here after killing Śambara by whom he had been abducted from your lying-in-chamber when he was but an infant boy.

37. This Māyāvatī is the chaste wife of your son. She is not the wife of Śambara. May the reason thereof be heard.

38. O Rukmiṇī, when Cupid was killed, his wife eagerly waiting for his nativity, deluded Śambara by assuming an illusory form.

39. In the course of enjoyment of conjugal and other pleasures, this lady of charming eyes showed only the splendid illusory form to the asura.

40-42. Kāma has incarnated as your son. This is Rati his beloved wife. You need have no doubt about this. This is your splendid daughter-in-law.

Vyāsa said :

Then Rukmiṇī and Keśava were fully delighted. The entire city said - "Well done, well done" On seeing Rukmiṇī who was rejoiced by her long-lost son, every citizen of Dvāravatī was surprised.

CHAPTER NINETYTWO

Rukmin is slain

Vyāsa said :

1-2. Rukmiṇī gave birth to eight sons, viz. Cārudeṣṇa, Sudeṣṇa, Cārudeha, Suṣeṇa, Cārugupta, Bhadracāru, Cāruvinda and Cāru who was the most excellent among the strong ones.

She gave birth to a daughter Cārumatī also.

3-5. Kṛṣṇa had seven other splendid wives. They were: Kālindī, Mitravindā, Satyā the daughter of Nagnajit, the gentle lady Jāmbavatī who was always contented, Rohiṇī another virtuous daughter of Madra king with good conduct, Satyabhāmā the daughter of Satrājit and Lakṣmaṇā of sweet and beautiful smiles. The discus-bearing lord had sixteen thousand other wives.

6-7. Pradyumna of great vigour married the splendid daughter of Rukmin in a Svayaṁvara ceremony. She loved the son of Hari. Aniruddha of great strength and exploits was born of her. He was an ocean of prowess and a suppressor of enemies but he was held (treacherously in Mahābhārata) war.

8. Kṛṣṇa chose the granddaughter of Rukmin as wife unto his grandson. Although Rukmin vied and contended with Kṛṣṇa he gave her to his daughter's son (i. e. Aniruddha)

9. O brahmins, to attend her marriage Rāma and other descendants of Yadu went to Rukmin's city named Bhojakaṭa, along with Lord Kṛṣṇa.

10. After the marriage of noble son of Pradyumna was concluded, Kaliṅga king and others spoke these words to Rukmin.

Kaliṅga king and others said:

11. Balarāma is not perfectly conversant with the game of dice; his indulgence in it is however, very great. Hence, O extremely lustrous one, we shall conquer him in the game of dice alone.

Vyāsa said :

12. "So be it" said Rukmin who possessed great strength, to those kings. He played the game of dice with Rāma, in the assembly.

13. A stake of a thousand Niṣkas (gold coins) was won by Rukmin from Bala. On the second day another thousand was won by Rukmin.

14. Then Rukmin the most excellent one among those who were conversant with the game of dice, put up a stake of ten thousand gold coins againts Baladeva who was desirous of victory.

15. Then, O brahmins, exhibiting all his teeth, the foolish overlord of Kaliṅga laughed at Bala. The haughty Rukmin spoke then:

Rukmin said :

16. O members of the assembly, this Balarāma devoid of learning has been defeated by me in the game of dice. He is not conversant with either the manner of fighting or the lore of the game.

Vyāsa said :

17. On seeing the king of Kaliṅga with the teeth in his mouth fully exhibited, and Rukmin indulging in harsh words, Balarāma became infuriated.

18. With his mind full of fury Balarāma put up the stake at a crore of gold coins. Rukmin too accepted it. He threw the dice for that purpose.

19. Baladeva won the stake. He said to him loudly "This is won by me".

"The victory is mine" loudly proclaimed Rukmin to Bala in false words.

20. "It is true that this stake was announced by you. But it had not been accepted or approved of by me. That being the case if (you say) you have won how (can't I say that) I have won ?

21. Then loud resonant words rose up in the sky aggravating the fury of noble Baladeva.

22. The speech in the firmament said : "The stake is won by Baladeva. What is uttered by Rukmin is false. Certain things are accepted through actions even without mentioning words."

Vyāsa said :

23. Then Bala of great strength got up with his eyes turned red due to fury. With the dice board itself he hit and killed Rukmin.

24. With great force he held the king of Kaliṅga who was throbbing and trembling. In his fury he broke his teeth with which he had openly laughed at him.

25. The infuriated Bala seized a great column of gold and killed those kings who belonged to his side.

26. When Bala was angry thus, O brahmins, the entire assembly of kings became eager to flee crying out "Alas, Alas".

27. On hearing that Rukmin was killed by Bala, Kṛṣṇa did not utter a single word for fear of offending Rukmiṇī or Bala.

28. Then, O excellent brahmins, the descendants of Yadu, accompanied by Kṛṣṇa returned to Dvārakā taking Aniruddha with them after his marriage rites were concluded.

CHAPTER NINETYTHREE

Naraka is killed

Vyāsa said :

1-2. O sages, seated on the back of the inebriated Airāvata, Indra the lord of the three worlds came to meet Lord Kṛṣṇa at Dvāravatī. After entering the city he approached the lord and mentioned to him the vicious activities of the asura Naraka.

3. O lord, all miseries have been subdued by you, the lord of Devas, though stationed in the form of a human being.

4-5. For affording protection to those people who perform penance, the following asuras have been killed by you—Ariṣṭa, Dhenuka, Keśin, Pralamba and others. Those who harassed the universe were destroyed by you, namely, Kaṁsa, Kuvalayāpīḍa, the child-slayer Pūtanā and many others.

6. When the three worlds have been saved by your excellent intellect as well as brawny baton-like arms, the heaven-dwellers partook of oblations in the sacrifice and became gratified.

7. O lord, it behoves you to pursue efforts and counter-measures after listening to the reason for which I have come now.

8. O suppressor of enemies, this son of Bhūmi named Naraka

who is the king of Prāgjyotiṣa harasses and destroys all living beings.

9. After killing Devas, Siddhas, kings, and others, that Asura imprisoned their daughters in his own palace.

10. He has taken away the umbrella of Pracetas, that exudes water. He has removed the Maṇiparvata, peak of the Mandara.

11. That Asura has taken away the illustrious ear-rings of my mother Aditi, the ear-rings that exude nectar. He now desires to take possession of my elephant Airāvata.

12. O lord, I have told you about his evil activities. What steps should be taken by way of remedy may be pondered over by yourself.

Vyāsa said :

13. On hearing this, lord Kṛṣṇa, son of Devakī, smiled and caught hold of the hand of Indra. He then got up from the excellent seat.

14. He then rode on Garuḍa who traversed through the sky. He kept Satyabhāmā also on its back and went to the city of Prāgjyoṭiṣa.

15. Even as the residents of Dvārakā watched him, the delighted Indra mounted his elephant Airāvata and went to heaven.

16. For a hundred Yojanas all round the city of Prāgjyotiṣa, the entire place was covered with terrible nooses in order to ward off the army of enemies.

17. Lord Kṛṣṇa hurled his discus Sudarśana and cut off those nooses. Then the asura Mura got up. Keśava killed him.

18. By the fire from the sharp edges of his discus Hari burned seven thousand sons of Mura as though they were mere moths.

19. O brahmins, after killing Mura, Hayagrīva and Pañcajana the intelligent lord hastened to Prāgjyotiṣa.

20. There Kṛṣṇa fought with Naraka who had a great army. In that battle Lord Kṛṣṇa killed thousands of asuras.

21. By hurling his discus the discus-bearing lord, the powerful destroyer of asuras, split Naraka into two, Naraka, son of the Earth, who was hurling weapons and missiles on him.

22. When Naraka was killed, the Earth approached the lord of the universe taking with her the earrings of Aditi. She spoke these words :—

The Earth said :

23. O lord, when I was lifted up by you in the form of a Boar, this son had been born of me as a result of my contact with you.

24. He had been given to me by you and now has been struck down by you. Take back these two ear-rings and protect his children.

25. It is for reducing my own burden that O lord of gentle and pleasant face, you have come to this worlds a part of yours.

26. You are the creator, re-creator, annihilator, eternal source of origin and one whose form is identical with that of the universe. O Acyuta, how am I to eulogise you ?.

27. You are the one all-pervading and the pervaded; deed, the doer and the thing done. You are the Ātman, the inner soul of all living beings. O Acyuta, how can I eulogise you?

28. You are the Supreme Ātman, the innermost soul, the soul of living beings, the eternal lord. These are not your praises. They are the statements of facts. How shall anyone go about (this act of eulogy)?

29. O lord, the soul of all-living beings, be pleased. May what is done by Naraka be excused for making him free from defects. My son has already been struck down.

Vyāsa said :

30. "So be it", the lord said to the Earth. O excellent sages, the conceiver and creator of the living beings took up jewels from the residence of Naraka.

31. The lord of unequalled exploits saw sixteen thousand one hundred virgins in the harem, O excellent brahmins.

32-35. He saw six thousand terrible elephants with four tusks and two million and one hundred thousand Kamboja horses. Immediately the lord despatched those girls, elephants and horses to Dvārakā through the servants of Naraka. The umbrella of Varuṇa and the jewel mountain were put on the back of Garuḍa the lord of birds. Accompanied by Satyabhāmā, Kṛṣṇa mounted Garuḍa and went to Heaven to restore ear-rings to Aditi.

CHAPTER NINETYFOUR

The prayer by Indra

Vyāsa said :

1. Playfully carrying the umbrella of Varuṇa, the jewel mountain and bearing lord Kṛṣṇa on his back accompanied by his wife, Garuḍa went ahead.

2. Lord Kṛṣṇa reached the gateway of heaven and blew the conch. Then Devas approached the lord along with the vessels full of materials of worship.

3. After being worshipped by Devas, Kṛṣṇa entered the abode of the mother of Devas that had the shape of the peak of white mountain. After entering it he saw Aditi.

4. Accompanied by Indra he bowed to her. The lord gave her the excellent earrings and intimated to her the death of Naraka.

5. Then Aditi the mother of Devas was pleased. Unruffled, she directed her mind to the lord who is the creator of the worlds and eulogised him.

Aditi said :

6. Obeisance to you, O lotus-eyed one, O lord causing fearlessness to devotees, O lord, the eternal Ātman, O Ātman of living beings, O Ātman of everything, O creator of living beings.

7-10. You are of the nature of vital airs, soul and mind, intellect and sense-organs. You are beyond three attributes. O pure one, you are devoid of mutually clashing opposites. O lord stationed in the heart of all, O lord devoid of all conceptions such as those of whiteness, and length. You are untouched by birth, You are devoid of dreamy state. You are all these—dusk, night, day, Earth, firmament, wind, water, fire, mind, intellect and subtle elements. You are Acyuta, the cause of creation, sustenance and destruction; you are the lord of makers and doers. With your forms named Brahmā, Viṣṇu and Śiva, you are the lord of all. This universe consisting of mobile and immobile beings is pervaded by your Māyā.

11. O lord, if one takes the non-Ātman to be the Ātman, this misconception is your Māyā. It is from this that the ideas of 'I', 'Mine' etc. emerge.

12-19. O lord, this is the activity of your Māyā amid the ocean of worldly existence.

Those men who are devoted to their own Dharmas and by whom you have been propitiated, surmount all this Māyā and proceed to self-liberation.

Brahmā and Devas, human beings and animals are enveloped by the darkness of delusion. They are involved in the great whirlpool of your Māyā.

O lord, these men bound by your Māyā desire to obtain all desires when rebirths of the Ātman cease, after propitiating you.

You were propitiated by me with a longing for sons and for the extermination of the hosts of foes. It was not for liberation. Indeed, it is the activity of Māyā.

It is like the longing for loin-cloth and similar things from the wish-yielding Kalpa tree. This kind of guilt happens in the case of those who perform meritorious deeds deriving worldly fruits. It originates from their own defects.

Hence, be pleased, O unchanging lord, who cause illusory delusion into the entire universe. Destroy our ignorance, O lord of all living beings having perfect knowledge and good intention.

Obeisance to you, to the discus-armed one, obeisance to you who have the conch in your hand. Obeisance to the deity holding the ironclub. O Viṣṇu, obeisance to you, having lotus in your hand.

I see your form rendered splendid by gross signs and symbols. I do not know the greatest principle. O Supreme lord be pleased.

Vyāsa said :

20-23. Thus eulogised by Aditi the lord laughed and spoke to Aditi.

Śrīkṛṣṇa said :

O gentle lady, you are our mother. Be pleased. Be one that bestows boons.

Aditi said :

Let it be as you wish. O tiger among men, you will be unconquerable by Devas, Asuras and human beings.

Vyāsa said :

Immediately thereafter, Satyabhāmā accompanied by Śacī bowed to Aditi and said again and again—'Be pleased'.

Aditi said :

24. O lady of fine eye-brows, due to my favour you will never have old age or deformity. O lady of blameless limbs, you will enjoy all worldly pleasures.

Vyāsa said :

25. Permitted by Aditi, the king of Devas duly worshipped the lord with adequate reverence.

26. Then, O excellent ones, Kṛṣṇa accompanied by Satyabhāmā visited the divine gardens and parks such as Nandana.

27-28. There Keśava, the lord of the Universe, the destroyer of Keśin saw the Pārijāta tree which put forth bunches of excessively fragrant flowers, which was divine, which caused cool comfort and delight, which was beautified by tender sprouts, which had the lustre similar to that of gold and which was produced when the milk ocean was churned for getting nectar.

O excellent brahmins, on seeing the Pārijāta tree, Satyabhāmā spoke to the lord.

Satyabhāmā said :

29-32. O Kṛṣṇa, why is not this tree taken to Dvārakā ?

If these words of yours are true—"Satyā is my most beloved one", let this tree be taken to my house for beautifying my garden. O Kṛṣṇa, these pleasing words are often mentioned by you to me—"O Satyā, neither Jāmbavatī nor Rukmiṇī is so much desired by me as you are". If, O lord, those are not mere complimentary flattering words, if they are really meant, let this Pārijāta be an ornament to my house.

I shall appear very splendid amongst my co-wives if I wear the bunch of its flowers on my braid of hair. Hence I desire for it.

Vyāsa said :

33. The lord who was requested thus laughingly placed the Pārijāta tree on Garuḍa. Then the guards of the park said.

The guards of the park said :

34. O lord, Śacī is the crowned queen of Devas. It does not behove you to take away the Pārijāta tree specially adopted by her.

35. When the milk ocean was being churned for obtaining nectar, this tree had been adopted by Devas for embellishing Śacī. If you take this, you will not go safe and secure.

36. You seek for this Pārijāta out of foolishness. Who will go out safe and secure if he takes this with him? O Kṛṣṇa, the lord of Devas will indeed be furious over this.

37. The immortal ones will follow Indra with the thunderbolt raised up in his hand. Hence, O Acyuta, enough of your attempts to quarrel with Devas. Scholars do not praise that action which is very bitter in its result.

Vyāsa said :

38-44. When this was mentioned by him, the infuriated Satyabhāmā said :—

Satyabhāmā said :

Who is Śacī and who is Indra the lord of Devas, in regard to this Pārijāta tree ? This Pārijāta tree is common to the worlds. It originated formerly (as common to all). Why should Indra alone take it? Just like the wine, moon or Śrī, O guards of the park, this tree born of the ocean is common to all.

If Śacī clings to this, on account of her pride in the mighty arms of her husband, go quickly to her and mention these words—Satyabhāmā says in words couched in her pride over her husband, "If you are the beloved of your husband, if you are fond of him, prevent my husband from removing this tree. I know your husband Indra. I know the lord of Devas. Still I, a human being, shall remove this Pārijāta."

Vyāsa said :

45. The guards of the park who were addressed thus, went to Śacī and told her what they were told. Śacī then encouraged her husband the over-lord of Devas.

46. Then, O brahmins, Indra who was surrounded by the armies of Devas began to fight over the Pārijāta tree.

47. Then Indra stood ready with the thunderbolt in his hand. Devas also stood in readiness holding their weapons such as iron clubs, sword and tridents.

48-50. On seeing Indra seated on his lordly elephant, surrounded by Devas and approaching him for a battle, the lord blew on his conch. He filled the quarters with sounds. He discharged thousands and ten thousands of arrows. On seeing the quarters and the firmament covered with hundreds of arrows, Devas discharged many missiles and weapons.

51. Then lord of the worlds playfully split each of the missiles and weapons discharged by Devas, into a thousand bits.

52. Garuḍa snatched the noose of the king of waters (i.e. Varuṇa), split it into bits like the body of a young serpent and moved about.

53. The lord, the son of Devakī, struck down on to the ground the staff discharged by Yama. It was broken when he hurled his iron club at it.

54. The lord Kṛṣṇa smashed the palanquin of the god of wealth into minute bits like gingelly seeds. The sun and the moon lost their prowess as it was destroyed by a single glance of the lord.

55. The fire god was split into hundreds by means of arrows. The Vasus were made to flee in all diretions. The tips of the tridents of Rudras were split by the discus and the Rudras themselves were struck down on to the ground.

56. The Sādhyas, Viśvedevas, Maruts and Gandharvas were sent up into the sky like the cotton bits from a Śālmali tree by the Śārṅga-bearing lord through his arrows.

57. Garuḍa killed and ate Devas and Upadevas by means of his beak, wings and claws.

58. Then Indra, the lord of Devas, and lord Kṛṣṇa, the slayer of Madhu showered each other with a thousand arrows like two clouds by heavy downpours.

59. In the utter confusion obtaining there, Garuḍa fought with Airāvata and lord Kṛṣṇa with Devas accompanied by Indra.

60. When weapons and missiles were split and scattered, Indra hastily seized the thunderbolt and Kṛṣṇa took up his discus Sudarśana.

61. On seeing the king of Devas and Śrī Kṛṣṇa holding up their thunderbolt and discus respectively the whole of the universe consisting of mobile and immobile beings raised a hue and cry.

62. Lord Kṛṣṇa caught hold of thunderbolt hurled by Indra. Without releasing his discus he told him 'stay, stay'.

63. As the king of Devas lost his thunderbolt, as his vehicle was wounded by Garuḍa, he became inclined to run away then. Satyabhāmā spoke to him.

Satyabhāmā said :

64. O lord of three worlds, it is not proper for the husband of Śacī to run away. Śacī will honour you with a big garland of Pārijāta flowers.

65. Of what nature is your divine realm ? You are unable to see Śacī approaching you lovingly as before shining with the Pārijāta garlands.

66. O Indra, enough of your endeavour. It does not behove you to be ashamed. Let this Pārijāta tree be taken away. Let Devas be rid of pain.

67. On account of her excessive pride and arrogance Śacī did not view me with reverence as I went to her house. Nor did she honour me.

68. Being a woman, my mind is very light. I was devoted to the praise of my husband. Therefore, O Indra I picked up a quarrel with you.

69. Hence, enough of this Pārijāta which is another man's property. Why should it be taken away? Which woman does not become proud due to beauty and fame.

Vyāsa said :

70. O brahmins, when addressed thus the king of Devas returned and said to her :

O my angry friend, stop from expatiating on a sorrowful fact.

71-73. I do not experience any shame on being conquered by that lord of universal form who is the cause of creation, sustenance and annihilation of the universe.

He is without a beginning or a middle or an end. The worlds are resting in him. They originate from him. He is the cause of origin, protection and annihilation. O gentle lady, if I am routed by him how can I feel ashamed of it?

Who can conquer him? His form is the entire world. It is subtle and minute. It is known only to those who have understood the Vedas. He is unborn, and unmade. He is the permanent lord. He is the primordial lord who can remove universe if he pleases. Who can conquer him?

CHAPTER NINETYFIVE

Lord Kṛṣṇa marries sixteen thousand and one hundred virgins

Vyāsa said :

1. O excellent brahmins, eulogised thus by the king of Devas, lord Kṛṣṇa laughed and spoke in an emotionally majestic manner.

The lord said :

2. You are Indra, the king of Devas. O lord of the universe, we are mortals. The crime committed by me should be excused by you.

3. May this Pārijāta tree be taken to its proper site. O Indra, it was at the instance of Satyā that it was taken by me.

4. Take back this thunderbolt which had been hurled at me by you. O Indra, it is your own weapon that pierces enemies.

Indra said :

5. O Lord, why do you try to delude me by saying "I am a mortal". We know you; we are conversant with the infinite happiness.

6. As you are, so you are, O lord of the universe. O lord, you are firmly fixed in your work. O slayer of Asuras, you remove thorns of the universe.

7. O Kṛṣṇa, may this Pārijāta tree be taken to Dvāravatī. Except with you this will not remain anywhere else in the mortal world.

Vyāsa said :

8. After saying "So be it" to the lord of Devas Śrī Kṛṣṇa came to the Earth, eulogised by the liberated Siddhas, Gandharvas and sages.

9. Taking the excellent tree with him, Kṛṣṇa hastened. He then reached the aerial space over Dvārakā and blew the conch.

10. O brahmins, getting down from Garuḍa in the company of Satyabhāmā he delighted the residents of Dvārakā.

11. He fixed the great tree Pārijāta in his garden. People who approached it were able to remember their previous birth.

12-18. The ground three Yojanas all round it was rendered fragrant by the sweet scent of its flowers. Coming and looking at it, the Yādavas saw divine and superhnman scents on that tree.

Kṛṣṇa took possession of elephants, horses, and other wealth brought by the servants from the collection of Naraka.

Kṛṣṇa, on an auspicious day married damsels brought from Naraka's residence.

O excellent brahmins, with a separate body for each of these, Kṛṣṇa married them in accordance with piety. There were sixteen thousand and one hundred women or even more. Lord Kṛṣṇa took up as many forms. But those virgins considered him as their sole lord individually, thinking, "Kṛṣṇa married me alone."

During the nights, O brahmins, Kṛṣṇa the creator of the universe, Kṛṣṇa of universal forms, stayed in the abodes of all of them.

CHAPTER NINETYSIX

Vyāsa said :

1. Pradyumna and other sons of Kṛṣṇa born of Rukmiṇī, have already been mentioned. O brahmins, Satyabhāmā gave birth to Bhānu and other sons.

2. Prapakṣa and others were the brilliant sons of Rohiṇī and Kṛṣṇa. Sāmba and others of mighty arms were born to Jāmbavatī.

3. Bhadravinda and other powerful sons were born to Nāgnajiti. The sons the chief of whom was Saṅgrāmajit were born as sons of Saibyā.

4. Mādrī's sons were Vṛka and others. Lakṣmaṇā had sons the chief of whom was Gotravān. Śruta and others were the sons of Kālindī.

5. The discus-bearing lord had sons in other wives too. On the whole, he had eightyeight thousand and one hundred sons.

6. Among them Pradyumna was the eldest. He was the son of Rukmiṇī. Aniruddha was the son of Pradumna and Vajra was born to him.

7. O excellent brahmins, Aniruddha of great strength who had been held as a prisoner of war, married Uṣā, the Daughter of Bāṇa and the grand-daughter of Bali.

8. In the course of events, Kṛṣṇa and Śaṅkara fought with each other during which the thousand arms of Bāṇa were cut off by the discus-bearing lord.

The sages said :

9-10. O holy brahmin, how did the fight between Śaṅkara and Kṛṣṇa take place for the possession of Uṣā ? How did Hari destroy the arms of Bāṇa ? O highly blessed one, it behoves you to mention all this to us. Our curiosity to hear this splendid story is great.

Vyāsa said :

11-12. O brahmins, on seeing Pārvatī sporting about with Śambhu, Uṣā the daughter of Bāṇa too desired it very much. Gaurī conversant with the workings of everyone's mind spoke to that beautiful damsel—"Enough of your yearning too much. You will also sport about with your husband".

Vyāsa said :

13. Thus consoled by Pārvatī, she thought within herself—"When ? Who will be my husband ?" Pārvatī then said to her again.

Pārvatī said :

14. "O princess, that person will be your husband, the person who will molest you in your dream on the twelfth day in the bright half of the month of Vaiśākha".

Vyāsa said :

15. On that day, in the manner mentioned by the goddess a man molested her in the course of her dream. She too loved him. When she woke up she did not see the man. She became very eager.

Uṣā said :

16-18. "Where have you gone ?" said Uṣā without bashfulness. O brahmins, she said to her friend. The minister of Bāṇa was Kumbhāṇḍa. Citralekhā, his daughter was the friend of Uṣā. She asked her "Who is being mentioned by you ? In her bashfulness she at first denied everything. Her friend thereupon created confidence in her and heard everything through her own words. After mentioning everything when everything was known by her Uṣā said :—"Immediately do somethihg by way of employers to attain him as mentioned by the goddess."

Vyāsa said :

19-22. Citralekhā then drew the pictures of Devas, asuras, Gandharvas, and human beings, on a cloth and showed them to Uṣā. She turned her face from Gandharvas, Suras and Asuras. She began to look at human beings especially at Andhakas and Vṛṣṇis. On seeing Kṛṣṇa and Balarāma the lady of fine eyebrows became bashful. O brahmins, on seeing Pradyumna she turned her bashful glance away from him. When her real lover, the son of Pradyumna was seen, she said—"It is he, It is he. He is my husband." Citralekhā then consoled Uṣā and went to Dvāravatī traversing the path by her Yogic power.

CHAPTER NINETYSEVEN

Uṣā and Aniruddha were brought back

Vyāsa said :

1-2. Bāṇa bowed down in front of the three-eyed lord and said—O lord, without any battle (to fight) I am disgusted with my thousand arms. Will there be any battle at all, making my arms fruitful ? Without a battle they are conducive to be burdensome. Of what avail are they to me ?

Śaṅkara said :

3. O Bāṇa, when there is an unprecedented breakage in your flagstaff you will have a war that will delight the flesh eating asuras.

Vyāsa said :

4. Joyously he bowed down to Śambhu and returned to his mansion. On seeing breakage in his flagstaff he was very much delighted.

5-6. In the meantime, by virtue of her yogic power, Citralekhā the excellent friend (of Uṣā) brought Aniruddha to the harem of virgins. The guards came to know that he was indulging in sexual intercourse with Uṣā. They went to their king and intimated everything to him.

7. Aniruddha the destroyer of heroic enemies seized a great iron beam and killed the army of servants sent against him by that noble king.

8-10. When they were killed, Bāṇa himself came there seated in his chariot. He endeavoured to slay him. Fighting to his ability (Bāṇa) was defeated by the heroic (Aniruddha). Thereupon Bāṇa fought with him by means of his Māyā. Discharging a serpent missile by means of mantras he bound the scion of the family of Yadu. At Dvāravatī the members of the family of Yadu began to cry aloud—"Where has Aniruddha gone?" Nārada told them that he had been imprisoned by Bāṇa.

11-12. The Yādavas had already heard that Aniruddha was carried off by a woman who was an expert in Yogic lore, to Śoṇitapura[1] the capital city of the asura monarch Bāṇa. Hence, they believed in what Nārada said. Accordingly lord Kṛṣṇa mounted Garuḍa who came to him immediately on being remembered and went to Bāṇa's city accompanied by Balarāma and Pradyumna.

13. At the entrance to the city he had a fight with the very powerful Pramathas. After destroying them, he went near Bāṇa's city.

14. Then the great Jvara (Fever) pertaining to Maheśvara who had three feet and three heads, fought severely with the Śārṅga-bow-bearing lord for the sake of protecting Bāṇa.

15-18. Due to contact with Kṛṣṇa's body Balarāma too experienced the heat originating from a touch of its Bhasman. Hence, he kept his eyes closed together with him. He began to fight with the Śārṅga-bearing lord. But (the Jvara of Maheśvara)

6. *Śoṇitapura* : This capital city of Bāṇa was protected by Śiva, Kārttikeya, Bhadrakālī, Agni and other divinities. In the battle between Śrīkṛṣṇa and Bāṇa, the former defeated all the sentries and entered the city through the northern gate. Within the fort Bāṇa was defeated. Śrīkṛṣṇa, then released Aniruddha and Uṣā from their prison.

was dispelled from the body of Kṛṣṇa by the Jvara pertaining to Viṣṇu. On seeing him (i. e. Maheśvara Jvara) agitated due to the painful blow of Nārāyaṇa's arms, lord Pitāmaha said "kindly excuse him." Thereupon saying— "O I have already forgiven", lord Kṛṣṇa dissolved the Vaiṣṇava Jvara within himself.

19. Lord Kṛṣṇa said thus to Maheśvara Jvara—"Those who remember our fight between us shall be free from fever. After saying this lord Kṛṣṇa went away.

20. Then the lord defeated and destroyed the five fires. Viṣṇu playfully smashed the army of Asuras.

21. Then the son of Bali, Śaṅkara and Kārttikeya assisted by the entire army of asuras fought with Kṛṣṇa.

22. The fight between Kṛṣṇa and Śaṅkara was very terrible. The worlds were agitated when they were harassed by weapons and missiles.

23. The battle raged furiously. Then Devas thought :— "Certainly the dissolution of the universe has arrived".

24. Kṛṣṇa made Śaṅkara burst open Jṛmbhaṇa missile. Thereby the Pramathas and Daityas perished all round.

25. Śaṅkara who was attacked by Jṛmbhā (Yawning) sat within his chariot. He could not fight with Kṛṣṇa of unimpaired activities.

26. Guha's vehicle was destroyed by Garuḍa. He himself was affected by Pradyumna's missile. His trident was blown off by a hissing angry sound of Kṛṣṇa. So Guha fled away from the field.

27-28. When Śaṅkara burst open, (?) when the army of the asuras perished, when the army of the Pramathas was destroyed by the lord with the bow named Śārṅga and when Guha was defeated, Bāṇa came there to fight with the soldiers of Kṛṣṇa's son. He was seated in a great chariot where the horses were managed by Nandīśa.

29. Balarāma of great prowess hit the army of Bāṇa by means of many arrows. Pradyumna did not go astray from virtue. He abided by the rules of war as laid down in the śastras.

30. Bāṇa saw his army crushed and suppressed by Bala by means of his iron club after being dragged by the tip of his

ploughshare, as well as by the arrows of the discus-bearing lord.

31-32. Then there was a brief encounter of Kṛṣṇa with Bāṇa. They hurled blazing arrows at each other piercing through their armour. Kṛṣṇa cut off those arrows discharged by Bāṇa by means of his own arrows. Bāṇa hit and pierced Kṛṣna and the discus-bearing lord pierced Bāṇa.

33. Then, O brahmins, Bāṇa and Kṛṣṇa were eager to conquer each other. They hurled missiles and iron clubs at each other.

34-35. When all the weapons were being cut off, when the miraculous missiles became ineffective, Kṛṣṇa decided to kill Bāṇa with a massive use of force. Thereupon, lord Kṛṣṇa whose splendour was like that of a hundred suns and who was the enemy of Asuras took up Sudarśana, his discus.

36. Even as Kṛṣṇa, the enemy of Madhu, was going to hurl discus for the destruction of Bāṇa, the naked goddess Koṭarī, the demoniac lore, appeared before him.

37. On seeing her in front Kṛṣna closed his eyes and discharged Sudarśana against Bāṇa in order to cut off the thousand arms of his enemy.

38-40. Hurled by Acyuta, the discus gradually cut off the arms of Bāṇa. When the arms were cut off the discus immediately returned to the hands of the lord. Because of the hurling of many weapons and missiles by the Asura, Kṛṣṇa decided to hurl the discus at Bāṇa for slaying him. When this was known by the enemy of Tripuras, the husband of Umā, he rushed at Kṛṣṇa. On seeing the blood gushing out from the body of Bāṇa because his arms had been cut off, Rudra spoke with gentle words of overtures.

Rudra said :

41. O Kṛṣṇa, O Kṛṣṇa, O lord of the universe, I know that you are Puruṣottama the great lord, the great Ātman the greatest being without beginning or without end.

42. Your sport inasmuch as you take up physical forms among Devas, animals and human beings, is characterised by the slaying of Daityas.

43. Be pleased, O lord, fearlessness (freedom from fear) has been offered to Bāṇa by me. The words uttered by me should not be falsified by you.

44. He has grown old in serving me and having my support. O unchanging one, it is not your fault. (?) Boons have been granted to this Daitya by me. Hence, I request fo, your forbearance.

Vyāsa said :

45. Thus requested, Kṛṣṇa became delighted as evidenced by his bright face. His anger towards the Asura disappeared. He spoke to the Trident-bearing lord of Umā.

The lord said :

46. O Śaṅkara, may Bāṇa live (since) he has been granted boons by you. The discus has been withdrawn by me out of deference for your words.

47. The freedom from fear granted by you is the freedom from fear granted by me. O Śaṅkara, it behoves you to see yourself not different from me.

48-49. It is those men who had been deluded by ignorance that see all these differences. What I am, so you are. (We are identical with) this universe including Devas, Asuras and human beings.

Vyāsa said :

50. After saying this Kṛṣṇa went to that place where the son of Pradyumna had been imprisoned. When dried up by the winds of Garuḍa the serpents that fettered him perished.

He made Aniruddha sit on Garuḍa alongwith his wife. Thus Balarama, Kṛṣṇa and Pradyumna came to Dvārakā.

CHAPTER NINETYEIGHT

The burning of Kāśī

The sages said :

1-2. Kṛṣṇa who assumed human form performed great deeds. Playfully he defeated Indra, Śaṅkara and Devas. May his other activities too withstanding the divine intercession, be mentioned. We are very eager to hear.

Vyāsa said :

3. O excellent sages, even as I narrate, let this be listened to with great attention how Vāraṇasī was burned by Kṛṣṇa during his incarnation as a human being.

4. (Defective) Pauṇḍraka, king of Vārāṇasī was told by the people deluded by ignorance—"Vāsudeva has taken incarnation on the Earth. You are that incarnation."

5. Accordingly, he thought that he was the incarnation of Vāsudeva on the Earth. He who lost all faculty of reasoning adopted the symbols of Viṣṇu. O excellent brahmins, he sent a messenger to Kṛṣṇa.

6-7. "Leave off the discus and other symbols that pertain to me. O foolish one, eschew everything pertaining to Vāsudeva. For the sake of your sustenance bow unto me".

When he was addressed thus, Kṛṣṇa said to the messenger.

The lord said :

8-12. Go and tell Puṇḍraka thus : "I shall leave my symbol, the discus on you (I shall hurl it against you) O messenger, may these words be mentioned as mine.

"The good intention behind your words has been understood. May what should be done be carried out. I shall come to your city taking the symbols with me. I shall discharge discus certainly towards you. Since you have commanded me to come I shall carry it out tomorrow without delay. O king, seeking refuge in you, I will do that whereby there will not be further fear from you."

Vyāsa said :

13. When the messenger who had been instructed thus,

had gone away, Kṛṣṇa rode on Garuḍa who came to him on being remembered, and hastened to that city.

14. On hearing about the endeavour of Kṛṣṇa and that of his (Pauṇḍraka's), the lord of Kāśī came as his supporting ally, with all his armies surrounding him.

15. With a great army (of his own) and that of the king of Kāśī, Pauṇḍraka Vāsudeva marched against Kṛṣṇa.

16-18. From a distance Kṛṣṇa saw him seated in an elegant chariot. He carried discus, conch and iron club in his hands and he held a lotus with another hand. He wore a garland and held the bow Śārṅga. The emblem of Garuḍa adorned his banner. Kṛṣṇa saw the scar Śrīvatsa marked on his chest. He wore a crown on his head and earrings too. He was clad in yellow robes. On seeing him, lord Kṛṣṇa laughed heartily.

19. O brahmins, he fought with his army that was very strong in elephants and horses and that contained swords, daggers, maces, tridents, javelins and bows.

20. Instantaneously he slew the army by means of arrows discharged from his bow and blazing like fires, and by means of hits and blows with the iron clubs and discus.

21. After destroying the army of the king of Kāśī also, Kṛṣṇa spoke to Pauṇḍraka who was deluded and who bore his own characteristic marks.

The lord said :

22. O Pauṇḍraka, through the messenger you had told me "Leave the symbols." I shall now accomplish it.

23. This discus is left off; this iron club is discharged against you. This Garuḍa has been directed. Let him mount your banner.

24. After saying this, he discharged his discus by which Pauṇḍraka was torn asunder. He was then threshed with his iron club. Garuḍa of Pauṇḍraka was smashed by his own Garuḍa.

25. When there was a great hue and cry the overlord of Kāśī stood ready for avenging the slaughter of his friend. He fought with Vāsudeva. If Kṛṣṇa cut off his head with the arrows discharged from his bow, he hurled it into the city of Kāśī, causing wonderment amongst the people.

27. After killing Pauṇḍraka and the king of Kāśī alongwith his followers Kṛṣṇa returned to Dvārakā and sported like an immortal being staying in heaven.

28. On seeing the head of the king of Kāśī fallen in his city the wonder-struck people said—"What is this? By whom is this heinous crime committed?

29. On understanding that he was killed by Vāsudeva, his son propitiated Śaṅkara assisted by his priest.

30. Śaṅkara was propitiated by him at the great holy centre 'Avimukta'. The lord then said to the Prince, "Choose your boon".

31. He chose thus—"O lord, O Maheśvara, by your favour, may a Kṛtyā (female deity of destruction) rise up for destroying Kṛṣṇa who slew my father."

Vyāsa said :

32. When this was uttered "It will be so", a great Kṛtyā rose up from the chamber of sacrificial fire at a spot beyond Dakṣiṇāgni.

33. It had an awful face blazing terrible with flames of fire. The tresses were dishevelled and blazing. Angrily shouting 'Kṛṣṇa Kṛṣṇa' it went to Dvāravatī.

34. On seeing the terrible Kṛtyā with hideous eyes, the people of Dvārakā sought refuge in Śrī Kṛṣṇa who is worthy of being the refuge to the worlds.

The people said :

35. After propitiating the bull-emblemed deity this great Kṛtyā has been created by the son of the king of Kāśī for killing you, the discus-bearing lord. Kill this terrible Kṛtyā having a confused mess of matted hair blazing like flame of fire.

Vyāsa said :

36-41. Sudarśana, the discus of Viṣṇu was playfully hurled down amongst the dice as he had been engaged in the game. It became very terrible, spitting flames of fire. Clusters of fiery flames appeared like matted hair. It pursued Kṛtyā quickly. When hit and smashed by the discus Kṛtyā rushed along quickly. The discus too followed her. Kṛtyā hurriedly entered Vārāṇasī. O excellent sages, its prowess was restrained by the discus of

Viṣṇu. Then the vast army of Kāśī and the army of Pramathas (attendants of Śiva) marched against discus. They were equipped with various weapons and missiles. They were discharging missiles and weapons.

After burning that army with its own prowess, the discus went to Vārānasī. It burnt citizens, their servants, horses and elephants.

42-43. It burnt the entire city with all its chambers and forts. Flames of fire surrounded the outer walls and arched gateways of all abodes. It was an unbearable sight even to Devas. Still the fury of discus did not abate. It was as indifferent as though very little had been accomplished. Shining and blazing as before, the discus went back to the hand of Viṣṇu.

CHAPTER NINETYNINE

Glory of Balarāma

The sages said :

1. O sage, we wish to hear again about the exploits of the intelligent Balarāma. It behoves you to recount his heroism unto us.

2. His exploits, such as dragging Yamunā have already been heard by us here. Hence, O blessed one, kindly recount anything else which Bala performed.

Vyāsa said :

3. O sages, listen to the activities carried out by Rāma the infinite one, the unmeasurable one, the incarnation of Śeṣa, the holder of the Earth.

4. Sāmba the heroic son of Jāmbavatī forcefully abducted Duryodhana's daughter whose Svayaṁvara was awaited.

5. Then the infuriated Karṇa, Duryodhana and others including Bhīṣma and Droṇa of great prowess bound him after conquering him.

6. On hearing about it, O sages, the Yādavas became

furious with Duryodhana and made efforts to kill the Kauravas by way of retaliation.

7. Bala stopped them and spoke to them although his words were indistinct through inebriation :—

"I alone will go unto the Kauravas. At my instance they will let him off".

8. Then Balarāma went to Hastināpura. He camped in the middle of a park at the outskirts of the city. He did not enter it.

9. On coming to know that Balarāma had arrived, Duryodhana and others brought unto him by way of presents, greetings, along with Arghya and water for drinking.

10. After duly accepting those things he said to the Kauravas—"It is Ugrasena's order—Release Sāmba quickly".

Vyāsa said :

11. O excellent brahmins, on hearing his words, Bhīṣma, Droṇa, Karṇa, Duryodhana and others became angry.

12. Bāhlīka and all other kings too, were angry on seeing Balarāma who had the threshing rod for his weapon and realizing that the race of Yadu did not deserve a kingdom, they said :—

The Kauravas said :

13. O Balarāma, what is it that you say ? Which Yādava will pass an order on those who are born of Kuru's family ?

14. If even Ugrasena can pass orders on Kauravas, enough of the white umbrellas and ornaments befitting kings.

15. Hence, go back, O Balarāma. Neither at your bidding will we release Sāmba whose activities are unjust.

16. Formerly, Kukuras and Andhakas used to bow unto us, for we are worthy of that honour. Now-a-days that usual obeisance is not made. What is this commanding attitude of a servant towards a master ?

17-18. (Defective) You have become haughty because you have been invited for feasts and offered seats on the basis of equality. It is not your fault that good polity pleases only when it is not expected (hopefully). He who has been mentioned by you, O Bala, is worthy of being worshipped by us and treated with love. But that has not been acquired by your family from ours.

Vyāsa said :

19. After saying this the Kauravas remained adamant. They did not release Kṛṣṇa's son. After making this unanimous decision they entered Hastināpura.

20. Maddened by the anger originating from the insult, Balarāma lifted up his rugged ploughshare and rolled it.

21. Then the ground was pierced as the noble Balarāma kicked it with his heel. He clapped his hands filling the quarters with the sound with his eyes turned copper-coloured and knitting the eyebrows in the face he said :

Balarāma said :

22. Alas, the insignificant wicked haughty Kauravas wish to rule over us. It is brought about by adverse time.

23-24. The behest of Ugrasena cannot be transgressed. It is virtually awaited by Indra along with Devas. Still these people do not care for Ugrasena's command.

Ugrasena always occupies a seat in the divine assembly hall of Indra. But fie upon the satisfaction these people derive from the ordinary throne of a king that had been enjoyed by hundreds of men and then left over like the leavings of food.

25. The womenfolk of the servants of Ugrasena wear bunches of flower, of Pārijāta tree, still he is not a king for these people.

26. Let Ugrasena, the lord of kings stay by. I shall go to that city after making the Earth devoid of Kauravas.

27-29. I shall kill all these viz. Karṇa, Duryodhana, Droṇa, Bhīṣma, Bahlīka, Duḥśāsana, Bhūriśravas, Somadatta, Śala, Bhīma, Arjuna, Yudhiṣṭhira, the twin-borns Nakula and Sahadeva, and others along with their horses, elephants and chariots. I will take the heroic Sāmba accompanied by his wife to Dvārakā and inform Ugrasena and other kinsmen.

30-33. O I shall hurl Hastināpura immediately into Gaṅgā along with the Kauravas. I have been urged by the king of Devas to reduce the burden of the Earth.

Vyāsa said :

After saying this, Balarāma, whose emblem was a palm tree and whose weapon was ploughshare, placed it with its face downwards on the top of the city outer wall and pulled. Suddenly, the city of Hastināpura rolled. On seeing it the Kauravas were agitated in their hearts. They cried out :—

The Kaurvas said :

34-35. O Rāma, of great arms, let (everything) be forgiven by you. May the fury be restrained. Be pleased (O lord) with the threshing rod for your weapon. Sāmba is released along with his wife. O Bala, your strength is realized. Let the guilt of those who have not understood your prowess be forgiven.

Vyāsa said :

36-39. O leading sages, the Kauravas came out of their city immediately and released Sāmba along with his wife.

When Bhīṣma, Droṇa, Kṛpa and others bowed to him and spoke pleasing words, Bala the most excellent among the strong ones, said—"I have forgiven".

O brahmins, even today that city appears as though it had been tossed about. Such is the power of Rāma. He was fully endowed with strength and vigour.

Then the Kauravas duly honoured Sāmba along with Balarāma. They bade farewell to him after offering him the appropriate dowry and sending his bride along with him.

CHAPTER ONE HUNDRED

The Monkey Dvivida is slain

Vyāsa said :

1-4. O sages, listen ye all. O brahmins, may the other activities of Bala the powerful be heard.

There was a monkey of great prowess named Dvivida. He was a friend of Naraka the leader of Asuras, one who was opposed to Devas. That powerful monkey nursed continuous animosity towards Devas.

Dvivida said :

Kṛṣṇa killed Naraka who was proud of his strength. Hence I shall take revenge on all Devas.

Vyāsa said :

5-10. He destroyed Yajñas and annihilated men. Deluded by ignorance he damned and demolished sacrificial rites. He violated bounds of decency. He destroyed embodied beings. The fickle fellow burnt territories, cities and villages. At places he hurled mountains and powdered villages. He uprooted mountains and hurled them into oceans. Standing in the middle of the ocean he made it agitated. Thereby, O brahmins, the ocean was excessively stirred up and it overflew the shores, flooding the villages and cities nearby. He used to assume different forms as he pleased and crushed down plants and trees as he wandered here and there. The monkey reduced everything to powder. This entire universe was thus ruined and ravaged by that wicked monkey.

11-14. O brahmins, self-study of the Vedas and repetition of the Vaṣaṭkāra Mantras ceased. Everyone was extremely miserable.

Once Balarāma, the highly blessed Revatī and other excellent ladies were seated in the Raivata garden and engaged in drinking wine. Elegant ladies were singing in the midst of highly elegant and charming assembly. The chief and the most excellent among the descendants of Yadu sported like Kubera on the Mandara mountain.

At that time the monkey came there, seized the ploughshare and the threshing rod of Balarāma and began to emulate him standing in front of him. The monkey stood in front of the womenfolk also and chattered and laughed.

15-20. He struck and hit the bowls and jugs filled with beverages. Thereupon Bala, with great fury surging up in his soul, rebuked him. In spite of that the monkey disregarded him and made tinkling chattering noise. Thereat, Bala got up in anger and seized his iron club. The excellent monkey seized a terrible rocky boulder, and hurled it (against Bala). The most excellent Yādava split it into a thousand bits by his iron club. The rocky boulder fell on the Earth. The monkey dodged the iron club and fell down. On getting up in great anger and gathering up his strength he struck him on his chest. Then the monkey was hit on his head with his fist by Bala. Thereupon Dvivida vomited blood and fell down. His life became extinct. As his body fell down the peak of the mountain crumbled.

21-23. O sages, the peak split into a hundred pieces as though it had been struck down by the thunder-bolt of Indra. Then Devas discharged showers of flowers over Rāma. They approached him and praised him "Well done. A great task has been accomplished. O heroic one, the universe had been harassed by this wicked monkey who used to render help unto asuras. Fortunately, he has been destroyed."

Vyāsa said :

Thus the activities of Balarāma, the incarnation of Śeṣa, the supporter of the Earth, cannot be measured and stipulated. There were many.

CHAPTER ONE HUNDRED AND ONE

Śrīkṛṣṇa returns to his abode

Vyāsa said :

1-4. Thus Kṛṣṇa performed the task of annihilating asuras with Balarāma to assist him. Similarly, for the sake of universe, he destroyed the wicked kings as well. Accompanied by Arjuna, the lord disburdened the Earth by slaying Akṣauhiṇīs of soldiers. After reducing the burden of the Earth, after killing the kings, Kṛṣṇa, exterminated his own family under the pretext of the curse of brahmins. Thereupon, lord Kṛṣṇa left off Dvārakā and his human form which had been his own part. He entered his own abode of Viṣṇu.

The sages said :

5. How did Kṛṣṇa exterminate his family under the pretext of the curse of brahmins ? How did he give up his human form ?

Vyāsa said :

6-7. The great sages Viśvāmitra, Kaṇva and Nārada were seen by some young men of the Yādava family in the great holy centre Piṇḍāraka.

Elated due to their blooming youth, and urged by the inevitability of the future events they embellished and dressed Sāmba, son of Sāmbavatī in the guise of a woman, and said to the sages after approaching and making obeisance to them.

The young men said :

8-13. O saintly lords, this woman is desirous of a son. What will she give birth to ?

Vyāsa said :

O sages of good holy rites, the brahmins were endowed with divine wisdom. Hence, though an attempt was made by the young men to deceive them they could not be deceived. Those brahmins cursed them to their doom. The infuriated sages replied—"She will give birth to an iron club whereby the entire family of Yādavas will perish.

Thus warned by those brahmins the young men mentioned everything precisely to Ugrasena.

An iron club came out of the belly of Sāmba. Ugrasena powdered that iron club and scattered the powder into ocean. It grew into an Airaka reed. O brahmins, when the iron club was powdered, there remained a piece which could not be reduced to powder by the Yādavas. It had the shape of a miniature iron club.

14-17. It was also cast off into the ocean. A fish swallowed it. When it was killed by the fishermen the iron piece came out of its belly which a hunter immediately caught hold of. Though Kṛṣṇa understood the truth, and though he was all-powerful, he did not wish to alter the course of events as brought about by the fate.

A certain messenger, sent by Devas visited Kṛṣṇa and said : "O lord I have been sent as a messenger by Vasus, Aśvins, Maruts, Ādityas, Rudras, Sādhyas and other Devas. O lord, Indra submits to you. O lord may it be listened to.

Devas said :

18-21. The lord has incarnated for reducing the burden of the Earth. More than a hundred years have gone by. You have been propitiated by Devas since Daityas of evil conduct have been killed. The burden of the Earth has been brought down. Let Devas with you as their leader go back to heaven. O lord of the universe, you have spent more than a hundred years on this Earth. If it pleases you, kindly repair to heaven. Our lord is intimated thus by Devas—If you still desire to be here we, your followers and servants, too, will have to be here alone for the requisite period of time.

The lord said :

22. O messenger, I know fully well what you say. But the destruction of Yādavas is only just started by me.

23. If they remain unexterminated, they will constitute a great burden unto the Earth. Hence I shall hurriedly bring that down within seven nights.

24. In the same manner as it had been taken from the ocean I shall replace Dvārakā in the ocean, exterminate Yādavas and then return to heaven.

25. I shall cast off my human body too, assisted by Saṁkarṣaṇa. It should be considered by the leader of Devas that I have come there.

26-27. The burden of Yādavas on the Earth is greater than the burden of Jarāsandha and others who have been killed. Hence, after bringing down this very great burden of the Earth, I shall go over there in order to protect the world of immortal beings. Please tell them thus.

Vyāsa said :

28. Thus informed by Vāsudeva O sages, the divine messenger bowed to him and went to heaven near the king of Devas.

29. Day and night the lord witnessed evil omens in heaven, on Earth and in the sky as well, indicating the destruction of Dvārakā.

30. On seeing them he said to Yādavas—"See the extremely terrible evil omens. In order to subdue these, we shall go to Prabhāsa. Do not delay".

31-32. Uddhava the great devotee of the lord bowed down to Kṛṣṇa and said :

"O lord, mention to me. What has to be done by me now ? O lord, command me now. I think the lord will annihilate this entire family. O Acyuta, I see evil signs for the destruction of this family.

The lord said :

33-34. Equipped with the divine facility of movement originating from my favour, go to the holy hermitage of Badarikāśrama, on the mountain Gandhamādana. It is the most sacred spot on Earth as it is the abode of Nara and Nārāyaṇa. Keeping your mind in me, you will attain Siddhi there, due to my favour.

35. After finishing this family I shall go to Heaven. The sea will engulf Dvārakā in its flood when it has been abandoned by me.

Vyāsa said :

36. Thus advised and urged by Kṛṣṇa, Uddhava bowed to him and went to the abode of Nara and Nārāyaṇa.

37. Then Yādavas, O brahmins, got into fast moving chariots and went to Prabhāsa alongwith Kṛṣṇa, Balarāma and others.

38. After reaching Prabhāsa, the Kukuras and Andhakas were sanctified and delighted. As it was approved of by Vasudeva, they indulged in drinking bouts.

39. As Yādavas went on drinking a mutual struggle ensued amongst them giving rise to a conflagration of quarrel that led to their destruction.

40. Urged by the divine fate, they struck at one another by means of weapons. When they had exhausted their weapons they took up Erakā reed nearby.

41. When the Erakā was grasped by them, it appeared as though it had turned adamantine. With this they hit one another with terrible blows.

42-43. O brahmins, Pradyumna, Sāmba, Kṛtavarmā, Sātyakī, Aniruddha, Pṛthu, Vipṛthu, Cārudeṣṇa, Subāhu, Akrūra and others hit and struck one another with the adamantine pieces of Erakā reeds.

44. Kṛṣṇa restrained them. They thought that he was one who had come to assist them. They bit and struck one another.

45. The infuriated Kṛṣṇa seized a fistful of Erakā from them. Thus the iron club became the fistful of iron for their destruction.

46. As an Assailant he killed all Yādavas. Suddenly they too approached him and hit one another. Others also did likewise.

47. Then O excellent brahmins, even as Dāruka went on watching, observing, Jaitra, the chariot of the discus-bearing lord was dragged by the horses through the middle of the ocean.

48. The discus Śārṅga, quivers, conch and the sword circumambulated him and went away along the solar path.

49. O excellent brahmins, within a moment Yādavas were destroyed except the mighty-armed Kṛṣṇa and Dāruka.

50. While taking their rounds both of them saw Balarāma seated at the root of a tree. A great serpent was coming out of his mouth.

51. After wriggling out of his mouth that serpent of huge dimension went towards the ocean. It was worshipped by Siddhas as well as Nāgas.

52. Taking Arghya with him the ocean came face to face with Balarāma. Worshipped by the excellent Nāgas he entered the water. On seeing the passing away of Bala, lord Kṛṣṇa said to Dāruka.

The lord said :

53-58. Mention all this to Vasudeva and Ugrasena viz.—the passing away of Balarāma, the destruction of Yādavas.

I shall remain in yogic posture and cast off this physical body. The residents of Dvārakā and Āhuka should be informed that the ocean will flood this city. Hence all of you should stand ready with well equipped chariots and wait for Arjuna's arrival. When the Pāṇḍava prince comes you must not stay in Dvārakā. You must go along with him wherever Arjuna, that descendant of Kuru, may go. After going there tell Arjuna, son of Kuntī these words of mine. "These are my people. They should be protected by you in accordance with your ability".

Thus you shall accompany Arjuna taking the people of Dvārakā. Vajra shall become the king of Yadus.

CHAPTER ONE HUNDRED AND TWO

Lord Kṛṣṇa ascends Heaven

Vyāsa said :

1. Thus directed, Dāruka bowed to and circumambulated Kṛṣṇa and went away as instructed.

2. After going to Dvārakā he did as he was bid. He brought Arjuna there and made Vajra the king of Yadus.

3. Lord Kṛṣṇa reinstated the greatest Brahman of the nature of Vāsudeva into the Ātman and held it in all living beings.

4. O excellent ones, honouring the words of brahmins and Durvāsas, the lord remained in the yogic posture keeping one of his feet over the other knee.

5. The hunter Jarā came there, holding a great arrow fitted with the last remnant bit of the iron club.

6. O excellent brahmins, on seeing the foot of the lord having the shape of a deer the hunter stopped. With the same remnant of the iron club he hit the lord.

7-8. On going up (to the victim) the hunter saw a man with four arms. He bowed to him again and again and said, "Be pleased. This has been committed by me out of ignorance suspecting you to be a deer. I may be excused. It does not behove you to burn me as I am already burned by my own sin.

Vyāsa said :

9-13. Then the lord said to him—"You need not have even the least bit of fear. O hunter, go to heaven, the resort of happiness, by the virtue of my grace".

Vyāsa said :

Immediately after he had uttered these words, an aerial chariot arrived there by virtue of his grace. The hunter got into it and went to heaven. When he had gone the lord cast off that mortal body and united his Ātman with the supreme Ātman, the Brahman, the unchanging, unimaginable, pure, unborn, unaging, undying, immeasurable soul of all identical with Vāsudeva. Then he attained heaven.

CHAPTER ONE HUNDRED AND THREE

The episode of Kṛṣṇa concluded

Vyāsa said :

1. Arjuna found out the cast off physical bodies of Kṛṣṇa and Balarāma and performed the requisite consecratory rites. He did the same for others too.

2. The eight crowned queens of Kṛṣṇa, Rukmiṇī and others, took the dead body of Kṛṣṇa and entered fire.

3. Revatī the excellent lady, embraced the body of Balarāma and entered the blazing fire which cooled and delighted her by the mere touch of her body.

4. On hearing about this, Ugrasena, Ānakadundubhi, Devakī and Rohiṇī entered fire.

5. Arjuna performed their funeral rites in accordance with the injunctions. Taking all the people and Vajra with him he left Dvārakā.

6. Thousands of wives of Kṛṣṇa went out of Dvāravatī. Looking after Vajra and the people, the son of Kuntī went ahead slowly.

7. O brahmins, the assembly chamber Sudharmā, that had been brought to the mortal world by Kṛṣṇa went back to heaven. So also the Pārijāta tree.

8. It was on the day on which Kṛṣṇa left the Earth and went to heaven that the Kali age, with time for its body set in.

9. The great ocean flooded Dvārakā. The sea did not engulf the house of the most excellent one among the descendants of Yadu. This was the only thing it did not envelop in its waters.

10. Since Kṛṣṇa the lord, is permanently present there, O brahmins, the great ocean does not even today, go beyond the limit (of this house).

11. It is an abode of great merit. It destroys all sins. It is a place where Viṣṇu sports about. On seeing it one is liberated from sins.

12. O excellent sages, in the land of Pañcanada (watered by five rivers), equipped with much of wealth and foodgrains, Arjuna made arrangements for the residence of all the people.

13-14. The ladies whose husbands had been killed in the battle-field were being led by Arjuna who had the bow in his hand. On seeing them led by Arjuna, robbers felt greedy. The Ābhīras (cowherds) who were very haughty, who committed sinful deeds and whose minds were afflicted by covetousness gathered together and consulted one another.

The Ābhīras said:

15-17. Here is Arjuna armed with his bow. Alone he is leading the women-folk whose husbands had been killed. He is taking them beyond us. Let his strength be reduced and ridiculed. By killing Bhīṣma, Droṇa, Jayadratha, Karṇa, and others he has become arrogant. He is not aware of the strength of the rural folk. He treats others with contempt regarding them inferior to him in strength, especially the people of villages.

Vyāsa said:

18. Tnereafter Dasyus who hurled lumps of clay and who struck with their staffs rushed at those womenfolk whose husbands had been killed. They attacked them in their thousands. Turning back, the son of Kuntī spoke to the Ābhīras laughingly :

Arjuna said :

19-24. "Return, O unrighteous ones, if you are not desirous of dying".

Vyāsa said :

They disregarded his words and seized the wealth and the womenfolk from the son of Kuntī, the womenfolk who had been the wives of Kṛṣṇa.

Then Arjuna began to string up his bow Gāṇḍīva that never became infirm in battle. But that powerful hero could not string it up.

With great difficulty he tied up the string but it became loose again. Although he racked his brain the son of Pāṇḍu could not remember the mantras with which they had to be discharged.

Arjuna discharged the remaining arrows against these. But, though they were discharged from the Gāṇḍīva bow they did not inflict any injury. The everlasting arrows received from the god of fire became exhausted. Thus when he fought with the cowherds Arjuna was defeated and exhausted.

25-26. Arjuna thought—"It was really Kṛṣṇa's strength whereby the various kings were conquered by me through volleys of arrows".

Even as the son of Pāṇḍu was watching with wide open eyes, those excellent ladies were abducted by Ābhīras. Others went away as they desired.

27. When the arrows were exhausted Arjuna struck them with the tip of his bow. O brahmins, at the blow the Dasyus laughed derisively.

28. Even as Arjuna was watching, O excellent sages, those Mlecchas seized the excellent women of Vṛṣṇis and Andhakas and carried them to their places all round.

29. Arjuna became dejected saying—"Alas; Alas, I have been abandoned by that lord." He lamented.

Arjuna said :

30. That bow, those miraculous missiles, that chariot and those horses—all these are destroyed at one stroke like the charitable gift to one who is not learned in the Vedas.

31. O, fate indeed is very powerful. Without that Ātman, I am devoid of all efficiency. I have been led to ignoble defeat.

32. These are the same arms as before; this is the same fist of mine. This is the same spot. I am the same Arjuna but without merit everything has gone worthless.

33. My superior powers and those of Bhīma were certainly effected by Lord Kṛṣṇa. Without him, I have been conquered by the cowherds. How can it happen otherwise ?

Vyāsa said :

34. Saying thus, Arjuna went to Indraprastha. There he crowned as king, the Yādava scion Vajra.

35. Arjuna saw there the highly blessed sage Vyāsa with his abode in the forest. He approached him humbly and saluted the sage.

36-41. As Arjuna bowed down to his feet, the sage closely looked at him. He spoke "Why are you so exceedingly pale and colourless ? Did you follow a column of dust kicked up and raised by goats ? Was the murder of a brahmin committed by you ? Are you miserable because your hopes of victory have been shattered ? Surely you don't have brilliant lustre (in your face) now. Were your offsprings and others rebuked while they were begging ? Have you taken any lustful interest in any woman who cannot be carnally approached ? You are lacking lustre thereby. Are you in the habit of eating sweets alone without giving a portion to brahmins ? Or were the riches of any miser removed by you ? I hope, O Arjuna, you have not been affected by the glare of the sun or the gust of wind ? Has the evil eye struck you ? How can you be devoid of splendour otherwise ? Are you defiled in the water from the nail or have you been sprinkled by the water from a jar ? Why do you very much lack in lustre ? Or have you been defeated by base men in battle."

Vyāsa said :

42. Arjuna who was thus addressed took a deep breath and said. "O holy sir, may it be heard". O brahmins, he mentioned about his mortification precisely.

Arjuna said :

43. He who had been our strength, our splendour, our prowess, our exploit, our glory, our lustre—lord Kṛṣṇa—has left us.

44-45. Without him, O sage, we are like stumps and pegs. He had been one who used to speak smilingly to us. He, the best of men, had been the cause of strength of our missiles, of our arrows and of my bow Gāṇḍīva.

46. It was due to his supervision that glory, victory and increase of wealth never forsook us. But to our misfortune, the lord himself has forsaken us now.

47. It was through the power of Kṛṣṇa that Bhīṣma, Droṇa, Karṇa, Duryodhana and others were destroyed. But that Kṛṣṇa has left off the Earth.

48. To me the Earth appears like a lady who has lost her blooming youth, whose splendour is destroyed and whose lustre has vanished. O dear one, I am not the only one to suffer from the bereavement of the discus-bearing lord.

49. Due to the power and magnificence of Kṛṣṇa I was able to kill Bhīṣma and others. I was like fire and they were like moths. But today, without lord Kṛṣṇa, I have been defeated by cowherds.

50. My bow Gāṇḍīva is well known in the three worlds due to his magnificence. But without him, it has been slighted by the cowherds by means of mere sticks.

51. O great sage, thousands of helpless ladies have been carried off, in spite of my endeavour, by the Dasyus who had batons for their weapons.

52. All the womenfolk of Kṛṣṇa, while being brought over here by me, have been carried away by the cowherds who carried sticks as their weapons.

53. It is not surprising that I am devoid of splendour. The fact that I am alive is miraculous. I have been marked by the mud in the form of insults at the hands of base men. I have been ashamed, O grand-father.

Vyāsa said :

54. On hearing the words of the noble-minded Arjuna, who

was dejected and miserable, O excellent brahmins, I spoke thus :

55. Enough of your being ashamed, O Arjuna, it does not behove you to bewail. Understand that the working of time in all living beings is like this.

56. O Arjuna, Kāla is conducive to the nativity of living beings as well as to their non-existence. Knowing that Kāla is at the root of everything, be steady-minded.

57-58. Rivers, oceans, mountains, Earth, Devas, human beings, animals, trees and reptiles are created by Kāla and later they attain dissolution through Kāla. Knowing that all this is of the nature of Kāla you shall attain mental peace.

59. O Arjuna, the greatness of Kṛṣṇa is just as you say. He had taken up incarnation on Earth for reducing its burden.

60. Formerly, the Earth that had been afflicted by burden had gone to Devas. It was for that purpose that Viṣṇu who could assume any form that he desired had taken up incarnation.

61. That task has been achieved, the kings have been killed. The family of Vṛṣṇis and Andhakas has been duly finished.

62. O Arjuna, there was nothing else to be done by him on the face of the Earth. So the contented lord went away as he wished.

63. This lord of Devas performs creation at the beginning and sustains during its maintenance. He is competent to annihilate as well, as has been done now.

64. Hence, O Arjuna, you must not feel aggrieved due to this discomfiture. At the moment of creative activity men will have exploits.

65. It is exemplified by the fact that Bhīṣma, Droṇa and other beings were killed by you alone. O Arjuna, is not this attack a deficiency in their case, as brought about by Kāla ?

66. Just as their mortification was brought about by the magnificence of Viṣṇu and through you, so also is your mortification at the hands of Dasyus. It is caused by the magnificence of Viṣṇu.

67. That lord, the lord of the universe, permeates other bodies and performs the task of dissolving all living beings in the end.

68. During the origin of this creative process the lord was your ally, O son of Kuntī. At the close of created beings those who are viewed with sympathy by the lord had been your adversaries.

69. Who could have believed at the beginning that you could kill Kauravas including Bhīṣma? Who could have believed your discomfiture at the hands of cowherds?

70-71. Arjuna, this is only a peculiar type of activity of Kṛṣṇa in respect of all living beings. The fact that Kauravas and others were defeated by you in the battle and that the women under your protection were carried away by Dasyus—this is only the lord's sport.

I shall tell you an anecdote, O Arjuna, in the manner it had occurred.

72. O Arjuna, formerly the brahmin Aṣṭāvakra was interested in staying under water for many years even as he was worshipping the eternal lord.

73. When Asuras had been defeated, there was a great festival on the top of Meru. The celestial damsels saw him on their way to the festival.

74. O Arjuna, Rambhā, Tilottamā and hundreds and thousands of other ladies eulogised and praised that great soul.

75. They praised the sage who wore weighty matted hair and who was standing immersed in water upto his neck. With humility they bent down their heads. They were eager in repeating the hymns.

76. They eulogised him so much that he became pleased with them. O most excellent among the descendants of Kuru, they eulogised that most excellent brahmin.

Aṣṭāvakra said:

77. O highly blessed ladies, I am delighted. Whatever is wished for by you, may be requested for from me. I shall grant it even if it is very difficult to grant.

Vyāsa said:

78-82. Rambhā, Tilottamā and other celestial damsels said:

The Apsaras said :

If you are pleased, O brahmins, grant what is not achieved by us ?

Others said—"O brahmin, if you are pleased we wish to obtain Kṛṣṇa as our husband".

Vyāsa said :

Saying, "It will be so", the sage got up from water. As he got up they saw that he was deformed with crookedness in eight ways

O scion of the family of Kuru, on seeing the deformed sage the celestial damsels laughed. Some concealed their laughter. But some laughed openly. The infuriated sage cursed them.

Aṣṭāvakra said :

83-85. Considering me ugly and deformed you have laughed derisively at me. Hence I curse you.

Due to my favour, you will obtain Kṛṣṇa as your husband. But afflicted by my curse, you will fall into the hands of Dasyus.

Vyāsa said :

86. On hearing these words, the sage was propitiated by them. He said, "You will go once again to the world of the lord of Devas."

87. Hence, O Arjuna, even the least bit of sorrow need not be felt by you. Everything has already been ordained by the lord of all.

88. Your strength, splendour, prowess and greatness have been condensed by the lord desirous of annihilating you all.

89. Death is inevitable to one who is born; fall is a sequal to rise. Close contact leads to separation in the end; hoarding leads to destruction.

90-92. After knowing all these things the learned men neither feel sorry nor elated. There are others like them who derive lessons from such events.

Hence, O excellent among men, know this. Eschew the entire kingdom. Alongwith your brothers, go to the forest for performing penance.

Hence go. Intimate to Dharmarāja (Yudhiṣṭhira) these words of mine. O heroic one, day after tomorrow attain the ultimate goal along with your brothers.

Vyāsa said :

93-95. Thus advised, Arjuna approached his elder brother and informed him and the other brothers including the twins Nakula and Sahadeva what he had seen and experienced. On hearing the words of Vyāsa uttered by Arjuna, the sons of Pāṇḍu crowned Parīkṣit in the kingdom and went to the forest.

Thus, O excellent sages, the activities of Vāsudeva, born in the family of Yadu, have been mentioned by me in detail.

CHAPTER ONE HUNDRED AND FOUR

The glorification of different Manifestations of the lord

The sages said :

1. O excellent sage, the rare manifestation and the diverse activities of lord Kṛṣṇa as well as Balarāma in the world have been mentioned by you.

2. Listening to the story of the lord we are not contented. We wish to hear about the other manifestations of the lord of the universe.

3. There was a manifestation of Viṣṇu of unmeasured splendour, mentioned by good men in the Purāṇas. It has been heard by us as Varāha (Boar).

4. We do not know his full conduct nor the details of the process whereby the incarnation took place. We do not know the extent of the existence of Guṇas and Karmans in him. We do not know the extent of his will in the causation thereof.

5. Of what nature was this Varāha ? What was his form ? What is the deity ? What are his conduct and prowess ? What was performed by him then ?

6. The story of the great boar is conducive to the happiness of brahmins assembled at the sacrifice of those whose mind is always set on holy rites. It is pleasing to all the worlds.

7-9. O brahmin, we wish to know how Nārāyaṇa assumed the form of the Boar. How Viṣṇu, the suppressor of foes, lifted up the Earth that was within the ocean, by means of his curved fangs. It is our inclination to hear about the activities of the slayer of foes, in detail. We wish to hear about the manifestations of Viṣṇu alongwith his activities in due order. It behoves you to recount the nature of the lord, O holy brahmin.

Vyāsa said :

10. The burden of questions cited by you is indeed immense. I shall recount in accordance with my capacity. May the glory of Viṣṇu be heard about.

11. Fortunately your mind is inclined to listen to the prowess of Viṣṇu. O excellent brahmins, I shall recount to you the manifestations of Viṣṇu.

12-20. It is him that the brahmins conversant with the Vedic lore call with a thousand mouths, a thousand-eyed, thousand-footed, thousand-headed, the unchanging lord with thousand hands, thousand-tongued, brilliant lord with a thousand crowns. He is the bestower of a thousand, the devourer of a thousand, the unchanging one with a thousand arms. The various parts of the Yajña are mentioned as identical with him viz. Havana, Savana, Hotṛ, Havya, Holy vessels, altar, initiation, sacrificial twig, ladle, soma juice, winnowing basket, throbbing rod, prokṣaṇī vessel, Dakṣiṇāyana, Adhvaryu brahmin who sings sāman, Sādhya, Sadana, Sadas, Yūpa, Cakra, Dhruva, Darvi, Carus, Ulūkhalas, Prāgvaṁśa, the altar and whatever is beyond that. He is identical with the mobile and immobile beings whether short or huge in size. He is one with the rites of atonement, Arghya, Sthaṇḍila, Kuśa grass, fire that conveys the mantras and Yajñas, the share and he who conveys the share. They call him as one who partakes of his share at the outset, as the imbiber of Soma, as one who has put offering in flame, as one who has lifted up the weapon. The brahmins conversant with the Vedas call him the eternal lord of Yajña, thousands of manifestations of the lord of Devas, of Viṣṇu marked with the scar Śrīvatsa had taken place before; they will occur in future too—so says Brahmā.

21-22. O highly blessed ones, it is about this holy and divine story that you have asked. It is based on the incarnations of Viṣṇu. It is an auspicious story that dispels sins. O highly blessed ones, listen to this with your full concentration. May your wider soul be engrossed in the lord. O sinless ones, I shall recount in due order what you ask me.

23. I shall mention the greatness of Vāsudeva, the conduct of life of the highly intelligent one, for the welfare of Devas and mortal beings as well as the origin of the worlds.

24. The supreme Ātman manifests himself on many occasions. I shall recount the manifestations that are divine, sacred and endowed with good qualities.

25. The lord of Devas, the lord of universe, who sleeps for the period of a thousand sets of four Yugas, manifests himself against some (specific) task after the thousand sets of four Yugas are completed.

26-32. The ancient lord whose splendour was as brilliant as that of the well kindled fire created all these :- Brahmā, Kapila, the three-eyed Śiva, Devas, seven sages, Nāgas, Apsaras, Sanatkumāra of great magnificence and the noble Manu who was the lord and creator of subjects. When all the mobile and immobile beings had perished, when Devas, Asuras, human beings had perished, when Nāgas and Rākṣasas had perished, the lord remained in the middle of the ocean. (At that time) two Rākṣasas—Madhu and Kaiṭabha who were very powerful desired to win him. After boundless boons had been granted to them they were killed by the lord.

Formerly, as the lotus-umbilicused lord was sleeping in the waters of the ocean, Devas and sages were born in that lotus. This manifestation of the lord of the universe is the one which pertains to the lotus. In the course of this manifestation the Purāṇa is mentioned with the same concentration as the celestial Vedas. The manifestation of the great soul is mentioned in the Vedas. In this course this manifestation, Viṣṇu the most excellent of Devas assumed the form of a Boar.

Extra seven verses

[The Yajñavārāha (the Boar of the sacrificial form) appeared thus. The Vedas constituted his face. Sacrificial posts were his legs. Sacrifice was his tooth, sacrificial fire was his face, the fiery flame was his tongue, the Darbha grass constituted his hair; Brahmā was his head; he performed great penance (?) Day and night constituted his eyes; He was of a divine form; the ancillaries of the Vedas constituted his ear-ornaments; the clarified butter was his nose; the sacrificial ladle was his snout. The great Sāman songs were his loud snorting sounds. He was glorious and full of truthfulness and piety. He was duly greeted for his exploits in due order; the expiatory rites were his terrible nails (colours). He had the form of a sacrificial animal from knee to face. The intestines were the ancillaries, (?) the Homa was his symbol, the seeds and the medicinal plants constituted his great fruits, recitations were his inner soul; the Mantras were his loins; the Soma juice was his blood; the altar was his shoulder. Havis (offering) was his scent offering; Havyas and Kavyas constituted his velocity; Prāgvaṁśa was his physical body. He was lustrous, purified by different initiations. Dakṣiṇā was his heart. He was a Yogin in the form of a great sacrifice. The eight Upakarman rites constituted his golden ornaments round the neck; the Pravargya was his circular ornament. The different metres constituted his gait and paths; the secret doctrine of the Upaniṣads constituted his seat. He had his own shadow as his wife and assistant; he stood up like a mountain with a jewelled peak.]

33-36. The Earth extending upto oceans and consisting of mountains, tree-groves and forests got immersed in the vast sheet of water. The lord dived into the vast sheet of water and lifted the Earth by means of his curved fang, with a desire for the welfare of the worlds. The lord, the primordial cause of the world, the lord with a thousand heads reinstated the Earth once again. Thus the goddess Earth immersed into the waters of the ocean was lifted up formerly by Yajña-varāha, the one who sought the welfare of living beings.

Thus the incarnation of Varāha has been mentioned O brahmins. Thereafter (is the manifestation of) Narasiṁha

(Man-lion). In this incarnation, Hiraṇyakaśipu was killed by the lord who became a lion.

37-38. Formerly, O brahmins, in the Kṛtayuga, this enemy of Devas was the leader of asuras. He was proud of his strength. He performed great penance for ten thousand years. For a thousand years he was engaged in Japas and observance of fasts. For five hundred years he adopted the holy rite of silence.

39. Brahmā was delighted by his penance and observance of restraints by his mental control and subjugation of sense-organs and at his celebacy.

40-44. O brahmins, the self-born lord Brahmā came there on a shining aerial chariot with the lustre of the sun and fitted with a swan. He was accompanied and surrounded by all these Ādityas, Vasus, Maruts, Daivatas, Rudras, Viśvasahāyas, Yakṣas Rākṣasas, Kinnaras, Diśas (guardians of quarters), Pradiśas (guardians of the intermediary directions), deities of rivers, oceans, stars, Muhūrtas (the presiding deity of time units of 48 minutes), planets traversing firmament, celestial sages, persons grown old in performing penances, the learned Siddhas, the holiest saintly kings, Gandharvas, Apsaras and Devas. The glorious Brahmā, the preceptor of mobile and immobile beings, the most excellent one among the knowers of Brahman spoke to the asura.

Brahmā said :

45. O you of good holy rites, I am pleased wtih your penance. Welfare unto you. Choose a boon. Obtain your cherished desires.

Hiraṇyakaśipu said :

46-50. O grand-father of the worlds, none of these should curse me by imprecations—Devas, Asuras, Gandharvas, Yakṣas, Nāgas, Rākṣasas, infuriated sages and those who are endowed with penance. This the first boon I choose. I should not be killed by any of these things—weapons, missiles, mountains, trees whether dry or wet. I should not be killed above or below. He who is able to kill me at one blow of his hand along with my servants, armies and vehicles shall cause my death. I shall be all these : sun, moon, wind, fire, water, atmosphere, firmament, everything.

I must be anger, love, Varuṇa, Indra, Yama, Kubera, the presiding deity of riches as well as the over-lord of Yakṣas and Kimpuruṣas.

Brahmā said :

51. O dear one, all these divine and wonderful boons have been granted to you by me. O dear one, you will attain all these desires.

Vyāsa said :

52. After saying this, lord Brahmā immediately went to his abode frequented by the brahminical sage.

53. On hearing about the granting of boon, Devas, Nāgas, Gandharvas and sages approached him.

Devas said :

54. O lord, with this boon, that Asura will harass us. Hence, O lord, be pleased, let the manner of his destruction be also thought of.

55. O lord, you are the self-born lord, you are the cause of all living beings, you are the creator of Havyas and Kavyas. You are the unmanifest being. You are certainly Prakṛti.

Vyāsa said :

56. Then, on hearing these words conducive to the welfare of all, lord Brahmā spoke to Devas.

Brahmā said :

57. O Devas, the fruit of penance must of course be obtained by him. But as the benefits of penance are exhausted lord Viṣṇu will slay him.

Vyāsa said :

58. On hearing these words of the lotus-born Brahmā Devas felt joyous. They returned to their divine abodes.

59. Immediately after he had obtained the boon, the asura Hiraṇyakaśipu became haughty and he harassed his subjects.

60. He overpowered and insulted the highly blessed sages of holy rites, interested in truthfulness and piety and of subdued sense-organs.

61. That great Asura defeated Devas stationed in heaven. He kept the three worlds under his control and lived in heaven.

62. Whenever that asura became haughty due to his obtaining the boon he roamed over the Earth. He made asuras worthy of shares in the Yajñas and Devas, unworthy of shares in the same.

63-64. The Ādityas, Vasus, Sādhyas, Viśvedevas and Maruts sought refuge in Viṣṇu of great strength, worthy of being sought as refuge. They sought refuge in the eternal lord of Brahman identical with the Yajñas unto Devas and Brahman the lord of the past, present and future bowed to by all the worlds. They sought refuge in the omnipresent lord Nārāyaṇa worthy of being sought refuge.

Devas said :

65. O lord of Devas, save us today from the fear of Hiraṇyakaśipu. Indeed you are our greatest lord. You are our greatest preceptor.

66. O most excellent one among Devas, you are indeed the supreme creator of all of us, Brahmā and others. O lord, with the eyes resembling the petals of a full blown lotus devoid of impurities, O lord, the destroyer of the enemy hosts, be our refuge for the destruction of the race of Diti.

Vāsudeva said :

67. O immortal ones, cast off your fear. I grant you all, fearlessness. O Devas, you will regain heaven as before without delay.

68. I shall kill this asura along with his attendants. I shall kill this leading Dānava haughty on account of his acquiring the boon that he cannot be killed by the leading immortal ones.

Vyāsa said :

69. After saying this to the chiefs of Devas and bidding

them farewell, the lord of great strength came to the abode of Hiraṇyakaśipu.

70-74. The lord had half of his body human and half of the body leonine. Adopting the man-lion form, the lord clapped one hand with the other. He resembled the cloud; he had the voice and the brilliant prowess of the thick rain-bearing cloud; he was as impetuous as the cloud. On seeing the asura of great strength, guarded by the haughty asuras, the lord whose exploits were like those of a proud tiger hit and killed him with a single hand.

This manifestation of the Man-lion has been recounted. The next great manifestation is that of Vāmana. In the course of this manifestation, formerly, the powerful Viṣṇu adopted the form of a Dwarf destructive of Daityas. In the Yajña of the powerful Bali these great Asuras who could not be agitated by others were agitated by the three paces of Viṣṇu.

75-93. The following types of Asuras and Dānavas and those of the following names assailed Hṛṣīkeśa who had taken the steps. They were Vipracitti, Śiva, Śaṅku, Ayaḥśaṅku, Ayaḥśiras, Aśvaśiras, Hayagrīva, Vegavān, Ketumān, Ugra, the great Asura Ugravyagra, Puṣkara, Puṣkala, Aśvapati, Prahlāda, Kumbha, Saṁhrāda, Gamanapriya, Anuhrāda, Harihaya, Vārāha, Saṁhāra, Anuja, Śarabha, Śalabha, Kupatha, Krodhana, Kratha, Bṛhatkīrti, Mahājihva, Śaṅkukarṇa, Mahāsvana, Dīptajihva, Arkanayana, Mṛgapāda, Mṛgapriya, Vāyu, Gariṣṭha, Namuci, Śambara, Vikṣara the great, Candrahantā, Krodhahantā, Krodhavardhana, Kālaka, Kālakopa, Vṛtra, Krodha, Virocana, Gariṣṭha, Variṣṭha, Pralamba, Naraka, Indratapana, Vātāpī, Ketumān proud of his strength, Asilomā, Pulomā, Vāṣkala, Pramada, Mada, Svamiśra, Kālavadana, Karāla Keśi, Ekākṣa, Candramas, Rāhu, Saṁhrāda, Saṁvara and Svana were the Daityas. Some of them had Śataghnīs (hundred smashers) and discus in their hands; some carried iron clubs in their hands; some carried Aśvayantra weapons (mechanical devices driven by horses). Some had Bhindipāla variety of iron club as their weapons; some had tridents and mortars in their hands. Others were holding axes. Some had nooses, Mudgara iron clubs or Parigha iron clubs in their hands. The Dānavas used great rocky boulders as their weapons. They were armed with javelins. They were awful Dānavas with diverse kinds of weapons. They were very powerful and came from different lands. There were Dānavas with faces resembling those of tortoises, cocks, rabbits, owls, donkeys, camels, boars, cats, peacocks, crocodiles, rams, cows, goats, sheep, bulls, mountain lizards, porcupines, jackals, mice, frogs, wolves, sharks, Krauñca birds, Garuḍa, mules and peacocks. All of them were terrible and awful. Some were clad in the hides of big elephants. Some were clad in deer skins. Some covered their bodies with the barks of trees. Some had blue robes. Some had turbans or crowns. Some had rings. Some wore coronets, some had long loose tresses. They were refulgent with their necks resembling the conch. They wore various types of dress and garments. They had applied diverse kinds of unguents. They wore various kinds of garlands. They seized and wielded their respective blasting weapons and gathered round Hṛṣīkeśa.

94-96. With the soles of his feet and the palms of his hands he crushed Daityas. He assumed a great and terrible form and roamed over the Earth. As he grew in size and roamed over the Earth, the moon and the sun at first stood on a level with his chest. When he flew up in the sky they stood against his umbilicus. When he of unmeasured prowess further grew in size they stood on a level with his knees.

97-98. After killing the leading Asuras and seizing the entire Earth from them, Viṣṇu the most excellent among the strong ones granted the Earth unto Vāmana. Indra the manifestation of the great Ātman named Vāmana has been recounted to you. This glory of Viṣṇu is being recounted in detail by the brahmins who are conversant with the Vedas.

99. A further manifestation of Viṣṇu the great Ātman, in the nature of a living being, is well known as Dattātreya. He was equipped with great forbearance.

100-102. When the Vedas perished, when the holy rites and sacrifices became defunct, when the rigidity of discipline of the four castes became loose and when piety weakened, it was he who restored all these. When truthfulness got lost and when falsehood prevailed, when the subjects became shattered and scattered and when virtuousness became disarrayed, Vedas were restored by him along with the Yajñas and holy rites. The four castes were made by that great Ātman, free from admixture.

103. Boon was granted by the intelligent Dattātreya to Kārttavīrya the intelligent king of Haihayas.

104. O king, this pair of arms of thine which was placed at my service shall certainly become a thousand arms.

105. O lord of the Earth, you will protect the entire Earth. Engaged in battle you become so dazzling that you will not be stared at by the enemy.

106. This glorious and auspicious manifestation of Viṣṇu has been recounted to you. There is another manifestation of the great Ātman namely Jāmadagnya Paraśurāma.

107. In the course of this manifestation the lord Paraśurāma killed king Sahasrārjuna in battle. Previously he had been invincible to the enemies in battle by the prowess of his thousand arms.

108-109. King Sahasrārjuna was seated in the chariot. Paraśurāma struck him to ground. Sahasrārjuna was crying like the rumbling cloud. Paraśurāma assailed him. The scion of the family of Bhṛgu cut off his thousand arms by his refulgent axe. He slew him together with his kinsmen.

110. The Earth where crores of Kṣatriyas remained scattered about, the Earth that is adorned by the mountains Meru and Mandara was rid of Kṣatriyas twentyone times by the lord.

111. After making the Earth devoid of Kṣatriyas, Paraśurāma of great fame performed a horse sacrifice in order to dispel his sins.

112-116. In the course of this sacrifice, the scion of the family of Bhṛgu gave the Earth as gift unto Kaśyapa the son of Marīci. In this sacrifice precious articles were offered as gifts. Paraśurāma, the most excellent among those who fought gave elephants, horses, chariots, gold, and cows as gifts in that horse-sacrifice. For the welfare of the worlds, lord Jāmadagnya, the scion of the family of Bhṛgu, of great fame and great penance stays even today on the most excellent mountain Mahendra like a Deva. He is the manifestation of the great Ātman of Viṣṇu, the perpetual lord of Devas, the unchanging lord. He is well known as Jāmadagnya, son of Jamadagni.

117-120. In the twentyfourth cycle of four Yugas, the lord of large eyes resembling the blue lotus was born as the son of Daśaratha. Viśvāmitra preceded him in the course of this manifestation. The lord of great arms divided himself into four. The lord resembled the sun in refulgence. He became well known in the world as Rāma, son of king Daśaratha. The lord of great renown was born for augmenting piety, propitiating the people and curbing the wicked. They say that the lord of men engaged in the welfare of all living beings stayed in the forest for fourteen years. He was conversant with all holy rites and virtuous deeds.

121-122. Followed by Lakṣmaṇa, Rāma engaged in the welfare of all living beings, performed penance in the forest for fourteen years. Lakṣmī took the form of Sītā and followed her husband (to the forest) and remained at his side.

123-127. Living in Janasthāna,[1] the leader among men performed the task of Devas. Seeking the whereabouts of Sītā, the lord of great fame killed Rāvaṇa, the ruthless descendant of Pulastya, who had injured him. The lord killed Rāvaṇa the leader of Rākṣasas. The king of Rākṣasas was indestructible to Devas, Asuras, Yakṣas, Rākṣasas and Nāgas. He was in collaboration with crores of Rākṣasas. He was comparable to a mass of blue collyrium. He was invincible. He was incapable of being held. He was haughty and had exploits similar to that of a tiger. Devas dared not look at him. He was arrogant due to the boons that had been granted to him (by lord Śiva). Lord Rāma killed him along with his ministers and armies in the battle.

128. Rāma the lord of the living beings killed Rāvaṇa who had a huge body, who was very powerful and who resembled a mass of clouds.

129. For the sake of Sugrīva, Bāli the powerful lord of monkeys was killed in battle and Sugrīva was crowned in his place.

---

1. *Janasthāna* : A part of Daṇḍaka forest which lies in the basin of Godāvarī. Rāma had lived in this forest with Sītā and Lakṣmaṇa for a long time during the period of his exile.

130. The great Asura, the haughty son of Madhu, the Dānava named Lavaṇa, the heroic demon, proud of his boons was killed in the forest (named) Madhuvana.

131-132. Mārīca and Subāhu who were the most excellent ones among strong persons, who caused impediments in the Yajñas of the sages of purified souls, were killed by that great Ātman, an expert in battle in the course of the fight. Other Rākṣasas too were killed by him.

133. The tiger among men killed Virādha and Kabandha, the Rākṣasas of terrible exploits who had been formerly two Gandharvas deluded by imprecation.

134. In the battle Rāma killed his enemies by means of arrows, that had the lustre of fire, sun-rays and lightning streaks, that had the tail ends fitted with feathers of various kinds made of molten gold and the strength of which was like that of the thunderbolt of Mahendra.

135. Weapons were given to him by Viśvāmitra the intelligent sage for slaying the enemies who could not be assailed even by Devas.

136. Formerly, when a certain sacrifice was performed by Janaka the great Ātman, the great bow belonging to Maheśvara was broken by him even as he playfully and sportingly touched it.

137. After performing these tasks Rāma the most excellent among the virtuous performed ten horse-sacrifices where flesh was offered to the deities.

138. While Rāma was ruling over the kingdom people were not malicious or jealous. They did not speak inauspicious words. Winds blew without agitation. No wealth was stolen or taken by force.

139. No widow lamented. There were no calamities. Everything was auspicious when Rāma was ruling over the earth.

140. No living being had any fear from water, fire, wind or blows (of any sort). Old men never performed the funeral rites of boys (i.e. boys never died before old men).

141. The Kṣatriyas were devoted to the Brahmins. The Vaiśyas were devoted to the Kṣatriyas. The Śūdras served the three castes without any pride or egotism.

142. Women did not stray from their husbands; the husband did not stray from his wife. The entire universe was restrained and subdued. The earth was rid of robbers.

143-151. Rāma alone sustained the people. Rāma alone was the saviour. People lived for thousand years. They had thousand sons. When Rāma ruled over the earth all living beings were devoid of ailments; there was unity among the deities, sages and human beings everywhere on the Earth. The people who are conversant with ancient legends sing the following popular folk song thus—

People had a close and real bond of love with Rāma. The intelligent lord had greatness. He was a young man with red eyes and refulgent face. He spoke with limitation and restraint. His arms extended upto his knees. He had a gentle face. He had great arms and leonine shoulders. He ruled over the earth for ten thousand years. There were the following sounds continuously in his kingdom—the sound of the chanting of Ṛks, Sāmaṇ and Yajus Mantras; the twanging sound of the bow. This sound never ceased viz."Let this be given, let this be eaten." Rāma the son of Daśaratha richly possessed Sattva attributes and other qualities. He shone with his own brilliance, more brilliantly than the moon and the sun. He performed hundreds of holy sacrifices at the conclusion of which excellent gifts were offered to the Brahmins. He of great strength left Ayodhyā and went to Heaven. It was in this manner that the lord of great arms, the scion of the family of Ikṣvāku killed Rāvaṇa along with his attendants and went over to Heaven.

152. There was another manifestation of the great Ātman Kṛṣṇa for the welfare of worlds. It was well known in the Mathurā Kalpa (period of activity at Mathurā).

153-154. In the course of this mainfestation, the powerful lord in human form killed Daityas, Śālva, Śiśupāla, Kaṁsa Dvivida, Ariṣṭa, Vṛṣabha and Keśi, ogress Pūtanā, the elephant Kuvalayāpīḍa, Cāṇūra and Muṣṭika.

155. Thousands of arms of Bāṇa of miraculous activities were cut off. Naraka was killed in the war. So also Yavana of great strength.

156. All the jewels of the kings were taken away by him

due to his brilliance. The kings of the Earth whose conduct was wicked and sinful were killed.

157. The following manifestation of the great Ātman is conducive to the welfare of the world. It is the manifestation of Kalki named Viṣṇuyaśas also. It will occur in the village of Śambhala.

158-159. These and many other manifestations of the lord have taken place for the welfare of the worlds. In these manifestations, the lord of great renown was praised by Devas. These manifestations are sung about in the Purāṇas by the expounders of Brahman. Even Devas are deluded in enumerating these manifestations.

160. The Purāṇa is on a par with the Vedas and Śrutis (?) The enumeration of manifestation is but indicatory, not exhaustive.

161-163. The manifestations of the lord, the preceptor of the worlds, worthy of being glorified have been thus glorified. By the glorification of manifestations of the lord, the Pitṛs are pleased. He who listens to the (manifestations) of Viṣṇu of unmeasured prowess, with palms joined in reverence (attains happiness). By listening to the yogic Māyās of the lord of Yoga man is liberated from all sins. Due to the favour of the lord he obtains flourishing income, great prosperity and extensive pleasures quickly.

Thus, O excellent sages, the holy manifestations of Viṣṇu of unmeasured splendour have been glorified by me. They dispel all sins.

CHAPTER ONE HUNDRED AND FIVE

Review of the path of the world of Yama

The sages said :

1. O sage, we are not satiated by hearing about holy meritorious rites. Greatly sung by you they are like nectar. Our enthusiasm is further increased.

2. O sage, you know everything, origin and dissolution of living beings and the goal reached through actions. Hence, we ask you, O great sage.

3. It is heard that the path of the world of Yama is extremely impassable. It causes pain and misery. It is always a terror to living beings.

4. How do men go to the abode of Yama through that path ? O foremost among eloquent persons, tell us the magnitude and extent of the path.

5. O omniscient sage, we earnestly ask you to tell us entirely. O sage, how do men avert the miseries of hell ?

6. By what means do they prevent the hellish tortures ? By charitable gifts, holy rites and observances ?

What is the distance between the human world and the world of Yama ?

7. How do people attain the heavenly goal ? By what deeds do they go to hell ? How many are the abodes in heaven ? How many are the hellish abodes ?

8. How do men of good deeds go ? How do men of evil deeds go ? What is the form and what is the magnitude ? What is the caste of the two ? Even as an individual soul is being led to Yama's abode what is its form, shape and extent ?

Vyāsa said :

9. O leading sages, listen, even as I recount. O sages of good holy rites, the cycle of worldly existence is unageing. It has no permanent existence.

10. I shall decisively mention the path of Yama entirely. I shall recount everything in detail beginning from the time of departure. I shall recount it in a manner that no one else will be able to recount.

11. O excellent ones, I shall mention the form and nature of the path about which you have asked me and also the distance between the world of Yama and the mortal world.

12. That distance is 86000 Yojanas. That pathway is very hot like the red hot copper plate.

13. That pathway should of necessity be traversed by all living beings called individual souls. Meritorious men go to the meritorious sections and the sinful go to the sinful.

14-17. There are twentytwo hells in the realm of Yama. Men of evil deeds are cooked there in separate places. The chief among those hells are Raurava, Raudra, Śūkara, Tāla, Kumbhīpāka, Saṁdaṁśa, Śunabhojana, Śālmala, Vimohana, Kīṭāda, Kṛmibhakṣa, Lālābhakṣa, Bhrama, Agnijvāla, Asipatravana. There are rivers of putrescent and purulent matter. There are rivers of blood. There is the terrible Vaitaraṇī river of foetid matter.

18-20. On that great path there is no place where the person of great fatigue can rest. There is neither the shade of trees nor lakes nor tanks. There is neither a watering shed nor a well. There is no assembly or raised platform. There is no abode or hermitage. There are neither rivers nor mountains. That great path has of necessity to be traversed by all.

21-24. When the time arrives everyone has to leave off his friends, kinsmen, riches etc. and go along that great path. All living beings whether they are oviparous or viviparous, sweat-born or of vegetable kingdom that breaks open the ground and grows, whether they are mobile or immobile, will go along that path. Devas, Asuras and human beings are under the control of Yama and they follow him. All beings termed Jīvas whether a man or a woman or an eunuch have to traverse that path. All the people whether old, middle-aged or young have to traverse that path and the death may take place in the forenoon or afternoon, at midday or in the middle of the night, in the morning or at dusk.

25-28. Death may take place during childhood or in the womb. One may die at home as a householder or when one is on a journey away from home. A person may die in the forest or in water or on dry land; they may die in their abode or in a holy centre. That great journey has to be undertaken by the people who sit on the ground or on a chair or on a couch, whether asleep or awake. The creature enjoys the stipulated span of life here and at its close his vital airs cease to function even if he does not like it.

The embodied soul comes across some cause such as water, fire, poison, weapon, starvation, or sickness and thereby it is deprived of its vital airs.

29-33. The soul casts off the gross physical body made of the five elements and takes up another body from its own actions befitting the tortures undergone in hell.

For the sake of experiencing happiness and misery he derives a firm solid body. He who commits sins, reaps the adverse fruits. He who performs good deeds enjoys happiness and delight even in the abode of Yama.

The heat in the body becomes disturbed and displaced. When urged by the severe gust of wind it blazes even without fuel. It pierces the vulnerable vital spots. The organic wind Udāna begins to function, blowing upwards. It prevents the water and foodstuffs taken in from having a downward motion.

34. Those who make charitable gifts of water and cooked rice do not undergo any torture there along with their wives, sons and kins.

35. He who makes a charitable gift of cooked rice with the mind sanctified by faith derives satisfaction there even without (the presence of) cooked rice then.

36. The theist who has faith in God or holy scriptures, utters no falsehood and by whom severance of affection has not been effected, attains a happy death.

37. These men face a happy death :—those who are devoted to the worship of Devas and brahmins, those who are not jealous, those who have spotless character, those who are liberal in gifts and those who possess the attribute of modesty.

38. He who does not eschew virtue either due to lust or due to fury or out of hatred; he who carries out what is mentioned by elders and he who is gentle meets with a comfortable death.

39. Those who offer water to the thirsty, give food to the hungry, meet with timely death with ease and happiness.

40-45. Those who make gifts of riches conquer chillness; those who make gifts of sandal paste conquer scorching heat; those who dispel agonies and distresses of others conquer pain; those who impart perfect knowledge conquer delusion; those who make a gift of lights conquer darkness.

All these have death under delusion—the perjuror, he who tells lies, he who kills others and he who censures the Vedas.

The attendants of Yama are terrible. They have putrid odour. They have massive iron clubs in their hands. These persons are wicked in their designs. When they appear in front of him the dead man begins to tremble. He cries incessantly calling out his mother, father and brothers, O brahmins. That word Yama is indistinct. It appears as a single syllable. Due to fright, his eye rolls. There are convulsive movements in the body; he coughs and heaves a sigh. Thereafter he casts off that body afflicted by pain.

46. He attains another body having the same shape as the previous one. It is for experiencing the tortures caused by his bad Karman. This body does not originate from the parents.

47. Pain is derived by them in accordance with their magnitude, age, condition and manner of sitting.

Then the emissiry of Yama binds him with terrible nooses.

48-50. When the creature's death is imminent he is distressed due to the pain. The elements have abandoned his body. The vital air comes upto his neck. The soul is ejected out of the body. He laments excessively. Having come out of the body consisting of six sheathlike vestures he becomes gaseous in form. Then he is abandoned by the parents, brothers, uncles, wives, sons, friends and preceptors.

51. Watched by those people in distress, with their eyes full of tears he casts off his body, attains a gaseous form and goes ahead.

52-54. All such dead men are taken along the great path by the attendants of Yama. They are bound with nooses and dragged along and struck with iron clubs. They are led along the great path which is full of darkness. It is very terrible and endless. It yields both happiness and misery. To the persons of sinful activities it is impassable and unbearable. It is very difficult to traverse. It is always injurious to the sinful persons.

55. On seeing the living creature with the span of life extinct, the terrible emissaries of Yama come there desirous of taking him away.

56-57. These emissaries come there seated on various animals and birds at the departure of the dying man. The animals are bears, tigers, donkeys, camels, monkeys, scorpions, wolves, owls, serpents, cats, vultures, kites, Jackals, bees and herons.

58. The emissaries of Yama are excessively terrible and competent to frighten all living beings. They assume different forms and their faces resemble those of bears, buffaloes, vampires.

59. Some have long faces; some are hideous-faced; some have crooked nooses; some have three eyes. They have massive jaw bones, cheeks and faces. Some have hanging lips.

60. The limbs of some are smeared with blood and flesh. Their teeth come out of their mouths resembling spouts of shooting plants. They are very hideous in their shape. Their curved fangs are very fierce.

61. Their mouths resemble the nether worlds with blazing terrible tongues. The eyes are awful in their shape and size. They are shining, roving and tawny-coloured.

62. The eyes of some resemble fire or the eyes of the cat or owl. Some eyes are protruded like the eyes of the beetle. Some resemble the glowworm. Their hair are dishevelled and stand erect.

63. They are bedecked in garlands and skulls. Their limbs drip with blood (?). Their ornaments resemble terrible serpents tied up round their heads.

64. There are black serpents round their necks. They are very terrible due to their kissing sounds. Their tresses are coarse and stiff. They are terrible and they resemble fiery flames.

65. Their faces are covered with reddish brown moustaches and brown or tawny-coloured hairs. Their staff-like arms are very terrible. They hang down on either side and they resemble iron clubs.

66. Some of them have only two arms; others have four arms, still others have ten, sixteen or twenty arms.

67. There are still others with innumrable hands. Some of them have thousand arms. Terrible weapons of various forms shine in their hands.

68. These emissaries of great strength threaten the aying men with different brilliant weapons such as javelin, iron club, discus etc. or nooses, fetters and batons.

69. When the span of life of the men comes to an end these extremely terrible emissaries come to take away the creatures. All of them carry out the orders of Yama.

70. The creature assumes a physical body befitting tortures in the hell and originating from its own actions. It is this body of the creature that is taken away towards the abode of Yama.

71. With the nooses, adamantine fetters and iron chains, the creature is bound by the infuriated servants of Yama. He is beaten and taken over to the abode of Yama.

72-75. The dying man falters, cries and shouts frequently "Alas, my father, O my mother, O my son." He is defiled by his own evil actions. He is hit by sharp pointed javelins, keen-edged iron clubs and iron hammers. He is tortured with the blows of swords and javelins and terrible adamantine batons. He is threatened and rebuked with thundering shouts by the emissaries equipped with thunderbolts and javelins. One by one the creatures are led by the awful and infuriated servants who beat them on all sides. The creature is in agony. He faints and mutters in despair. It is dragged and taken along the path.

76-78. The man of sinful activities goes to Yama's abode along the terrible pathway full of Kuśa grass, thorns, ant-hills, pikes, pebbles and gravel. It is infested with blazing fires fiercer than hundreds of thunderbolts (soaked in) acid. He is scorched by the blazing sun. He is burnt by its rays. He is pulled and dragged by the emissaries of Yama terribly shouting like vixens. He is bitten and dragged by hundreds of those vixens.

79. That great path has to be traversed by these sinful persons frightened in some places, terrified in some places and faltering here and there. They are shouting and lamenting due to misery.

80. The living beings have to traverse the path even as they are rebuked and burnt in their bodies. They are agitated due to terror. They run about in great dejection and agitation.

81. Men who are devoid of charitable gifts are scorched and burnt by the heated sand. They have to go along the path strewn with thorns.

82. Those who are guilty of slaying living beings have to traverse the path with their bodies emitting putrescent odour of

fat and blood with faeces and urine smeared all over as though they were unguents. They will have their skin burnt or cracked everywhere.

83. The destroyers of living beings must of necessity go along the path shouting and lamenting, cooing and chirping out of tune. They shall be in agony due to their pain.

84. Those who are guilty of slaying living beings must of necessity go along the path even as they are being pierced and smashed by javelins, iron clubs, swords, maces and arrows or by the sharp pointed tridents.

85-89. Sinners must traverse the path even as they are eaten by dogs, tigers. wolves and herons.

Flesh-eaters must traverse the path even as they are cut and severed by a jumbled mass of bubble or sawn and torn by saws and scissors.

Those who habitually eat meat must traverse the path even as they are gored by the tips of horns of buffaloes and oxen and scraped by boars.

Those who are sinful by imbibing wine shall traverse the path even as they are being eaten and stung by the swarms of bees and flies with their needle-pointed antenae.

Those men who treacherously kill their trusting master, friend or woman must traverse the path in agony and distress even as they are split and pierced through by means of weapons. Those men who kill animals and strike guiltless persons traverse the path pertaining to Yama even as they are being swallowed by the Rākṣasas.

90-99. Those who take away the robes and covering cloths of other men's wives run about naked to the abode of Yama, when they turn into ghosts. They are chased by the servants of Yama.

Those wicked-minded and sinful persons who commit sinful deeds and take away cloths, foodgrain, gold, houses or fields have to traverse the path leading to Yama's abode even as they are beaten and shattered by stones, rods and batons. They shall shed profuse blood.

Those men who profess not to be afraid of hell and snatch away the wealth and property of brahmins and those base men who revile at and strike brahmins are tacked on to dry twigs. Their ears, eyes, and noses are cut off; they are smeared with putrid blood. they are struck at by the terrible and hideous servants of Yama as well as vultures and jackals of Yama: those sinners go to the abode of Yama shouting and lamenting.

Thus the path is extremely inviolable. It has the lustre of fire. It is terrible, impassable and inaccessible. It has been pointed out (as the path to be traversed by) men. It has the lustre and colour of heated copper. It emits sparks and flames of fire. It is strewn with thorns and yellow Amaranth twigs that are hideous and that strike and bit much. It is fully covered by javelins and thunderbolts. It blazes with severe thorns. It is mixed with sand burning like coal. It is impassable on account of fires and worms. It is terrible with clusters of flames. It is all the more scorched by the rays of the sun. The embodied soul is led along this path, being dragged by the ruthless servants of Yama.

100-102. Whenever a creature shouts in misery or falls anywhere he is hit with weapons by the servants of Yama. Thus the most covetous among the sinners, and he who has no right policy is beaten by the servants of Yama who cannot be checked or resisted. Helplessly the creature is led along the path. Everyone has to traverse that impassable path.

103-104. The dying man is led along the very impassable path contemptuously by the emissaries of Yama. O brahmins, the creature is then ushered into the terrible city of copper and iron. He is taken there by the servants of Yama. That city is very extensive in magnitude. It extends to a hundred thousand Yojanas.

105. It is mentioned as a square splendid city with four main gates. The outwalls are made of gold. They are ten thousand Yojanas in height.

106-108. That city is beautified by sapphires, lapis lazuli, the great blue stone and rubies. Agitated by terrible Devas, Dānavas, Gandharvas, Yakṣas, Rākṣasas and serpents that city is extremely awful.

The eastern gate of that city is splendid. It is beautified by hundreds of banners and festoons. It is adorned with diamonds, sapphires, lapis lazuli and pearls. It is full of Gandharvas and Apsaras singing and dancing.

109. The entry through this door is exclusively for Devas, sages, Yogins, Gandharvas, Siddhas, Yakṣas and Vidyādharas.

110. The excellent northern gate is adorned with bells and chowries. Umbrellas and chowries are placed there. It is studded with different sorts of jewels.

111. It is resonant with the sweet notes of flutes and lutes as well as charming and auspicious songs. The Sāman fills the air with sages in crowds everywhere.

112-118. Those who are conversant with virtue, those who are devoted to truthfulness and those who observe holy rites enter through this door. The following types of people too enter through this door : those who give water to the thirsty in the summer, those who offer warm fire during the winter; those who shampoo and rub gently (the feet of) tired persons ; those who are engaged in pleasing words, those who are devoted to charitable gifts, those who are the heroic ones, those who are devoted to their mothers and fathers ; those who serve the brahmins and those who worship guests continuously.

The western gate of the city is embellished with jewels. The steps are studded with wonderful jewels. The gate is beautified by bestoons in the shape of iron clubs. It is resonant with the sounds of drums, Bherī and Mṛdaṅga, conches and Kāhala pipes. It is full of auspicious chanting sounds raised by the delighted Siddhas.

It is through this gate that the delighted man, the devotees of Śiva, enter the city. The following also gain entry through this gate. Those who take holy dip in all sacred waters ; those who serve the five sacred fires ; those who die in the course of campaign ; those who die on the Kālañjara mountain; those who lose their lives in fires; those by whom the eternality has been achieved, those who are killed in the interest of their masters, friends and the general public or in the encounter with the thieves of cattle. O sages, all these people, the heroic men, enter the city through the western gate.

119-122. The southern gate of that city is very terrible. Its frightening cries of "Hā Hā" fill up the air. It is enveloped in darkness. It is infested with animals with dark-pointed horns. The place is strewn with thorns and is impassable. Scorpions, serpents & Vajrakīṭas (adamantine worms?) prick and pierce, (everyone). There are wolves, tigers, hares, lions, foxes, dogs, cats and vultures all having flame-filled mouths. It is through this gate that all men of sinful activities gain entry.

123-128. The following types of sinners enter through the southern gate : Those who kill brahmins, cows, boys, old men, sick men, persons who seek refuge, persons who have trusted, women, friends and persons who have no weapons ; those foolish persons who indulge in sexual intercourse with the forbidden women; those who steal other men's riches; those who misappropriate money deposited or kept in trust; those who poison others or commit arson ; those who rob others of their lands, houses, beds, clothes and ornaments; those who ruthlessly wound others in their vulnerable points ; those who are habituated to utter lies ; those who work havoc in villages, cities and in different places of the country ; those who commit perjury; those who sell their daughters ; those who invariably consume forbidden food, those who outrage the modesty of their daughters and daughter-in-laws; those who speak harsh words to their parents; all others who have been mentioned as people committing great sins—All these people enter through the southern door.